THE MONEY CHANGERS

Currency Reform from Aristotle to E-Cash

Edited by David Boyle

Earthscan Publications Limited
London • Sterling, VA

Dedicated to people involved in time banks and time dollars all over the world — and their practical solution to some of the problems of money

First published in the UK and USA in 2002 by
Earthscan Publications Ltd
Copyright © David Boyle, 2002

ISBN: 1 85383 895 0

Typesetting by JS Typesetting Ltd, Wellingborough, Northants
Printed and bound by Creative Print and Design (Wales), Ebbw Vale
Cover design by Andrew Corbett

For a full list of publications please contact:

Earthscan Publications Ltd
120 Pentonville Road
London, N1 9JN, UK
Tel: +44 (0)20 7278 0433
Fax: +44 (0)20 7278 1142
Email: earthinfo@earthscan.co.uk
http://www.earthscan.co.uk

22883 Quicksilver Drive, Sterling, VA 20166–2012, USA

A catalogue record for this book is available from the British Library

Library of Congress Cataloging-in-Publication Data

The money changers : currency reform from Aristotle to e-cash / edited by David Boyle.
        p. cm.
    Includes bibliographical references and index.
    ISBN 1-85383-895-0
        1. Money–History. 2. Currency question–History. I. David Boyle, 1958-
HG231 .M586 2002
332.4–dc21

2002015631

Earthscan is an editorially independent subsidiary of Kogan Page Ltd and publishes in association with WWF-UK and the International Institute for Environment and Development

This book is printed on elemental chlorine-free paper

CONTENTS

Part VII Create your own: free money   225

LIST OF ACRONYMS AND ABBREVIATIONS

ATM   automatic teller machine
BT   British Telecom
COMER   Committee on Monetary and Economic Reform
CWI   Centre for Mathematics and Computer Science
         (Amsterdam)
DTQ   domestic tradable quota
ECB   European Central Bank
ECU   the convergence mechanism
GATT   General Agreement on Tariffs and Trade
GDP   Gross Domestic Product
GM   General Motors
GNP   Gross National Product
GRC   Global Reference Currency
ICC   International Commodity Corporation
IMF   International Monetary Fund
IPO   Initial Public Offer
LETS   Local Exchange Trading System
OECD   Organisation for Economic Co-operation and Development
PURPA   Public Utility Regulating Practice Act
SDR   Special Drawing Rights
SEL   Système Échange Locale
SHARE   Self-Help Association for a Regional Economy
SLGEEA   State and Local Government Economic Empowerment Act
VAT   value added tax
WIC   Women with Infants and Children Programme (Berkshire,
         USA)
WIR   Wirtschaftsting

ACKNOWLEDGEMENTS

This book is either an exercise in economic archaeology or a treatise on heresy, or a serious rediscovery of a great reforming tradition, depending on your point of view. I hope it has a little of all of those in it, but it also probably betrays my background as an activist rather than an academic. I come at the subject of reforming the way we create money, as distinct from the more familiar debate about how to create wealth, from some years writing about new kinds of currency – local, electronic, barter, virtual, voluntary: you name it, I've dabbled in it.

I've noticed during that time a slow resurgence of interest by mainstream economists and politicians in those very practical issues. Probably the best known economist of the day, Paul Krugman, has even written recently how he applied his economic knowledge to rescue the rudimentary currency system launched by his local baby-sitting circle. This book is offered in the same spirit: it is full of practical complaints about the money-creation system, and practical proposals – some more feasible than others – about what can be done about it.

I am enormously grateful to Jonathan Sinclair Wilson, Pascale Mettam and Victoria Burrows at Earthscan for their advice and interest in the idea, and to those people who have given me their time or advice about the contents or the text. They include Pat Conaty, Caroline Hill, Bernard Lietaer, Michael Linton, James Robertson, Gill Seyfang, Ernie Yacub, and many others who have inspired me over the years to find out more about these now neglected corners of economics, which were once the very central issue of concern.

I must emphasize, though, that any mistakes and misjudgements, particularly about the structure of the book, and which passages belong where, are all mine. Having experimented with what seemed like an infinite set of variations, I came to the conclusion that there were arguments for almost any possible arrangement – so I am sure not to have satisfied everyone.

Finally, can I thank everybody at the New Economics Foundation and Time Dollar Insitute for their support, friendship and inspiration, helping me learn more about money over the years than I ever thought possible. And last, but not least, Sarah – for being so patient during the research and writing of this book.

David Boyle
Crystal Palace
January 2002

LIST OF SOURCES

References to all quoted sources are given in the text. Sources for which permission to quote was necessary are given below.

INTRODUCTION

John Ruskin, *Unto this Last: Four Essays on the First Principles of Political Economy*, Elder and Co, London (1862).

J M Keynes, *National Self-Sufficiency* in *Collected Works Vol 21* (ed Moggridge), Macmillan, London (1982). Reproduced with permission of Palgrave.

PART I

Benjamin Franklin, *A Modest Inquiry into the Nature and Necessity of Paper Currency*, Philadelphia (1729).

Robert Owen, *Report to the County of Lanark, of a Plan for Relieving Public Distress, and Removing Discontent, by giving Permanent, Productive Employment, to the Poor and Working Classes*, Glasgow University Press (1821).

Ignatius Donnelly, 'People's Party Platform', *Omaha Morning World-Herald*, 5 July (1892).

William Jennings Bryan, *Three Centuries of American Rhetorical Discourse*, edited by Ronald F Reid, Waveland Press, Prospect Heights (1988).

L Frank Baum, *The Wonderful Wizard of Oz* (1900).

Silvio Gesell, *The Natural Economic Order*, translated by Philip Pye, Peter Owen, London (1958). Reproduced with permission from Peter Owen Ltd, London.

C H Douglas, *The Monopoly of Credit* (4th edition), Bloomfield Books, Sudbury (1979). Reproduced with permission from Bloomfield Books, 26 Meadow Lane, Sudbury, Suffolk CO10 6TD.

William Krehm (editor), *Meltdown: Money, Debt and the Wealth of Nations*, Comer Publications, Toronto (1999). Reproduced with permission from Comer.

James Robertson, 'How to Make the New Economics Relevant', in *New Economics*, Winter, 1992. Reproduced with permission from James Robertson and the New Economics Foundation.

PART II

Daniel Defoe, *The Villainy of Stock-Jobbers Detected, and the Causes of the Late Run upon the Bank and Bankers Discovered and Considered*, London (1701).

Thomas Jefferson, letter to John Wayles Eppes Monticello, June 24 (1813).

Charles MacKay, *Memoirs of Extraordinary Popular Delusions and the Madness of Crowds*, London (1841).

Washington Irving, *A Time of Unexampled Prosperity* (1855).

John Kenneth Galbraith, *The Great Crash 1929*, Penguin/Hamish Hamilton, London (1961). Copyright © 1954, 1955, 1961, 1972, 1979, 1988 by John Kenneth Galbraith. Reproduced with permission from Penguin Books Ltd and Houghton Mifflin Company. All rights reserved.

Ralph Borsodi, *Inflation and the Coming Keynesian Catastrophe: The Story of the Exeter Experiments*, E F Schumacher Society/School of Living, Great Barrington (1989). Reproduced with permission from the E F Schumacher Society.

Paul Glover. Taken from *Ithaca Money*, January 1992 and from the Ithaca Hours website, www.ithacahours.org. Reproduced with permission from Ithaca Hours.

Earl of Caithness. Parliamentary copyright material from Hansard is reproduced with the permission of the Controller of Her Majesty's Stationery Office on behalf of Parliament.

George Soros, *Soros on Soros: Staying Ahead of the Curve*, John Wiley & Sons, New York (1995). Copyright © 1995 by George Soros. This material is used by permission of John Wiley & Sons, Inc.

PART III

Aristotle. Taken from *Aristotle's Politics*, translated by Benjamin Jowett, Book I, Part 10.

Francis Bacon, *Moral, Economical, and Political*, translated by Peter Shaw, M Jones, London (1802).

Jonathan Swift, 'Letter to the Tradesmen, Shop-Keepers, Farmers, and Common-People in General of Ireland, *Drapier's Letters*, March (1724).

Abraham Lincoln. Taken from Senate document No 23: National Economy and the Banking System of the United States.

Frederick Soddy, *The Arch-Enemy of Economic Freedom: What Banking Is, What First it Was and Again Should Be*, Enstone (1943).

Jane Jacobs, *Cities and the Wealth of Nations*, Viking, New York (1985). Copyright © by Jane Jacobs, 1984. Reproduced by permission of Penguin Books Ltd and Random House, Inc.

Margrit Kennedy, with Declan Kennedy, *Interest and Inflation Free Money: Creating an Exchange Medium that Works for Everybody and Protects the Earth*, New Society Publishers, Philadelphia (1995). Copyright © by Margrit Kennedy, 1995. Reproduced under licence from New Society Publishers

Joel Kurtzman. Taken from the author's preface to Joel Kurtzman, *The Death of Money*, Simon & Schuster, New York (1993). Copyright © 1993 by Joel Kurtzman. Reprinted with permission of Simon & Schuster.

Michael Rowbotham, *The Grip of Death: A Study of Modern Money, Debt Slavery and Destructive Economics*, Jon Carpenter Publishing, Charlbury (1998). Reproduced with permission from Jon Carpenter Publishing.

Part IV

Andrew Jackson. Taken from 'Veto of the Bill to Recharter the Second Bank of the United States', 10 July (1832).

C H Douglas, *Economic Democracy*, Cecil Palmer, London (1920). *Economic Democracy* is now published by Bloomfield Books, 26 Meadow Lane, Sudbury CO10 2TD, and permission to reprint this extract is acknowledged with thanks.

Henry Ford. Taken from the *New York Times*, 4 December (1921); quoted in *The Social Creditor*, vol 77, no 3, May–June (1998).

William Aberhart, *Social Credit Manual: Social Credit as Applied to the Province of Alberta*, Social Credit Association of the Province of Quebec, Montreal (1935). Reproduced with permission of the Social Credit Association of Canada.

B F Skinner, *Walden Two*, Allyn & Bacon, Boston (1976). Copyright © by B F Skinner, 1976. Reprinted by permission of Pearson Education, Inc, Upper Saddle River, NJ.

Sovereignty. Taken from the State and Local Government Economic Empowerment Act (HR 1452), currently before the United States Congress (1999).

James Robertson and Joseph Huber, *Creating New Money: A Monetary Reform for the Information Age*, New Economics Foundation, London (2000). Reproduced with permission from James Robertson and Joseph Huber.

PART V

Marco Polo, *The Book of Ser Marco Polo the Venetian concerning the Kingdoms and Marvels of the East*, translated and edited by Henry Yule, third edition revised by Henri Cordier, John Murray, London (1903).

John Law, *Money and Trade Considered: With a Proposal for Supplying the Nation with Money*, Edinburgh (1705).

Walter Bagehot, *A Practical Plan for Assimilating the English and American Money, as a Step Towards a Universal Money*, Longmans, Green & Co, London (1889).

Edward Bellamy, *Looking Backward: 2000–1887*, Ticknor & Co, Boston (1888).

William Morris, *News from Nowhere: Or, an Epoch of Rest, being some Chapters from a Utopian Romance*, Reeves & Turner, London (1891).

Fischer Black, *Banking and Interest Rates in a World without Money: The Effects of Uncontrolled Money*, Journal of Bank Research, Autumn (1970). Reproduced with permission from the Bank Administration Institute.

F A Hayek, *The Denationalization of Money – the Argument Refined: An Analysis of the Theory and Practice of Concurrent Currencies*, Institute of Economic Affairs, London, third edition (1990). Reproduced with permission from the Institute of Economic Affairs.

David Chaum, 'Achieving Electronic Privacy', *Scientific American*, August (1992). Copyright © by Scientific American, Inc, 1992. All rights reserved.

Lawrence H White, 'Competitive Payment Systems and the Unit of Account', *American Economic Review*, LXXIV(4), (1984). Reproduced with permission from the American Economic Association.

Edward de Bono, *The IBM Dollar*, Centre for the Study of Financial Innovation, London (1994). Reproduced with permission of the Centre for the Study of Financial Innovation.

David Birch and Neil McEvoy, 'Downloadsamoney' in *Demos* magazine, no 8 (1996). Reproduced with permission from Demos.

Mervyn King, 'A Future for Central Banks?' (1999). Taken from a speech by the author, Jackson Hole, Wyoming, 27 August. Reproduced with permission of Mervyn King.

PART VI

Pierre-Joseph Proudhon, 'Solution du Problème Social', in *Selected Writings of Pierre-Joseph Proudhon*, translated by Elizabeth Fraser, Macmillan, London (1970). Reproduced with permission of Palgrave Press.

Frederick Soddy, *Wealth, Virtual Wealth and Debt: The Solution to the Economic Paradox*, George Allen & Unwin, London (1926).

Robert Eisler, *The Money Maze: A Way Out of the Economic World Crisis*, Search Publishing Company, London (1931). Copyright © by Robert Eisler, 1931.

Jan Goudriaan, *How to Stop Deflation*, Search Publishing Company, London (1932). Copyright © by Jan Goudriaan, 1932.

Irving Fisher, *100% Money*, Adelphi, New York (1935). Reproduced with permission of George W Fisher.

Benjamin Graham, *World Commodities and World Currency*, McGraw-Hill, New York (1944). Reproduced under licence from McGraw-Hill.

E C Riegel, 'Toward a Natural Monetary System' in *Flight from Inflation: The Monetary Alternative*, edited by Spencer Heath MacCallum and George Morton, Heather Foundation (1978). Reproduced with permission from the Heather Foundation.

Ralph Borsodi, *Inflation and the Coming Keynesian Catastrophe: The Story of the Exeter Experiments*, E F Schumacher Society/School of Living, Great Barrington (1989). Published with permission from the E F Schumacher Society.

Nicholas Kaldor. Taken from the Preface to *Economic Stability is Attainable*, by L St Clare Grondona, Hutchinson, London (1975).

Shann Turnbull, 'Kilowatt Hour Currencies' (1977). Copyright © by Dr Shann Turnbull, 1977. See: http://members.optusnet.com.au/~sturnbull/index.html; email: sturnbull@mba1963.hbs.edu. Reproduced with permission of the author.

Robert Swann and Susan Witt, *Local Currencies: Catalysts for Sustainable Regional Economies*, E F Schumacher Society, Great Barrington, February (1995). Reproduced with permission from the E F Schumacher Society.

David Fleming. Taken from the Domestic Tradable Quotas website at: www.dtqs.org.

Bernard Lietaer, *The Future of Money: A New Way to Create Wealth, Work and a Wiser World*, Century, London (2001).

Part VII

Arthur Kitson, *A Scientific Solution of the Money Question*, Arena Publishing, Boston (1895). Copyright © by Arthur Kitson, 1895.

Silvio Gesell, *The Natural Economic Order*, translated by Philip Pye: Peter Owen, London (1958). Reproduced with permission of Peter Owen.

The Week, 17 May (1933).

Irving Fisher, *Mastering the Crisis*, George Allen & Unwin, London (1934).

Edgar Cahn, *Service Credits: A New Currency for the Welfare State*, Welfare State Programme discussion paper no 8, Suntory Toyota International Centre for Economics and Related Disciplines (STICERD), London (1986). Reproduced by permission of STICERD.

Margrit Kennedy, with Declan Kennedy, *Interest and Inflation Free Money: Creating an Exchange Medium that Works for Everybody and Protects the Earth*, New Society Publishers, Philadelphia (1995). Copyright © by Margrit Kennedy, 1995. Reproduced under licence from New Society Publishers.

Womanshare, February (1993). Reproduced with permission from Diana McCourt.

Joel Hodroff, *Re-inventing Money for the Information Economy* (1999). Reprinted with permission from Joel Hodroff.

Richard Douthwaite, *The Ecology of Money*, Green Books, Dartington (1999). Reproduced with permission from Green Books.

David Boyle, *Why London Needs its Own Currency*, New Economics Foundation, London (2000). Reproduced with permission from the New Economics Foundation.

Edgar Cahn, *No More Throwaway People: The Co-production Imperative*, Essential Books/Time Dollar Institute, Washington (2000). Reproduced with permission from the Time Dollar Institute.

Michael Linton and Ernie Yacub, *Open Money Manifesto*, taken from the website www.openmoney.org. Reproduced with permission of Landsman Community Services.

INTRODUCTION
THE FAILURE OF MONEY

There is no wealth but life

JOHN RUSKIN, UNTO THIS LAST

The world is full, on the one hand, of monetary cranks each with a patent panacea for setting all our ills to rights, and, on the other, of orthodox economists, so alarmed at the cranks' proposals as to be wholly unwilling to make any new discoveries at all, for fear of appearing to sanction some of their notions

G D H COLE, TOMORROW'S MONEY

There never was a profession so terrified of unorthodoxy as economics. Even in the summer of 2001, the Cambridge economics graduate students who signed the mild protest emerging from the Sorbonne against too much economic abstraction were so afraid for their future careers that they did so anonymously. Maybe this is because of its scientific pretensions; maybe because its tenets are so insubstantial. Whatever it is, mainstream economics lives constantly with the fear of insanity, of heresy, of a sudden strange untrained messiah arising to challenge the way the system works. It is a potent fear, especially, for some reason, amongst the British.

The trouble is, this is also a fear that stifles debate about fundamentals. It undermines imagination and reform and throttles big ideas at birth. As the Fabian economist G D H Cole put it in the quotation at the head of this introduction, it tends to make economics 'wholly unwilling to make any new discoveries at all'.

I'm not arguing that everyone included in this book is wholly wise, and certainly not that they are all correct in what they argue. I am arguing that the traditions they represent have something to teach us, and at the very least that it is important to listen to dissenting questions. Some have been immensely influential, some have developed practical solutions to intractable problems, but some were dismissed in their own lifetimes as cranks. But then, as another revolutionary economist, E F Schumacher, put it: 'A crank is a very elegant device. It's small, it's strong, it's lightweight, energy efficient and it makes revolutions.'

Cole's point of view is unusually liberal for a Fabian, because it was the Fabians – more than any other group of reformers – who spent the early years of the 20th century trampling on the millennarians, revolutionaries and vegetarians they saw as sucking attention away from the true path of steady progress towards state socialism. 'If only the sandals and pistachio-coloured shirts could be put into a pile and burnt, and every vegetarian, teetotaller and creeping Jesus sent home to Welwyn Garden City to do his yoga exercises quietly,' wrote George Orwell in the 1930s. Unfortunately, Orwell and Shaw and the Webbs put many of the great alternative ideas about money creation into the same pile, and it has taken nearly a century to drag some of them back into serious debate.

Paradoxically, the middle years of the 20th century were also a period of great monetary heresy, partly because the Great Depression made people wonder if there weren't better ways of creating money, and partly, perhaps, because economics had been so unformed in the previous century that it was hard to distinguish the heretics from the pioneers. Still, the ideas of Gesell, Douglas and Borsodi were still sent home to the equivalent of Welwyn Garden City – and apart from the occasional bleat about the power of bankers after the war, that's where they stayed.

But we are in a new century now, and the economic system we have inherited is – by relatively common consent – not working very well. The various players would certainly disagree about how serious the problems are. But the spread of currency crises around the world in the last years of the 20th century, the collapse of apparently secure financial institutions such as Barings and Long Term Capital Management, has made people – especially those at the radical end of politics – look again at the system, and wonder.

And when people started to wonder, they found a range of thinkers, often pulled together under the heading The Other Economic Summit (TOES) from the mid-1980s onwards, who had carried on a tradition of monetary dissent that stretched all the way back to the beginnings of economics. Some of them had been assistants to the great heretics of the mid-20th century, like Bob Swann. Some of them were idealists who had seen the inside of the system and realized that something had to be done, like George Soros, Bernard Lietaer and James Robertson. Some of them just had a practical idea of something that could be done here and now, like Edgar Cahn and Michael Linton.

They didn't necessarily agree about the means, and they still don't – nor do they agree what the fundamental problem is. Some of them are pragmatists, with more than one foot in the orthodox world; some of them continue the great tradition of heresy, and believe that their one change will usher in an era of peace and enlightenment all by itself. But all of them share something from a tradition of dissent that goes back via Ruskin and Morris to Franklin, Owen and even Aristotle.

It's a tradition that is outlined by the two introductory passages below, one from Ruskin and one from Keynes. Both of these in their own way remind us that the money system is simply a means to an end, and if it doesn't work, we can change it. There is no wealth but life, wrote Ruskin in 1860. It is, at one level or another, the battle cry of all the critics in this book.

This isn't intended to be a book about economics as a whole, just about money and its creation. It isn't intended to be exhaustive – I'm only too aware of all the other possible passages and people I could have included. But it is intended to raise some of the traditional questions about where money comes from that have dropped out of polite debate this past half century. As Richard Douthwaite says, the last big-name economists concerned about what form money should take were Keynes, Fisher and Simons in the 1930s.

But there is something stirring out there, which is why this book is likely to be of more interest than it was five or ten years ago. Writers like Bernard Lietaer or Michael Rowbotham aren't necessarily mainstream economists, but they are raising questions and attracting attention. New kinds of money like Local Exchange Trading Systems (LETS), time dollars, loyalty points and trade pounds aren't normally the stuff of serious economic discourse, yet they are out there in the real world – and they are making an impression. At least 10 per cent of world trade, and probably more, now uses barter currencies in one form or another, and there are at least 7000 local currencies circulating around the world.

Will they succeed in making changes in the way money works? It's hard to say and depends as much on the economic climate than anything else. But there is also a great irony in the tradition of money 'heresy', which is that – as Gershwin put it – 'just when you get what you want, you don't want it'. The climate changes, the money flows again and suddenly there's too much of it, and the heretics go back to the drawing board.

Some of them lean a little too far, perhaps, in their belief in the perfectibility of mankind. Some of them lean too far in their belief in the perfectibility of governments. But even the most cynical of the people included here probably share a sense that there must be some natural system of money creation that would bring people and planet back into some kind of harmony, with themselves and with each other. The dream of a sustainable system of money creation holds together the competing-currency free marketeers and those who want money-creation to be limited to governments and central banks alone.

Because of these common roots, the dividing lines between these reformers are blurred. I've tried to group them into broad themes, but I have to admit that every time I did so, it was clear I could have done it differently again. Any one of these passages could probably have belonged in any one of the other sections.

I settled on the current structure because there are still broad distinctions that can be drawn. There is a broad division between those whose prime concern is to provide more money in circulation, and those whose prime concern is to make sure that whatever medium we have in circulation is based on something real – between free money and real money. And generally speaking, that's a distinction between those who see the 'medium of exchange' function of money as the key issue, and those who are worried about its 'store of value' function. Behind that lies the age-old conflict between debtors and creditors: the former want to keep the value of their debt intact, while the latter want it to become irrelevant. In that sense, this is also the story of money. It's the secret history of economics.

Which side of this divide they settle on often depends on the economic environment they were living in. Radical critics battling with the gold standard were concerned about finding ways of putting more money into circulation; those battling with hyper-inflation or speculative binges were concerned about bringing the financial world back to reality.

But of course anyone who wants to design their own money system is going to need a little of both those functions – even if they might be combined differently to the way money is now. Even if they are advocating a multi-currency world of competing currencies, each one is going to need to be available enough to measure the value of purchases, or it will be useless. Each one is also going to need to de desirable and reliable enough to store value or it's going to be worthless.

In other words, you need both sides of the critique. Which is why a great economist like Irving Fisher finds himself urging more money as a 'medium of exchange' in his book *Stamp Scrip* (1934), and at the same time to urging us to root money to reality in his almost contemporaneous book *100% Money* (1935).

Fisher is also on both sides of the other distinction you might draw between these passages – between those who want to limit the creation of money to the state and those who want to broaden it out beyond banks to communities and individuals, between the democrats and the anarchists. But once again, money inventors need to have something of both – both state-issued money, local currencies and social currencies – to fill in some of the gaps where it fails to flow.

Although it is now fashionable again in some circles to argue that only nation states, or central banks, should have the right to create money, in practice, this is likely to be pretty fraught. If governments fail to create enough – and the history of governments includes centuries of misjudging the money supply – then we can expect people to take the law into their own hands. If governments don't provide it, people will lend money they don't own (probably with interest) to satisfy the demand, and they will once again create new means of exchange to bring needs and resources together again in communities.

It's easy for people to laugh at the idea that we can design our own currencies. You don't get these questions discussed much in the mainstream media. Yet, as I write, the new euro 'common currency' notes and coins are being sent out across the European Union, and the truth is that redesigning money is increasingly on the agenda. This is largely because we have recently lived through a series of currency crises, and found that the financial system has very few safeguards. One desperate finance minister phoned the International Monetary Fund in Washington in 1998, only to be told by the night porter that they were closed for the night and he would have to phone back in the morning. The world also witnessed the terrifying sight of hospital patients in Indonesia forced out of the building at bayonet point because the hospital had been drained of funds overnight.

Nor is the current prescription of linking national currencies together faring much better. Argentina is in a state of economic collapse after fixing the value of its currency to the US dollar, and has found itself inventing new paper currencies to provide a means of exchange in Buenos Aires. The days of the great currency innovators like John Law – briefly the richest and most powerful man in France – have not disappeared after all.

The job of linking Europe's currencies together is difficult enough. As many as 80 lorries a day for three months have been needed to shift the old coins in circulation to make way for the euro – and that's just in Belgium. But in Britain, the political issues – such as whether the Queen's head should be on the notes and coins – have overwhelmed attention to the gigantic economic uncertainties that large-scale international currencies throw up. Explaining his decision to put the pound back on the gold standard in 1925, Winston Churchill described international currencies that 'vary together, like ships in harbour whose gangways are joined and who rise and fall together with the tide'. He might equally well have been talking about the euro.

But while the euro has dominated monetary debate in Europe for the past decade, there are other new, unexpected kinds of money that are beginning to emerge. Here are three of them:

- Loyalty points programmes like beenz and air miles have been playing an increasing role in our lives. The latest loyalty card from the UK chemist Boots has space on it for more than 20 different loyalty currencies. And in case you don't think this is money, until recently Northwest Airlines in the USA used to pay their entire worldwide PR account in frequent flyer points.
- International barter is getting increasingly sophisticated, involving some of the biggest companies in the world, and increasingly using electronic barter currencies such as trade dollars. And when each local exchange can't immediately find what they need, they use an international currency called *universal* to barter it from elsewhere.
- If you have one of the dual-track HeroCards in Minneapolis, you can buy products at the Mall of America – the biggest mall in the USA – partly in dollars and partly in a local currency based on time earned by helping out in the local community, tutoring in schools or giving lifts to the elderly.

Even if we are just talking about technological change, it is pretty clear that the way we create and exchange money is due for a shake-up. All the internet currencies apart from one – e-gold.com – have disappeared in the great dot.com clear-out of 2001, but the widespread availability of new information technology in the form of computers, televisions and mobile phones seems likely to have a lasting effect on the form of money we use.

Only the most futuristic enthusiasts believe that electronic money will drive out what remains of cash altogether. But the technology does open up the possibilities of what else could be achieved, by bringing together the different kinds of currency that are out there in what is rapidly becoming a multi-currency world. Loyalty currencies such as air miles are being used to barter goods and services in the same way as barter currencies. Social currencies such as LETS are being developed to compete locally with barter currencies. Volunteer currencies such as time dollars are being used like loyalty cards to encourage people to behave in particular ways. As they do so, the technology that makes this convergence possible – the internet, smart cards, mobile phones and digital television – is being upgraded and made more available, and is carrying out a convergence of its own. Dual-card mobile phones that can replenish e-purses are already available; there are card slots on the set-top boxes that deliver digital TV.

If you accept the full range of electronic currencies as 'money', then a wide range of different sectors are now involved in issuing it. As well as banks, they include public transport systems issuing loyalty points and stored value cards, phone operators issuing smart cards and systems that allow customers to pay direct by phone, utilities issuing stored value cards, universities issuing smart cards and time credits, and much more.

In Finland, you can now pay for drinks or parking meters by phoning the machines, with the debit turning up on your phone bill. When corporates start investing in IT again – as they will – we will find retailers, utilities, phone companies and community organizations competing with the banks for the prize of controlling the new e-currencies. And the benefits will be worth winning. Branded electronic money will be able to tie customers further into a network of banks, supermarkets and other companies to encourage loyalty; customers will be that much less likely to shift suppliers if they have to change bank accounts, phone companies and money-type too. Money issuers may link themselves together in global *keiretsu*, to give customers as broad a buying power as possible.

A multi-currency future like this would imply a range of online broker-ages, helping people to shift from one kind of money to another – but using the rival currencies to underpin different aspects of their lives. It would mean corporate money backed by shares to store value, loyalty money backed by belief in brand to make purchases, local money backed by local trust to underpin local life. It could also mean a new generation of currency trading opportunities, between sectors or between regions, though some currencies will lose their entire *raison d'etre* without strict rules that you cannot use them to buy conventional cash.

As trade becomes more global, there looks like there's going to be an equal trend towards the local. Consumers are increasingly demanding fresh food, traditional services and local production. It seems likely that, as mainstream currencies get more international, there's going to be an increasing reliance on local currencies – some informal and some backed by local authorities and other local organizations. These have the potential to protect local economies against the uncertainties of the international markets, but they are likely to be used increasingly as methods of providing start-up finance to small businesses and encouraging local production, especially of fresh food.

And as the IT revolution throws up these new kinds of money, it is also throwing up new kinds of assets, any of which could be used as backing for new kinds of money. Some of these are complex, some of them very simple – such as the credits issued in the Brazilian city of Curitiba for recycling rubbish which can also be used to pay your bus fare. They could be anything from excess productive capacity, the loyalty of your customers, to the greenness of your electricity or your personal carbon debt. Many of the new currencies will be the result of accounting for assets differently, and giving the new totals buying power. This combination of multiple currencies, dematerialized assets and communications technology may mean any or all of the following – most of which exist already in some form or other – taking shape as part of mainstream life:

- Using virtual currencies as stores of value based on pollution permits, which are in turn created by international agreements like the carbon debt negotiations.
- Issuing pre-payment cards that can be denominated in a range of different units, including public transport trips, phone units, but also other commodities such as water, energy or food. These would not be subject to inflation.
- Using virtual currencies as collateral for hard currency loans by developing ways of getting them underwritten by a third party – either by regional government in the case of time dollars in the USA, or by insurance companies in the case of trade dollars.
- Providing alternatives to prison, fines and community service by converting debt into electronic money based on time, which must be paid off by helping out locally or doing training.
- Setting up local electronic currencies that allow people to buy excess capacity in the economy in return for the time they spend volunteering.
- Helping develop new supermarket and town centre loyalty schemes based on smart cards, and using them to provide backing for volunteer currencies such as time banks.
- Enabling brokers such as Comic Relief to turn corporate donations in time or loyalty points into goods or cash.
- Setting up new kinds of money systems, such as training pounds, which organizations use to boost the amount of training happening locally.

- Helping large organizations develop 'intellectual currencies' that encourage employees to share their knowledge or pass on their training.

A multi-currency world is difficult to envisage, even though the first signs of it are appearing already. It is not clear yet how people will cope with another level of complexity in their increasingly complex lives, but – assuming that the right regulatory framework is in place, and e-money issuers take their responsibility seriously for the whole of society – it should mean more currency stability. The new system could spread purchasing power to more people. It could broaden the definition of work to include a much wider range of activities than are currently recognized by the market, and reward them with buying power. It could usher in a period of monetary experimentation that might create a more sustainable economy – one that conserves natural resources and uses its waste as assets.

But, in line with the traditional way that monetary solutions create their own problems, there are dangers that a multi-currency economy could turn out to be more exclusive. It's certainly going to be considerably more complex. It offers the possibility that alliances of companies issuing their own cash will be able to design it in such a way that it circulates more to their favoured customers and less to the poor. There are privacy issues about electronic cash. There are social exclusion issues too: if physical cash disappears, it's going to be hard for beggars to get by without expensive smart-card readers.

That's a future shape for money, but there are still some big questions – raised again and again in passages included in this book – that remain unanswered about the way conventional money is created. Why, for example – despite unprecedented prosperity – does it seem so impossible to afford the simplest public services, health, post or education? My mother and stepfather live in a small Hampshire village, which during the austerity period of the late 1940s managed to boast two shops, a post office, two pubs, a butcher's, a village policeman, a doctor and district nurse, and a railway station connected to a massive local rail network, only a couple of miles away in the small town of Stockbridge. Now, when we are incomparably 'richer', all that's left is one pub and a very occasional bus.

The conventional reasons for this – high wages, over-regulation, fat cat salaries – don't really satisfy me and it's tempting to think there may be clues in the very design of money and it's issue. According to Victorian economists, after all, peasants in 1495 had to work 15 weeks to earn the money they needed to live for a year. By 1564, it was 40 weeks – and now look at us. We need to ask more fundamental questions about why money seems to have this built-in enslavement. Here are three more modern versions of big questions that simply won't go away:

- How can we sustain the financial system when speculation is now more than 20 times as powerful as trade, and has more than 20 times as much financial clout – and when the people who run the system in Tokyo, London and New York have more to gain from instability than they do from stability? How can we possibly organize a reliable system of global investment when the financial underpinning – the combined reserves of all the central banks in the world – could now be overwhelmed in just a few hours of foreign exchange trading?

- How can we create a free society when there is now less money in the economy – in the UK, about £100 billion less – than there is outstanding debt? Isn't the inevitable outcome of such a situation that the ownership of business, land and property will slip inexorably into the hands of the financial institutions, leaving people increasingly enslaved by their mortgages and credit cards?

- Why is it that a broadly similar percentage of the population has been considered poor for getting on for two centuries? The proportion of people in poverty in London is broadly similar to what it was in the 1880s, though it was measured differently – and the proportion of national income we spend on welfare is broadly similar to what it was in the 1820s, though it was administered differently. Isn't it possible that this continuing third of the population, and a third of the world's countries, are still considered poor due to some hitherto undiscovered economic 'law' about money creation?

It isn't really the business of this book to suggest answers to these questions, or even really to assert that there are answers. The purpose is much more to say that there are questions, and there have always been questions. And to argue that those questions have remained nagging away, even though the financial aristocracy may have persuaded almost everyone that the system we live with now is the way that God made it at the creation of the world.

At the very least, reading these passages – those complaining that there's no cash and those complaining about speculative mania – makes you realize the importance of historic context. For those of us brought up to believe that when people succeed or fail in business they somehow deserved it, these passages remind us that success or failure, wealth or poverty, has as much to do with whether you live at a moment of monetary expansion or contraction.

Whether you go into the historic lists of brilliant successes or impoverished fools depends as much on what the mood of the money creators happens to be at the time — and that often depends in turn on whether you are living through a period of population expansion or military spending. The shape of our lives, the ability to achieve our dreams, depends on money and how much there is around us.

We have lived through a period when the system that creates the money that allows us to connect with each other has reached a status that seemed unassailable. Where there was once a ferment of debate about how it might be organized differently, there seemed suddenly to be absolute silence. People who asked questions were dismissed as fools. The series of currency crises, the rickety state of the international financial system, the arrival of the euro, have all now played their part in making it possible to ask questions again. The purpose of this book is to show that there is a great tradition of creative questioning, and the signs are that it is beginning to revive itself.

And now it is reviving itself, it's worth remembering the other great tradition of monetary reform — that every solution throws up more problems. It's a good reason for staying vigilant about what is most important, as Ruskin and Keynes write below: that the money system should always be subservient to the human spirit. Our historic failure to take their advice means that money reform — when it has happened — traditionally makes us wonder, like William Morris did in *A Dream of John Ball*:

> *how men fight and lose the battle, and the thing that they fought for comes about in spite of their defeat, and when it comes turns out not to be what they meant, and other men have to fight for what they meant under another name.*

JOHN RUSKIN

Unto This Last (1860)

When the great art critic John Ruskin (1819–1900) turned his attention to economics, it was part of an integrated campaign that took him his whole life – battling against ugliness and industrial production and the degradation of people. *Cornhill* magazine in 1860 was under the editorship of the novelist W M Thackeray – the author of *Vanity Fair*, among other things. Thackeray commissioned Ruskin to write a series of essays which became a book two years later, under the title of *Unto This Last*.

A survey of the first Labour MPs found that the book had been more influential on them than Marx's *Das Kapital*. Even more important, a copy came into the hands of the young Mahatma Gandhi in 1904, and he read it on his train journey from Johannesburg to Durban, by the end of which it had changed his life and decided him to live by its principles.

Ruskin included in the book a newspaper report of a shipwrecked man who strapped all his gold to himself in an attempt to preserve it, leapt from the sinking vessel and promptly plunged to the bottom of the sea. Then, as part of his treatise on modern ideas of value and ownership, he asks the question: 'Does the man own the gold or does the gold own the man?'

At the start of *Unto This Last*, as he had done in *Modern Painters*, Ruskin took on the people who were supposed to be experts – and in this case, the new economists who believed that scarcity was the basic existence of humanity. 'No', says Ruskin to Malthus, Ricardo and Mill:

> *the real science of political economy, which has yet to be distinguished from the bastard science, as medicine from witchcraft, and astronomy from astrology, is that which teaches nations to desire and labour for the things that lead to life: and which teaches them to scorn and destroy the things that lead to destruction.*

From there it's a small step to his famous aphorism that 'there is no wealth but life'. For Ruskin, money is always subservient to this principle. If it doesn't promote life – if it doesn't create beauty and reality – it must be changed. It has been a key underlying theme of people who have wanted to change the way money works ever since.

* * *

Capital signifies 'head, or source, or root material' – it is material by which some derivative or secondary good is produced. It is only capital proper (*caput vivum*, not *caput mortuum*) when it is thus producing something different from itself. It is a root, which does not enter into vital function till it produces something else than a root: namely, fruit. That fruit will in time again produce roots; and so all living capital issues in reproduction of capital; but capital which produces nothing but capital is only root producing root; bulb issuing in bulb, never in tulip; seed issuing in seed, never in bread.

The Political Economy of Europe has hitherto devoted itself wholly to the multiplication, or (less even) the aggregation, of bulbs. It never saw, nor conceived, such a thing as a tulip. Nay, boiled bulbs they might have been – glass bulbs – Prince Rupert's drops, consummated in powder (well, if it were glass-powder and not gunpowder), for any end or meaning the economists had in defining the laws of aggregation. We will try and get a clearer notion of them.

The best and simplest general type of capital is a well-made ploughshare. Now, if that ploughshare did nothing but beget other ploughshares, in a polypous manner, – however the great cluster of polypous plough might glitter in the sun, it would have lost its function of capital. It becomes true capital only by another kind of splendour, – when it is seen 'splendescere sulco,' to grow bright in the furrow; rather with diminution of its substance, than addition, by the noble friction.

And the true home question, to every capitalist and to every nation, is not, 'how many ploughs have you?' but, 'where are your furrows?' not – 'how quickly will this capital reproduce itself?' – but, 'what will it do during reproduction?' What substance will it furnish, good for life? what work construct, protective of life? if none, its own reproduction is useless – if worse than none, (for capital may destroy life as well as support it), its own reproduction is worse than useless; it is merely an advance from Tisiphone, on mortgage – not a profit by any means. . .

This being the real nature of capital, it follows that there are two kinds of true production, always going on in an active State: one of seed, and one of food; or production for the Ground, and for the Mouth; both of which are by covetous persons thought to be production only for the granary; whereas the function of the granary is but intermediate and conservative, fulfilled in distribution; else it ends in nothing but mildew, and nourishment of rats and worms. And since production for the Ground is only useful with future hope of harvest, all essential production is for the Mouth; and is finally measured by the mouth; hence, as I said above, consumption is the crown of production; and the wealth of a nation is only to be estimated by what it consumes.

The want of any clear sight of this fact is the capital error, issuing in rich interest and revenue of error among the political economists. Their minds are continually set on money-gain, not on mouth-gain; and they fall into every sort of net and snare, dazzled by the coin-glitter as birds by the fowler's glass; or rather (for there is not much else like birds in them) they are like children trying to jump on the heads of their own shadows; the money-gain being only the shadow of the true gain, which is humanity.

The final object of Political Economy, therefore, is to get good method of consumption, and great quantity of consumption: in other words, to use everything, and to use it nobly. Whether it be substance, service, or service perfecting substance. The most curious error in Mr Mill's entire work, (provided for him originally by Ricardo) [referring to John Stuart Mill and David Ricardo, pioneering utilitarian economists] is his endeavour to distinguish between direct and indirect service, and consequent assertion that a demand for commodities is not demand for labour. He distinguishes between labourers employed to lay out pleasure grounds, and to manufacture velvet; declaring that it makes material difference to the labouring classes in which of these two ways a capitalist spends his money; because the employ-ment of the gardeners is a demand for labour, but the purchase of velvet is not. Error colossal, as well as strange.

It will, indeed, make a difference to the labourer whether we bid him swing his scythe in the spring winds, or drive the loom in pestilential air. But, so far as his pocket is concerned, it makes to him absolutely no difference whether we order him to make green velvet, with seed and a scythe, or red velvet, with silk and scissors. Neither does it anywise concern him whether, when the velvet is made, we consume it by walking on it, or wearing it, so long as our consumption of it is wholly selfish. But if our consumption is to be in anywise unselfish, not only our mode of consuming the articles we require interests him, but also the kind of article we require with a view to consumption. As thus (returning for a moment to Mr Mill's great hardware theory): it matters, so far as the labourer's immediate profit is concerned, not an iron filing whether I employ him in growing a peach, or forging a bombshell; but my probable mode of consumption of those articles matters seriously.

Admit that it is to be in both cases 'unselfish', and the difference, to him, is final, whether when his child is ill, I walk into his cottage and give it the peach, or drop the shell down his chimney, and blow his roof off.

The worst of it, for the peasant, is, that the capitalist's consumption of the peach is apt to be selfish, and of the shell, distributive; but, in all cases, this is the broad and general fact, that on due catallactic commercial principles, somebody's roof must go off in fulfilment of the bomb's destiny. You may grow for your neighbour, at your liking, grapes or grape-shot; he will also, catallactically, grow grapes or grape-shot for you, and you will each reap what you have sown.

It is, therefore, the manner and issue of consumption which are the real tests of production. Production does not consist in things laboriously made, but in things serviceably consumable; and the question for the nation is not how much labour it employs, but how much life it produces. For as consumption is the end and aim of production, so life is the end and aim of consumption.

I left this question to the reader's thought two months ago, choosing rather that he should work it out for himself than have it sharply stated to him. But now, the ground being sufficiently broken (and the details into which the several questions, here opened, must lead us, being too complex for discussion in the pages of a periodical, so that I must pursue them elsewhere), I desire, in closing the series of introductory papers, to leave this one great fact clearly stated. THERE IS NO WEALTH BUT LIFE. Life, including all its powers of love, of joy, and of admiration.

That country is the richest which nourishes the greatest number of noble and happy human beings; that man is richest who, having perfected the functions of his own life to the utmost, has also the widest helpful influence, both personal, and by means of his possessions, over the lives of others.

A strange Political Economy; the only one, nevertheless, that ever was or can be: all Political Economy founded on self-interest being but the fulfilment of that which once brought schism into the Policy of angels, and ruin into the Economy of Heaven.

JOHN MAYNARD KEYNES

NATIONAL
SELF-SUFFICIENCY (1933)

The lecture known as 'National Self-Sufficiency', from which this passage is taken, was John Maynard Keynes (1883–1946) at his most revolutionary. He was giving the first Finlay Lecture at University College, Dublin, on 19 April 1933, in front of leading members of an Irish government threatening to erect major trade barriers against British goods during the Depression. Much to the discomfort of British ministers, Keynes' strictures against Irish protectionism were outweighed by other parts of the speech. A more general version of the speech was published a few months later in the *New Statesman*.

Keynes' followers turned a blind eye to the speech, as conventional economics has done ever since. But it reflected his deep interest in the arts, and as such was no aberration, and is increasingly quoted in small sound bites by advocates of local economics and local currencies.

Keynes does have a localization message, but he is not against what is now known as 'globalization'. Instead, he is making a plea that the right aspects of life should be global and the right aspects kept local. Read like that, Keynes is echoing Ruskin – and this underpins the argument of currency reformers before and since. Money has a proper place. If it tries to break out and becomes a global monster, threatening the most important things in life, then the system must be redesigned. We should, he said, tentatively and experimentally, be 'disobedient to the test of an accountant's profit'. That is precisely what many of the writers in this book – economists, engineers, scientists and social critics – are urging us to do.

*   *   *

There may be some financial calculation which shows it to be advantageous that my savings should be invested in whatever quarter of the habitable globe shows the greatest marginal efficiency of capital or the highest rate of interest. But experience is accumulating that remoteness between ownership and operation is an evil in the relations between men, likely or certain in the long run to set up strains and enmities which will bring to nought the financial calculation.

I sympathize therefore, with those who would minimize, rather than with those who would maximize, economic entanglement between nations. Ideas, knowledge, art, hospitality, travel – these are things which should of their nature be international. But let goods be homespun whenever it is reasonably and conveniently possible; and, above all, let finance be primarily national. . .

The 19th century carried to extravagant lengths the criterion of what one can call for short the financial results, as a test of the advisability of any course of action sponsored by private or collective action. The whole conduct of life was made into a sort of parody of an accountant's nightmare. Instead of using their vastly increased material and technical resources to build a wonder-city, they built slums; and they thought it right and advisable to build slums because slums, on the test of private enterprise, 'paid', whereas the wonder-city would, they thought, have been an act of foolish extravagance, which would, in the imbecile idiom of the financial fashion, have 'mortgaged the future'; though how the construction today of great and glorious works can impoverish the future no man can see until his mind is beset by false analogies from an irrelevant accountancy.

Even today we spend our time – half vainly, but also, I must admit, half successfully – in trying to persuade our countrymen that the nation as a whole will assuredly be richer if unemployed men and machines are used to build much needed houses than if they are supported in idleness. For the minds of this generation are still so beclouded by bogus calculations that they distrust conclusions which should be obvious, out of reliance on a system of financial accounting which casts doubt on whether such an operation will 'pay'. We have to remain poor because it does not 'pay' to be rich. We have to live in hovels, not because we cannot build palaces, but because we cannot 'afford' them.

The same rule of self-destructive financial calculation governs every walk of life. We destroy the beauty of the countryside because the unappropriated splendours of nature have not economic value. We are capable of shutting off the sun and the stars because they do not pay a dividend. London is one of the richest cities in the history of civilization, but it cannot 'afford' the highest standards of achievement of which its own living citizens are capable, because they do not 'pay'.

If I had the power today, I would surely set out to endow our capital cities with all the appurtenances of art and civilization on the highest standards. . .

convinced that what I could create I could afford – and believing that money thus spent would not only be better than any dole, but would make unnecessary any dole. For what we have spent on the dole in England since the war we could have made our cities the greatest works of man in the world.

Or again, we have until recently conceived it a moral duty to ruin the tillers of the soil and destroy the age-long human traditions attendant on husbandry if we could get a loaf of bread a tenth of a penny cheaper. There was nothing which it was not our duty to sacrifice to this Moloch and Mammon in one; for we faithfully believed that the worship of these monsters would overcome the evil of poverty and lead the next generation safely and comfortably, on the back of compound interest, into economic peace.

Today we suffer disillusion, not because we are poorer than we were – on the contrary even today we enjoy, in Great Britain at least, a higher standard of life than at any previous period – but because other values seem to have been sacrificed unnecessarily. For our economic system is not, in fact, enabling us to exploit to the utmost the possibilities for economic wealth afforded by the progress of our technique, but falls far short of this, leading us to feel that we might as well have used up the margin in more satisfying ways.

But once we allow ourselves to be disobedient to the test of an accountant's profit, we have begun to change our civilization. And we need to do so very warily, cautiously and self-consciously. For there is a wide field of human activity where we shall be wise to retain the usual pecuniary tests. It is the state, rather than the individual, which needs to change its criterion. It is the conception of the Chancellor of the Exchequer as the chairman of a sort of joint-stock company which has to be discarded. Now if the functions and purposes of the state are to be thus enlarged, the decisions as to what, broadly speaking, shall be produced within the nation and what shall be exchanged with abroad, must stand high amongst the objects of policy.

PART I *INTRODUCTION*

THE TROUBLE WITH MONEY: THERE ISN'T ENOUGH OF IT

Experience, daily observation, minute and repeated personal enquiry and examination, have made me familiar with the state of the labouring poor, and, sir, I challenge contradiction when I say that a labouring man in England with a wife and only three children, though he never lose a day's work, though he and his family be economical, frugal, and industrious in the most extensive sense of these words, is not now able to procure himself by his labour a single meal of meat from one end of the year unto the other.

WILLIAM COBBETT

To enjoy the products of Factory 1, the public must build Factory 2. To enjoy the products of Factory 2, the public must build Factory 3 and so on ad infinitum.

WILLIAM HIXSON, A MATTER OF INTEREST, 1993

'Upon these steps where we stand has spread a carpet for the royal feet of a foreign princess, the cost of whose lavish entertainment was taken from the public Treasury without the consent or approval of the people,' said Jacob Coxey, having led the 'Industrial Army' of protest to the steps of the White House in May 1894. 'Up these steps the lobbyists of trusts and corporations have passed unchallenged on their way to committee rooms, access to which we, the representatives of the toiling wealth-producers, have been denied.'

It sounds so contemporary, it makes a shiver go down the spine, but it was actually over a century ago, at the height of the great monetary campaigns of the 1890s. Coxey was arrested for trespass a few minutes after this address, and – although his words sound familiar – his campaign for more money in circulation is not. He comes from a half-forgotten tradition of money heresy which is planted firmly in the central issue of why there isn't enough money. Of course there clearly is enough money for some people – more than enough – but consistently, and especially when the economy contracts, there doesn't seem to be enough for everyone.

Moments when that happens, after wartime expansions or during great depressions, are dangerous periods of history. They can result in sudden changes to the status quo. Even the American Revolution began with a terrible shortage of cash and British vetos on printing any more of it (see Franklin, p25). A contraction of the money supply throws people out of work and, even for those who survive the iciest winds, it can represent a frustration of dreams. There are the human needs ready and waiting to be fulfilled; there are the people to fulfil them; there are raw materials available – but there is suddenly no cash to bring them all together.

For much of the 19th century, the main focus for anger was the banks and the banking system and their habit of taking fright and calling in their loans. In North America especially, the demand for more money in circulation – money based on silver, for example, rather than the much scarcer gold – generated almost half a century of political rage, especially among farmers and shopkeepers. But in the 20th century, economic heretics like Keynes and Douglas were searching for the source of the problem in the structure of the money system itself.

For Douglas and the Social Credit movement, it was a problem of the interest bound up with money in the way it is created as loans by the banks. But history lay with Keynes and his campaign for governments to borrow more money, on the usual basis, in order to bring people back into employment. The alternative, he said, was 'a peregrination of the catacombs – with a guttering candle'. We are healthy children, he urged, we should spend – and there Douglas and the other heretics featured here would have agreed.

By the end of the 20th century, with the world's leading economists putting the defeat of inflation by contracting the money supply at the top of their priorities, the argument that there wasn't enough money became familiar again. But the powerful voices that we should tackle the system as a whole haven't been nearly so evident.

Maybe they knew that tinkering with the dodgy financial system – now our life support system – was too dangerous to risk. Maybe they felt that of all cranks, monetary cranks were the most abominable. Either way, there has been a strange silence on the subject until recently, when local currencies and Social Credit suddenly became more fashionable again – together with the understanding (see Krehm, p47 and Robertson, p49) that the financial system makes it impossible to find a happy balance that satisfies everybody's needs.

Of course there is a kind of original sin in the form of the Quantity Theory of Money. More money means higher prices and vice versa. The interesting question for money heretics of the future is whether we can expand the money supply in some sections of the economy without expanding it in others, an issue that local currency pioneers have been trying to answer since the 1930s.

Given the paradoxes that money forces us to live with, the problem of too much money is actually closely related to the problem of too little money – one tends to lead to the other. But they are battle cries that emerge in different forms according to the economic background of the time. This isn't a comprehensive trawl through the literature of too much money, but it does give a glimpse of some of the various ways in which it has been tackled – right back to Benjamin Franklin at home in Philadelphia with his money printing machine.

We now live in a period where the state of too much money lives cheek by jowl with its opposite, and poverty in the midst of plenty has always been upsetting. That is so especially when large sections of the world's population, having abandoned their villages in search of wealth and opportunity in the cities, simply can't earn enough to keep themselves and their families in anything other than desperation, no matter how hard they work.

Is that a problem embedded in the design of money? If it is, there are precious few people debating the issue in public these days. Yet there is a traditional critique that says so: that the way money is created in the form of loans, and the interest that has to be paid on about 97 per cent of the money in the economy – everything except notes and coins – is at least partly to blame. At least it needs to be debated.

THE BENEFITS OF PRINTING PAPER MONEY (1729)

'About this time there was a cry among people for more paper money, only fifteen thousand pounds being extant in the province, and that soon to be sunk,' wrote Benjamin Franklin (1706–1790) in his autobiography immediately before the Revolution.

> *I was on the side of an addition, being persuaded that the first small sum struck in 1723 had done much good by increasing the trade, employment, and number of inhabitants in the province, since I now saw all the old houses inhabited and many new ones building: whereas I remembered well, that when I first walked about the streets of Philadelphia, eating my roll, I saw most of the houses. . . with bills on their doors 'To be let.'*

In 1729 at the age of just 23, Benjamin Franklin wrote a little book with a long title, *A Modest Inquiry into the Nature and Necessity of Paper Currency*. Two years later he had a go at printing some himself for the first time. It wasn't his idea — Americans had been experimenting with money since arriving on the *Mayflower*, and the first Western paper money emerged there in the Massachusetts Bay Colony in 1690. Franklin was an enthusiastic supporter of the idea. His *Pennsylvania Gazette* apologized for not appearing on time because he was 'with the Press, labouring for the publick Good, to make Money more plentiful'. This passage is taken from his *Modest Inquiry* and makes the case for more money in circulation as a way to spread wealth through society.

Printing money was, of course, one of the causes of the rift with the British government which led to the Declaration of Independence — but that, as Rudyard Kipling might say, is another story. . .

✳ ✳ ✳

There is a certain proportionate Quantity of Money requisite to carry on the Trade of a Country freely and currently; More than which would be of no Advantage in Trade, and Less, if much less, exceedingly detrimental to it. This leads us to the following general Considerations.

First, A great Want of Money in any Trading Country, occasions Interest to be at a very high Rate. And here it may be observed, that it is impossible by any Laws to restrain Men from giving and receiving exorbitant Interest, where Money is suitably scarce: For he that wants Money will find out Ways to give ten per cent when he cannot have it for less, altho' the Law forbids to take more than six per cent.

Now the Interest of Money being high is prejudicial to a Country in several Ways: It makes Land bear a low Price, because few Men will lay out their Money in Land, when they can make a much greater Profit by lending it out upon Interest: And much less will Men be inclined to venture their Money at Sea, when they can, without Risque or Hazard, have a great and certain Profit by keeping it at home; thus Trade is discouraged.

And if in two Neighbouring Countries the Traders of one, by Reason of a greater Plenty of Money, can borrow it to trade with at a lower Rate than the Traders of the other, they will infallibly have the Advantage, and get the greatest Part of that Trade into their own Hands; For he that trades with Money he hath borrowed at eight or ten per cent cannot hold Market with him that borrows his Money at six or four.

On the contrary, A plentiful Currency will occasion Interest to be low: And this will be an Inducement to many to lay out their Money in Lands, rather than put it out to Use, by which means Land will begin to rise in Value and bear a better Price: And at the same Time it will tend to enliven Trade exceedingly, because People will find more Profit in employing their Money that Way than in Usury; and many that understand Business very well, but have not a Stock sufficient of their own, will be encouraged to borrow Money; to trade with, when they can have it at a moderate Interest.

Secondly, Want of Money in a Country reduces the Price of that Part of its Produce which is used in Trade: Because Trade being discouraged by it as above, there is a much less Demand for that Produce. And this is another Reason why Land in such a Case will be low, especially where the Staple Commodity of the Country is the immediate Produce of the Land, because that Produce being low, fewer People find an Advantage in Husbandry, or the Improvement of Land. On the contrary, A Plentiful Currency will occasion the Trading Produce to bear a good Price. . .

Thirdly, Want of Money in a Country discourages Labouring and Handicrafts Men (which are the chief Strength and Support of a People) from coming to settle in it, and induces many that were settled to leave the

Country, and seek Entertainment and Employment in other Places, where they can be better paid. For what can be more disheartening to an industrious labouring Man, than this, that after he hath earned his Bread with the Sweat of his Brows, he must spend as much Time, and have near as much Fatigue in getting it, as he had to earn it. And nothing makes more bad Paymasters than a general Scarcity of Money.

And here again is a Third Reason for Land's bearing a low Price in such a Country, because Land always increases in Value in Proportion with the Increase of the People settling on it, there being so many more Buyers; and its Value will infallibly be diminished, if the Number of its Inhabitants diminish. On the contrary, A Plentiful Currency will encourage great Numbers of Labouring and Handicrafts Men to come and Settle in the Country, by the same Reason that a Want of it will discourage and drive them out. Now the more Inhabitants, the greater Demand for Land (as is said above) upon which it must necessarily rise in Value, and bear a better Price.

[N]ow the Value of House Rent rising, and Interest becoming low, many that in a Scarcity of Money practised Usury, will probably be more inclined to Building; which will likewise sensibly enliven Business in any Place; it being an Advantage not only to Brickmakers, Bricklayers, Masons, Carpenters, Joiners, Glaziers, and several other Trades immediately employed by Building, but likewise to Farmers, Brewers, Bakers, Taylors, Shoemakers, Shopkeepers, and in short to every one that they lay their Money out with.

Fourthly, Want of Money in such a Country as ours, occasions a greater Consumption of English and European Goods, in Proportion to the Number of the People, than there would otherwise be. Because Merchants and Traders by whom abundance of Artificers and labouring Men are employed, finding their other Affairs require what Money they can get into their hands, oblige those who work for them to take one half, or perhaps two thirds Goods in Pay. By this Means a greater Quantity of Goods are disposed of, and to a greater Value. . .

As a plentiful Currency will occasion a less Consumption of European Goods, in Proportion to the Number of the People, so it will be a means of making the Balance of our Trade more equal than it now is, if it does not give it in our Favour because our own Produce will be encouraged at the same Time. And it is to be observed, that tho' less Foreign Commodities are consumed in Proportion to the Number of People, yet this will be no Disadvantage to the Merchant, because the Number of People increasing, will occasion an increasing Demand of more Foreign Goods in the Whole.

ROBERT OWEN

LABOUR AS A STANDARD OF VALUE (1820)

Reading the laborious *Report to the County of Lanark*, getting on for two centuries since it was delivered on 1 May 1820, you are immediately struck by two thoughts. First, just what an old windbag the pioneer socialist Robert Owen (1771–1858) was, and second what a practical man he was.

Owen had bought the factory holdings in New Lanark in 1799 – and married the daughter of the vendor at the same time. His socialist experiments there proved the truth that still seems to elude so many employers today, that if you improve the conditions people work in, then productivity tends to go up.

This passage covers the turbulent period during and after the Napoleonic Wars, during which it was clear to Owen and others that gold wasn't an adequate basis for money – because there wasn't nearly enough of it. The government's solution from 1797 and 1815 was known as 'the restriction', and is very similar to the situation today: it abandoned the gold standard and allowed banks to issue almost as much paper currency as they wanted.

The trouble came after the Battle of Waterloo when the banks started to call in their loans – in response to the Bank of England calling in their own notes – and the money stock began to dwindle, prices collapsed and thousands of farms went bankrupt. The year before Owen was speaking, the pound then returned to the gold standard, with even more devastating effects and accompanied by terrible poverty.

So what should be the basis of the value of money, asks Owen? And here he comes up with the radical notion that it should be based on human labour. In Trier in Germany, Karl Marx was then just two years old, but the idea would later form the basis of his own thinking on Adam Smith's Labour Theory of Value – the idea that, as Smith put it, 'labour . . . is the real measure of the exchangeable value of all commodities'. It was a less successful notion for Robert Owen. Five years later, he bought 21,000 acres in Illinois for his utopian settlement New Harmony – intended to demonstrate that his 'natural standard of value' would work. Three years later, he sold out at a massive loss. His National Equitable Labour Exchange, based on the ideas of the 17th century Quaker John Bellers – he invented 'labour notes' – closed just two years after it opened in 1832.

*   *   *

One of the measures which he (the speaker) thus ventures to propose, *to let prosperity loose on the country* (if he may be allowed the expression), *is a change in the standard of value.*

It is true that in the civilized parts if the world gold and silver have been long used for this purpose; but these metals have been a mere artificial standard, and they have performed the office very imperfectly and inconveniently.

Their introduction as a standard of value altered the *intrinsic* values of all things into *artificial* values; and, in consequence, they have materially retarded the general improvement of society. So much so, indeed, that, in this sense, it may well be said, 'Money is the root of all evil.' It is fortunate for society that these metals cannot longer perform that task which ignorance assigned to them. The rapid increase of wealth, which extraordinary scientific improvements had been the means of producing in this country prior to 1797, imposed upon the Legislature in that year an overwhelming necessity to declare virtually by Act of Parliament that gold ceased to be the British standard of value. Experience then proved that gold and silver could no longer practically represent the increased wealth related by British industry aided by its scientific improvements.

A temporary expedient was thought of and adopted, and Bank of England paper became the British legal standard of value – a convincing proof that society may make any artificial substance, whether possessing intrinsic worth or not, a legal standard of value.

It soon appeared, however, that the adoption of this new artificial standard was attended with extreme danger, because it placed the prosperity and well-being of the community at the mercy of a trading company, which, although highly respectable in that capacity, was itself, in a great degree, ignorant of the nature of the mighty machine which it wielded. The Legislature, with almost one voice, demanded that this monopoly of the standard of value should cease. But it was wholly unprepared with a remedy. The expedient adopted was to make preparations for an attempt to return to the former artificial standard, which, in 1797, was proved by experience to be inadequate to represent the existing wealth of the British Empire, and which was, of course, still more inadequate to the purpose when that wealth and the means of adding to it had been in the interim increased to an incalculable extent.

This impolitic measure involved the Government in the most formidable difficulties, and plunged the country into poverty, discontent, and danger.

Seeing the distress which a slight progress towards the fulfilment of this measure has already occasioned, by the unparalleled depression of agriculture, commerce, and manufactures, and the consequent almost total annihilation of the value of labour, it is to be hoped that the Government and the Legislature, and the enlightened and reasonable part of society, will pause while they are about to precipitate the prosperity and safety of themselves and the country.

The Meeting may now justly ask of the Reporter, what remedy he has to offer, and what standard of value he proposes to substitute for gold and silver? . . .

To understand the subject on which your Reporter is now about to enter requires much profound study of the whole circle of political economy. A knowledge of some of its parts, with ignorance of the remainder, will be found to be most injurious to the practical statesman; and it is owing to this cause, perhaps, more than to any other, that the world has been so wretchedly governed; for the object of this science is to direct how the whole faculties of men may be most advantageously applied; whereas those powers have been combined, hitherto, chiefly to retard the improvements of society.

Your Reporter, then, after deeply studying these subjects, practically and theoretically, for a period exceeding 30 years, and during which his practice without a single exception has confirmed the theory which practice first suggested, now ventures to state, as one of the results of this study and experience, THAT THE NATURAL STANDARD OF VALUE IS, IN PRINCIPLE, HUMAN LABOUR, OR THE COMBINED MANUAL AND MENTAL POWERS OF MEN CALLED INTO ACTION.

And that it would be highly beneficial, and has now become absolutely necessary, to reduce this principle into immediate practice.

IGNATIUS DONNELLY

THE POPULISTS (1892)

Thanks to a financial panic and declining farm prices, the 1870s in the USA were tough times for farmers and small business people, especially in the Midwest – who blamed the currency policies of bankers on the east coast for their predicament. The Greenback Party – backing President Lincoln's paper money issued during the American Civil War – had failed, but had been replaced by a range of farmers' alliances in the 1880s. Their campaign came together in Cincinnati in 1891, which led the following year to the formation of the Populist Party, linking Southern and Midwestern farmers – and campaigning for what had become known as the Free Silver Movement.

The problem with the gold standard of the day, again, was that the amount of money in circulation was limited by the government's gold reserves. Free silver supporters wanted them to use silver as a standard as well, which could reflate the money supply. It was a concept known as 'bimetallism'.

This passage is taken from the preamble to *The Omaha Platform*, the introductory manifesto for the party agreed on 4 July 1892, and was composed by Ignatius Donnelly (1831–1901), a former Republican Congressman from Minnesota who – as well as writing early books about Atlantis and the theory that Shakespeare was actually written by Francis Bacon – had become a leading figure in the party.

This passage also provided the basis for thinking for a political party founded to campaign for silver money. Apart from the central issue of silver, which has disappeared from polite political discourse, the Populist platform might also sound very familiar to modern campaigners against globalization.

✳   ✳   ✳

The conditions which surround us best justify our cooperation; we meet in the midst of a nation brought to the verge of moral, political and material ruin. Corruption dominates the ballot box, the legislatures, the Congress, and touches even the ermine of the bench. The people are demoralized; most of the states have been compelled to isolate the voters at the polling places to prevent universal intimidation or bribery. The newspapers are largely subsidized or muzzled; public opinion silenced; business prostrate, our homes covered with mortgages, labour impoverished and the land concentrating in the hands of capitalists. The urban workmen are denied the right of organization for self-protection; imported pauperized labour beats down their labour; a hireling standing army, unrecognized by our laws, is established to shoot them down, and they are rapidly disintegrating to European conditions.

The fruits of the toil of millions are boldly stolen to build up colossal fortunes, unprecedented in the history of the world, while their possessors despise the republic and endanger liberty. From the same prolific womb of governmental injustice we breed the two great classes – tramps and millionaires.

The national power to create money is appropriated to enrich bond-holders; a vast public debt payable in legal-tender currency has been funded into gold-bearing bonds, thereby adding millions to the burdens of the people. . .

We have witnessed for more than a quarter of a century the struggles of the two great political parties for power and plunder, while grievous wrongs have been inflicted upon the suffering people. We charge that the controlling influences dominating both these parties have permitted the existing dreadful conditions to develop without serious effort to prevent or restrain them.

Neither do they now promise us any substantial reform. They have agreed together to ignore, in the coming campaign, every issue but one. They propose to drown the outcries of a plundered people with the uproar of a sham battle over the tariff, so that capitalists, corporations, national banks, rings, trusts, watered stock, the demonetization of silver, and the oppression of usurers, may all be lost sight of. They propose to sacrifice our homes, lives, and children on the altar of mammon; to destroy the multitude in order to secure corruption funds from the millionaires.

Assembled on the anniversary of the birthday of the nation, and filled with the spirit of the grand general and chieftain who established our independence, we seek to restore the government of the Republic to the hands of the 'plain people', with which class it originated. We assert our purposes to be identical with the purposes of the National Constitution; to form a more perfect union and establish justice, insure domestic tranquillity, provide for the common defence, promote the general welfare, and secure the blessings of liberty for ourselves and our posterity. . .

WILLIAM JENNINGS BRYAN

CRUCIFYING MANKIND

(1896)

When the Democrats adopted bimetallism, it was all up for the Populist Party. It was a crucial moment in the campaign, when the Democrat nominee for the presidency, 36-year-old William Jennings Bryan (1860–1925), made one of the most famous speeches of the 19th century at the party convention on 8 July 1896.

When he reached the crescendo about crucifying 'mankind upon a cross of gold,' Bryan slowly lowered his arms from the air until they were outstretched into the shape of a cross. It was an electrifying moment – but not so electrifying that he actually won the presidency.

Bryan lost twice to McKinley and once more to Taft before throwing in the towel. He ended his life as the lawyer on the wrong side of the Tennessee Monkey Trial nearly three decades later. Bimetallism lost out as a worldwide political creed whenever anybody discovered new gold deposits – making it a little less scarce – and Bryan's era was no exception. The Gold Standard Act of 1900, combined with an increase in world gold production, was enough to end the argument in mainstream US politics.

✤   ✤   ✤

I call your attention to the fact that some of the very people who are in this convention today and who tell us that we ought to declare in favour of international bimetallism – thereby declaring that the gold standard is wrong and that the principle of bimetallism is better – these very people four months ago were open and avowed advocates of the gold standard, and were then telling us that we could not legislate two metals together, even with the aid of all the world.

If the gold standard is a good thing, we ought to declare in favour of its retention and not in favour of abandoning it; and if the gold standard is a bad thing why should we wait until other nations are willing to help us to let go?

Here is the line of battle, and we care not upon which issue they force the fight; we are prepared to meet them on either issue or on both. If they tell us that the gold standard is the standard of civilization, we reply to them that this, the most enlightened of all the nations of the earth, has never declared for a gold standard and that both the great parties this year are declaring against it. If the gold standard is the standard of civilization, why, my friends, should we not have it?

If they come to meet us on that issue we can present the history of our nation. More than that; we can tell them that they will search the pages of history in vain to find a single instance where the common people of any land have ever declared themselves in favour of the gold standard. They can find where the holders of the fixed investments have declared for a gold standard, but not where the masses have.

Mr Carlyle said in 1878 that this was a struggle between 'the idle holders of idle capital' and 'the struggling masses, who produce the wealth and pay the taxes of the country' and, my friends, the question we are to decide is: Upon which side will the Democratic party fight; upon the side of 'the idle holders of idle capital' or upon the side of 'the struggling masses?' That is the question which the party must answer first, and then it must be answered by each individual hereafter.

The sympathies of the Democratic party, as shown by the platform, are on the side of the struggling masses who have ever been the foundation of the Democratic party. There are two ideas of government. There are those who believe that, if you will only legislate to make the well-to-do prosperous, their prosperity will leak through on those below. The Democratic idea, however, has been that if you legislate to make the masses prosperous, their prosperity will find its way up through every class which rests upon them.

You come to us and tell us that the great cities are in favour of the gold standard; we reply that the great cities rest upon our broad and fertile prairies. Burn down your cities and leave our farms, and your cities will spring up again as if by magic; but destroy our farms and the grass will grow in the streets of every city in the country.

My friends, we declare that this nation is able to legislate for its own people on every question, without waiting for the aid or consent of any other nation on earth; and upon that issue we expect to carry every State in the Union. I shall not slander the inhabitants of the fair State of Massachusetts nor the inhabitants of the State of New York by saying that, when they are confronted with the opposition, they will declare that this nation is not able to attend to its own business. It is the issue of 1776 over again.

Our ancestors, when but three millions in number, had the courage to declare their political independence of every other nation; shall we, their descendants, when we have grown to seventy millions, declare that we are less independent than our forefathers? No, my friends, that will never be the verdict of our people.

Therefore, we care not upon what lines the battle is fought. If they say bimetallism is good, but that we cannot have it until other nations help us, we reply that, instead of having a gold standard because England has, we will restore bimetallism, and then let England have bimetallism because the United States has it.

If they dare to come out in the open field and defend the gold standard as a good thing, we will fight them to the uttermost. Having behind us the producing masses of this nation and the world, supported by the commercial interests, the labouring interests, and the toilers everywhere, we will answer their demand for a gold standard by saying to them: You shall not press down upon the brow of labour this crown of thorns, you shall not crucify mankind upon a cross of gold.

L FRANK BAUM

THE WIZARD OF OZ (1900)

What does the Wizard of Oz have to do with all of this? The answer lies in depression-hit Chicago, where the author Frank Baum (1856–1919) moved in 1891, steeped in Populist Party politics and taking part in regular torchlight processions in support of William Jennings Bryan.

Baum wasn't really a political activist, but he did feel strongly on the issue. This fairy tale, *The Wonderful Wizard of Oz*, from which this passage is taken, was published during Bryan's second abortive bid for the presidency. And hidden away is a subtle tract for more money.

Dorothy sets out on the Yellow Brick Road wearing the Witch of the East's magic silver shoes (they were red in the Judy Garland film) – shoes that neither she, nor the Witch of the North, nor the Munchkins understand the power of: 'All you have to do is knock the heels together three times and command the shoes to carry you wherever you wish to go,' she is told at the end. The poor residents of Oz were required to wear green-tinted glasses fastened by gold buckles.

The journey is a kind of folk memory of the 1894 march of Coxey's Army, a group of unemployed demanding the public issue of 500 million greenbacks, which ended with Coxey himself arrested for trespass on the steps of the White House. Oz, of course, was the well-known measure of gold – the abbreviation for ounces – and the Wonderful Wizard, the personification of the gold standard, is finally revealed as a fraud.

* * *

Promptly at nine o'clock the next morning the green-whiskered soldier came to them, and four minutes later they all went into the Throne Room of the Great Oz. Of course each one of them expected to see the Wizard in the shape he had taken before, and all were greatly surprised when they looked about and saw no one at all in the room. They kept close to the door and closer to one another, for the stillness of the empty room was more dreadful than any of the forms they had seen Oz take.

Presently they heard a solemn Voice, that seemed to come from somewhere near the top of the great dome, and it said: 'I am Oz, the Great and Terrible. Why do you seek me?'

They looked again in every part of the room, and then, seeing no one, Dorothy asked, 'Where are you?'

'I am everywhere,' answered the Voice, 'but to the eyes of common mortals I am invisible. I will now seat myself upon my throne, that you may converse with me.' Indeed, the Voice seemed just then to come straight from the throne itself; so they walked toward it and stood in a row while Dorothy said: 'We have come to claim our promise, O Oz.'

'What promise?' asked Oz.

'You promised to send me back to Kansas when the Wicked Witch was destroyed,' said the girl.

'And you promised to give me brains,' said the Scarecrow.

'And you promised to give me a heart,' said the Tin Woodman.

'And you promised to give me courage,' said the Cowardly Lion.

'Is the Wicked Witch really destroyed?' asked the Voice, and Dorothy thought it trembled a little.

"Yes,' she answered, 'I melted her with a bucket of water.'

'Dear me,' said the Voice, 'how sudden! Well, come to me tomorrow, for I must have time to think it over.'

'You've had plenty of time already,' said the Tin Woodman angrily.

'We shan't wait a day longer,' said the Scarecrow.

'You must keep your promises to us!' exclaimed Dorothy.

The Lion thought it might be as well to frighten the Wizard, so he gave a large, loud roar, which was so fierce and dreadful that Toto jumped away from him in alarm and tipped over the screen that stood in a corner. As it fell with a crash they looked that way, and the next moment all of them were filled with wonder. For they saw, standing in just the spot the screen had hidden, a little old man, with a bald head and a wrinkled face, who seemed to be as much surprised as they were.

The Tin Woodman, raising his axe, rushed toward the little man and cried out, 'Who are you?'

'I am Oz, the Great and Terrible,' said the little man, in a trembling voice. 'But don't strike me – please don't – and I'll do anything you want me to.'

Our friends looked at him in surprise and dismay. 'I thought Oz was a great Head,' said Dorothy. 'And I thought Oz was a lovely Lady,' said the Scarecrow. 'And I thought Oz was a terrible Beast,' said the Tin Woodman. 'And I thought Oz was a Ball of Fire,' exclaimed the Lion.

'No, you are all wrong,' said the little man meekly. 'I have been making believe.'

'Making believe!' cried Dorothy. 'Are you not a Great Wizard?'

'Hush, my dear,' he said. 'Don't speak so loud, or you will be overheard – and I should be ruined. I'm supposed to be a Great Wizard.'

'And aren't you?' she asked.

'Not a bit of it, my dear; I'm just a common man.'

'You're more than that,' said the Scarecrow, in a grieved tone; 'you're a humbug.'

'Exactly so!' declared the little man, rubbing his hands together as if it pleased him. 'I am a humbug.'

'But this is terrible,' said the Tin Woodman. 'How shall I ever get my heart?'

'Or I my courage?' asked the Lion.

'Or I my brains?' wailed the Scarecrow, wiping the tears from his eyes with his coat sleeve.

'My dear friends,' said Oz, 'I pray you not to speak of these little things. Think of me, and the terrible trouble I'm in at being found out.'

'Doesn't anyone else know you're a humbug?' asked Dorothy.

'No one knows it but you four – and myself,' replied Oz. 'I have fooled everyone so long that I thought I should never be found out. It was a great mistake my ever letting you into the Throne Room. Usually I will not see even my subjects, and so they believe I am something terrible.'

'But, I don't understand,' said Dorothy, in bewilderment. 'How was it that you appeared to me as a great Head?'

'That was one of my tricks,' answered Oz. 'Step this way, please, and I will tell you all about it.'

He led the way to a small chamber in the rear of the Throne Room, and they all followed him. He pointed to one corner, in which lay the great Head, made out of many thicknesses of paper, and with a carefully painted face.

'This I hung from the ceiling by a wire,' said Oz. 'I stood behind the screen and pulled a thread, to make the eyes move and the mouth open.'

But how about the voice?' she inquired.

'Oh, I am a ventriloquist,' said the little man. 'I can throw the sound of my voice wherever I wish, so that you thought it was coming out of the Head. Here are the other things I used to deceive you.' He showed the Scarecrow the dress and the mask he had worn when he seemed to be the lovely Lady. And the Tin Woodman saw that his terrible Beast was nothing but a lot of skins, sewn together, with slats to keep their sides out. As for the Ball of Fire, the false Wizard had hung that also from the ceiling. It was really a ball of cotton, but when oil was poured upon it the ball burned fiercely.

'Really,' said the Scarecrow, 'you ought to be ashamed of yourself for being such a humbug.'

SILVIO GESELL

WHY MONEY HAS TO RUST

(1 9 1 3)

Silvio Gesell (1862–1930) is a fascinating figure in alternative economics. Keynes
approved of him, his influence is still being felt, and his insight followed directly
from his experience running an export business in Argentina during the economic
instability of the 1880s.

Gesell was born near the German–Luxembourg border, and after his South
American experience retired to Switzerland to be a farmer and formed what he
called the Free Economy Movement to further his economic ideas – which were
based on the idea that the way money could attract interest by staying idle made it
chronically scarce (see p233).

That was an almost mainstream insight in comparison to his solution. Gesell
wanted money to have a negative interest rate. He wanted it to 'rust', just as money
would have done in its 'natural' state when it was represented by stocks of grain or
other foodstuffs. And in 1919, he was offered the chance to test it out, when he
was asked to be Finance Minister in the revolutionary Munich government.

Unfortunately for Gesell, the government was forced out by local communists
before he could achieve anything: he was arrested by reactionaries, tried for treason
and eventually acquitted. It was left to the next generation to put his ideas into
practice (see Worgl, Part VII, p236).

This passage is taken from his book *The Natural Economic Order* and explains why
he wants to end the control that speculators have over money, so that it can become
more available.

*   *   *

In short, our worthy experts when considering the currency question forgot
the goods – for the exchange of which the currency exists. They improved
money exclusively from the point of view of the holder, with the result that
it became worthless as a medium of exchange. The purpose of money
evidently did not concern them, and thus as Proudhon put it, they forged 'a
bolt instead of a key for the gates of the market'.

The present form of money repels goods, instead of attracting them. People do, of course, buy goods, but only when they are hungry or when it is profitable. As a consumer everyone buys the minimum. No one desires to have stores, in planning a dwelling house the architect never includes a storeroom. If every householder were today presented with a filled storeroom, by tomorrow these stores would be back on the market. Money is the thing people want to own, although everybody knows that this wish cannot be fulfilled, since the money of all mutually neutralizes itself.

The possession of a gold coin is incontestably more agreeable than the possession of goods. The 'others' have the goods. But who, economically speaking, are these others? We ourselves are these others; all of us who produce the goods. So if, as buyers, we reject the products of the others, we really all reject our own products. If we did not prefer money to the products of our fellows, if instead of the desired yet unattainable reserve of money, we built a storeroom and filled it with the products of our fellows, we should not be obliged to have our own products offered for sale in expensive shops when they are, to a great extent, consumed by the cost of commerce. We should have a rapid and cheap turnover of goods.

Gold does not harmonize with the character of our goods. Gold and straw, gold and petrol, gold and guano, gold and bricks, gold and iron, gold and hides! Only a wild fancy, a monstrous hallucination, only the doctrine of 'value' can bridge the gulf. Commodities in general, straw, petrol, guano and the rest can be safely exchanged only when everyone is indifferent as to whether he possesses money or goods, and that is possible only if money is afflicted with all the defects inherent in our products. That is obvious. Our goods rot, decay, break out, rust, so only if money has equally disagreeable, loss-involving properties can it effect exchange rapidly, securely and cheaply. For such money can never, on any account, be preferred by anyone to goods.

Only money that goes out of date like a newspaper, rots like potatoes, rusts like iron, evaporates like ether is capable of standing the test as an instrument for the exchange of potatoes, newspapers, iron and ether. For such money is not preferred to goods either by the purchaser or the seller. We then part with our goods for money only because we need the money as a means of exchange, not because we expect an advantage from the possession of money.

So we must make money worse as a commodity if we wish to make it better as a medium of exchange.

As the owners of goods are always in a hurry for exchange, it is only just and fair that the owners of money, which is the medium of exchange, should also be in a hurry. Supply is under an immediate, inherent constraint; therefore demand must be placed under the same constraint.

Supply is something detached from the will of owners of goods, so demand must become something detached from the will of owners of money.

If we decide to abolish the privileges enjoyed by the owners of money and to subject demand to the compulsion to which supply is by nature subject, we remove all the anomalies of the traditional form of money and compel demand to appear regularly in the market, independently of political, economic, or natural conditions. Above all, the calculations of speculators, the opinions or caprices of capitalists and bankers will no longer influence demand. What we term the 'tone of the Stock-Exchange' will be a thing of the past. As the law of gravity knows no moods, so the law of demand will know of none. Neither the fear of loss nor the expectation of profit will be able to retard or accelerate demand.

C H DOUGLAS

Purchasing Power (1931)

Clifford Hugh Douglas (1879–1952), known rather disconcertingly as 'Major Douglas', was the man behind the Social Credit movement which caused such a stir between the wars in the last century. Douglas wasn't a fluent writer, and his ideas were consistently ignored by mainstream politicians and economists, yet he could fill stadiums of supporters around the world, and Social Credit administrations were elected in no less than two Canadian provinces.

Social Credit grew out of Guild Socialism, a romantic amalgam of medievalism and trade unionism pioneered by the journalist A R Orage in the magazine *The New Age*, the forerunner of the *New Statesman*. Orage serialized Douglas' first book *Economic Democracy* in 1919, warning that the financial system is unstable because it is completely dependent on new lending by banks and on constant growth.

The key point was the problem he identified, which came to him as a revelation while he was working as an engineer at the aircraft factories in Farnborough – for some reason, many of those who want to change the fundamental creation of money have been engineers. The problem is that companies need to cover their costs, pay the interest on the money needed to set up in the first place, pay for the raw materials and pay their staff. The money they pay on their loans just goes back to the banks for what he calls 'extinction'. Only the money paid in wages is available to actually buy the company's products – and it isn't enough.

Douglas called this the A+B Theorem. Imagine this problem extrapolated across all companies – there is then a fundamental mismatch. There is always a tendency for the money to be too scarce – a fatal gap between purchasing power and prices – and only constant 'growth' can keep the machinery of the economy turning.

More about the remedy proposed by Social Credit later (see p124). The A+B Theorem flew in the face of the classic economic dictum known as Say's Law, which said that producing things automatically generated the income to pay for them – and that was enough to earn the dismissal of conventional economics.

Douglas campaigned against Keynes and the idea of employment as the solution to what he saw as a much more fundamental problem – the way that money was created by banks, carrying interest. Keynes – who also rejected Say's Law – was mildly interested in his ideas, but regally dismissed him as 'having scarcely established an equal claim to rank – a private, perhaps, but not a major in the brave army of heretics – with Mandeville, Malthus, Gesell and Hobson'.

As the years went by, Douglas became increasingly enraged by the way the establishment failed to engage with his claims – even after the 1929–30 Macmillan Committee was set up to examine the workings of the financial system and listened to his evidence. For Douglas at the end of his life, the world was in the grip of an international conspiracy of bankers. And for some reason, those who believe in such conspiracies are usually just a hairsbreadth away from believing it to be a Jewish conspiracy too – and the campaign fizzled out in an unpleasant mix of anti-Semitism and paranoia. While other groups who believed in strong central state paraded on the streets – Hitler's Brownshirts, Mosley's Blackshirts, even the Blueshirts of Ireland – Social Crediters formed themselves into a political party known as the Greenshirts.

It has taken half a century for people to forget that mistake and there is now a revival of interest in Social Credit, thanks to the efforts of academics like Frances Hutchinson and polemicists like Michael Rowbotham (see Part III, p108) – and there is clearly a great deal we can still learn from Douglas' insights. But like many monetary 'heretics' at the time, Douglas had rather a concrete writing style. The future Labour leader Hugh Gaitskell claimed it helped him say his ideas had never been refuted. This passage is taken from his 1931 book *The Monopoly of Credit* (Douglas, 4th edition, 1979) and it puts his famous A+B Theorem into slightly simpler terms.

✳   ✳   ✳

Let us imagine a capitalist to own a certain piece of land, on which is a house, and a building containing the necessary machinery for preparing, spinning, and weaving linen, and that the land is capable of growing in addition to flax, all the food necessary to maintain a man. Let us further imagine that the capitalist in the first place allows a man to live free of all payment in the house and to have the use of all the foodstuffs that he grows on condition that he also grows, spins, and weaves a certain amount of linen for the capitalist. Let us further imagine that after a time this arrangement is altered by the payment to the man of £1 a week for the work on the linen business, but that this £1 is taken back each week as rent for the house and payment for the foodstuffs.

Let us now imagine that from the time the flax is picked to the time that the linen is delivered to the capitalist, a period of six weeks elapses. Obviously the cost of the linen must be £6, and this will be the price, plus profit, which the capitalist would place upon it. Quite obviously only one-sixth of the purchasing power necessary to buy the linen is now available, although 'at some time or other' all the £6 has been distributed. It should also be noticed that the arrangement is a perfectly equitable arrangement. The employee obtains definite return for his services in the form of bed, board, and clothes, which quite probably he might not have been able to obtain had not the knowledge and organization of the capitalist brought together housing, flax, food, and machinery. In other words, the problem disclosed is not a moral problem, it is an arithmetical problem.

Let us now imagine that half of the employee's time is devoted to making a machine which will do all the work of preparing and manufacturing linen, and that the manufacture of this machine takes twelve weeks. We may therefore say that the machine costs £6, the total value of the production of machine and flax being still £1 per week. At the end of this period the machine is substituted for the man, the machine being driven, we suppose, by the burning of the food which was previously consumed by the man, and the machine being housed in the house previously occupied by the man, and being automatic.

The capitalist will be justified in saying that costs of the operation of the machine is £1 per week as before, and if there is any wear, he will also be justified in allocating the cost of this wear to the cost of the linen. It should be noticed, however, that he will now not distribute any money at all, since it is obviously no use offering a £1 note a week to a machine. He will merely allocate this cost, and once again the allocation will be perfectly fair and proper, but no one will be able to pay the price, because no one has received any money.

In the modern industrial system, this process can be identified easily in the form of machine charges. For instance, a modern stamping plant may require to add 600 per cent to its labour charges to cover its machine charges, this sum not being in any true sense profit. In such a case, for every £1 expended in a given period in wages, £6, making £7 in all, would be carried forward into prices. Although this is an extreme case, the constant, and in one sense desirable, tendency is for direct charges to decrease and for indirect charges to increase as a result of the replacement of human labour by machinery. . .

The essential point is that when a given sum of money leaves the consumer on its journey back to the point of origin in the bank it is on its way to extinction. If the extinction takes place before the extinction of the price value created during its journey *from* the bank, then each such operation produces a corresponding disequilibrium between money and prices. For these causes and others of a similar character, it seems to me quite beyond argument that the production of such a quantity of intermediate products, including plant, machinery, buildings, and so forth, as is physically necessary to maintain a given quantity of consumable products, will not provide a purchasing power sufficient to buy these consumable products. This would be true even if prices and costs were identical. But since prices can and do rise much above costs, additional purchasing power from intermediate production is rapidly absorbed.

WILLIAM KREHM

BULGARIAN TENORS AND CENTRAL BANKERS (1989)

Something about Canada has made it a hotbed of monetary heresy. Canadians elected two Social Credit administrations, in Alberta and British Columbia. They developed green dollars and LETS (see Linton, Part VII, p263). Money and its creation has been central to political dialogue in Canada for a century or more. So perhaps it isn't surprising that one of the most trenchant critics of the current accepted way of doing things should start there.

The Committee on Monetary and Economic Reform (COMER) emerged in the mid-1980s to look at the way the world's central banks had swallowed the 'monetarist' ideas of Milton Friedman – and were almost universally raising interest rates to bring down inflation, as if it was the only economic issue remaining in the world.

Of course, they have largely succeeded in the rich industrialized countries, but the cost of making money scarce was felt primarily by the poor rather as it was in England after the Napoleonic War. Yet strangely enough, the wealthy in society managed at the same time to create a stock-market boom that gave the impression that money was actually widely available.

When the new governor of the Bank of Canada, John Crow, was appointed in 1988, he proclaimed that 'zero inflation' was his central objective. COMER, under the leadership of Waterloo University economics professor John Hotson, launched their newsletter *Economic Reform* in response. This article by William Krehm (1913–), who took over the newsletter from Hotson shortly after it began, is an early example of the COMER style.

* * *

I recall a lecture some time ago by the great accompanist Gerald Moore. He told of his experience with a famous Bulgarian tenor. Having some discomfort with the high notes of a song they were performing, he turned to Moore and asked, 'Could you transpose it down half a tone?'

Moore obliged. But then the tenor was in trouble with the low notes. After a moment in deep thought, he surfaced with a solution, 'Don't you have anything in between?' As I follow the efforts of our central bank, I am tempted to believe that our tenor abandoned singing to become a central banker.

For the Bank of Canada, too, has been trying to find something 'in between'. Last February Governor John Crow proclaimed that 'any degree of inflation is unacceptable'. That is a pretty tight groove, when you consider that not once in the past 35 years, that is since our mixed economy came into existence, have we experienced a year when our prices have not moved forward – slowly or fast. The Governor then has little to base himself on in his search of those green pastures between C and B.

This process of 'fine tuning' with a complete disregard of scales must lead to ever more bizarre results. This was evident from the stock market crash of October 1987. Repeatedly before it happened, the Bank upped the bank rate – because Ottawa and some of the provinces had raised some of their taxes. And when the Governor increased the rates once too much, the market not only fell – but collapsed. Immediately the Bank of Canada – along with the US Fed – pulled back a full point and a half.

Although the Bank has subsequently dictated reams of self-congratulation about its vigilance in 'heading off inflation', a few cynics ask why it had to bring the roof down on our heads, before pulling rates back a per cent and a half. Couldn't it have left them where they were in the first place?

Worse yet: Why is it shoving them up again?

JAMES ROBERTSON

Chickenfood and Horsefood (1992)

William Krehm and COMER were arguing that it was impossible to find a mid-point between too much and too little money, because getting the balance right for the rich – as central banks tend to do – will starve the poorest of cash. Their simile of the Bulgarian tenor has a parallel in James Robertson's horses and chickens in this article, first published during the political fall-out from the Maastricht treaty in 1992. The point is the same, but the argument ends up somewhere else – looking ahead to ideas of multiple currencies (see Part VII).

Robertson (1928–) is himself a fascinating study in heresy. He was a member of Harold Macmillan's staff in Downing Street when he was Prime Minister, and in fact drafted the famous 'Winds of Change' speech during Macmillan's critical African tour. But via his directorship of inter-bank research in the 1970s, he emerged as one of Britain's foremost alternative economists, and was co-founder of the UK answer to COMER, the New Economics Foundation.

This passage comes from an article in their magazine *New Economics* about Stop-Go economics. It is included as a way of demonstrating that the argument that there's too little money is inextricably related to the argument that there's too much.

❊   ❊   ❊

Here is a fable. Once upon a place it is taken for granted that chickens must be allowed to feed only from the grains of corn they can find in horse manure. The result is that to give their chickens enough to eat, farmers must give their horses too much. And when they stop giving their horses too much, their chickens get too little.

Farm management policy is in a stop-go trap, for ever swithering between wasting corn on horses already too fat, and allowing too little food to chickens already too thin. From time to time farming experts come up with 'supply side' proposals to alter the metabolism of horses. But these miss the point.

When the food available to chickens depends on the amount given to horses, it is impossible for both to get the right amount.

Eventually one farmer's son secretly allows his father's chicks to forage for food that has not 'trickled down' through horses. Horses and chickens both flourish on that farm. The experts suggest all sorts of far-fetched reasons why. But eventually the truth comes out. Reluctantly the conventional wisdom shifts.

A single-level system of control, determining the food supplied to chickens by what is given to horses, is not after all a sensible system of farm management. Decoupling control of chickenfood from control of horsefood gives better results all round.

The point is not simply that much conventional economic wisdom is, in the American idiom, 'horseshit' — though that is undoubtedly the case. The point is that post-modern economic polices must disconnect dependencies that gum up the workings of the economic system, not reinforce them.

In the Maastricht context this means that, instead of a centralized economic management at a single level, whether European or national, only a multi-level system — the levels being European and national and also local, and perhaps eventually global — will provide a framework of effective control that encourages freedom and flexibility.

There is no doubt that some form of further European economic integration is both desirable and inevitable. But it must take the form of a multi-level, not a unitary, system. Instead of arguing whether or not national currencies should be replaced by a *single* European currency which everyone would have to use, we must work for a *common* European currency which can be used by those who wish to use it.

PART II INTRODUCTION
THE TROUBLE WITH MONEY: THERE'S TOO MUCH OF IT

Lenin. . . declared that the best way to destroy the Capitalist system was to debauch the currency. . . Lenin was certainly right. There is no subtler, no surer way of overturning the existing basis of society.

JOHN MAYNARD KEYNES

My father's generation grew up with certain beliefs. One of those beliefs is that the amount of money one earns is a rough guide to one's contribution to the welfare and prosperity of society. It took watching his son being paid 225 grand at the age of twenty-seven, after two years on the job, to shake his faith in money.

MICHAEL LEWIS, LIAR'S POKER, *DESCRIBING HIS LIFE ON WALL STREET DURING THE 1980S' BOOM*

The problem with money isn't just that there isn't enough of it. There is another, possibly related, radical position to take – as many reformers have done over the centuries: the idea that there is too much cash, and it is plummeting society into an impoverished world where nothing is real and nothing is reliable. Those who have used this critique of the money system tend to be distinguished from those who thought there wasn't enough money by the boom times or the inflation they lived through, but it must also partly have been a matter of personality. But actually the two attitudes are sometimes pretty close together.

For some of them, the problem of too much money means that – at least in great exchanges of the world – there is wild speculation, which is necessarily followed by collapse and poverty. For others, the problem is inflation, caused by over-extending the money supply – usually, but not always, by the government. For both, the underlying demand is that money should be real: if it loses touch with underlying reality — either because it isn't underpinned by anything or because it is inflated by speculative froth — then disaster is likely to follow. Real money is stable and meaningful; unreal money could — and often does — disappear tomorrow.

There is a basic division of money reformers between those who want 'free money', to make it more available, and those who want 'real money', to root it to reality. In practice, they have tended to make common cause with each other, but both are actually emphasizing the different functions that are bound up in money. While the free money advocates are emphasizing the need for money to be a medium of exchange, the real money advocates are emphasizing the need for a store of value. And without some realistic foundation in the world, without some backing to the currency — even if it is, as now, a widespread belief that governments will honour their debts — currencies are at best wildly unstable, and at worst worthless.

The following passages — from Daniel Defoe in the 18th century to George Soros at the end of the 20th — are all in their different ways pleas for stability.

DANIEL DEFOE

THE VILLAINY OF
STOCK-JOBBERS (1701)

The essence of the argument that there's too much money is often the horror of the markets. With recent memory of the internet stocks bubble, when a website like Yahoo! was suddenly worth more than American Airlines, it's easy to forget that this isn't a new phenomenon. The problem of bubbles, where money and credit is frighteningly plentiful, and which then burst with devastating consequences for everybody, has been with us since before the South Sea Bubble in 1720.

That took place during the lifetime of the author of *Gulliver's Travels*, Daniel Defoe (1660–1731), but even by the time the South Sea Bubble had burst, he had long since identified the London 'stock-jobbers' as the object of his disdain. His 1719 tract, *The Anatomy of Exchange Alley*, another full-frontal assault on the markets, incorporated his previous writings on the subject, and were published almost on the eve of the Bubble, and also put him in serious danger of arrest. This passage is taken from an even earlier pamphlet on *The Villainy of Stock-Jobbers*, which refers back to the dubious record of Sir Josiah Child, who made himself a fortune provisioning the Navy, and then – as a director of the East India Company – on the markets.

Defoe was writing immediately before the satirical tract aimed at the Anglican church which led to his imprisonment, and subsequent release – probably on the condition that he act as government informer.

Child had died in 1699, just before Defoe wrote this, but the passage is almost as relevant today. The techniques he accuses Child of using were used to similar effect on the anonymous internet bulletin boards that hyped the great internet stocks bubble of the late 1990s.

✻   ✻   ✻

If we may believe the report of those who remember the machines and contrivances of that original of stock-jobbing, Sir Josiah Child, there are those who tell us, letters have been ordered, by private management, to be written from the East-Indies, with an account of the loss of ships which have been arrived there, and the arrival of ships lost; of war [with] the great Mogul, when they have been in perfect tranquillity, and of peace with the great Mogul when he has come down against the factory of Bengal with one hundred thousand men: just as it was thought proper to calculate those rumours for the raising and falling of the stock, and when it was for his purpose to buy cheap, or sell dear.

It would be endless to give an account of the subtilties of that capital ch—t, when he had a design to bite the whole Exchange. As he was the leading hand to the market, so he kept it in his power to set the price to all the dealers. The subject then was chiefly the East India stock, though there were other stocks on foot too, though since sunk to nothing; such as the Hudson's Bay Company, the linnen manufacture stock, paper stock, salt-petre stock and others, all at this day worse than nothing, though some of them jobbed up to 350 per cent, as the two first in particular.

But the East India stock was the main point, every man's eye, when he came to market, was upon the brokers who acted for Sir Josiah. Does Sir Josiah sell or buy? If Sir Josiah had a mind to buy, the first thing he did was to commission his brokers to look sower, shake their heads, suggest bad news from India; and at the bottom it followed, 'I have commission from Sir Josiah to sell out whatever I can,' and perhaps they would actually sell ten, perhaps twenty thousand pound.

Immediately, the Exchange (for they were not then come to the Alley) was full of sellers; nobody would buy a shilling, 'till perhaps the stock would fall six, seven, eight, ten per cent, sometimes more; then the cunning jobber had another set of men employed on purpose to buy, but with privacy and caution, all the stock they could lay their hands on, 'till by selling ten thousand pound, at four or five per cent lost, he would buy a hundred thousand pound stock at ten or twelve per cent under price; and in a few weeks by just the contrary method, set them all a buying, and then sell them their own stock again at ten or twelve per cent profit.

These honest methods laid the foundation, we will not say of a fine great stone house, on a certain forest, but it certainly laid the foundation of an opulent family, and initiated the crowd of jobbers into that dexterity on tricking and cheating one another, which to this day they are the greatest proficients in that this part of the world ever saw.

THOMAS JEFFERSON

SHOULD WE HAVE BANKS?

(1813)

The suspicion with which the third president of the USA, Thomas Jefferson (1743–1826), regarded banks probably stemmed from his experience as a farmer. And unlike his near contemporary Benjamin Franklin (see Part I, p25), he was also deeply suspicious of any money that wasn't, as he saw it, absolutely real. 'Paper is poverty,' he said in a letter written in 1788. 'It is only the ghost of money, and not money itself.'

These attitudes have formed a powerful strand in American politics ever since – though the same tradition transmuted as the decades wore on to demand that the government actually issues more money, like the greenbacks issued by Abraham Lincoln during the Civil War (see Part III, p94), and gave birth to the Greenback Party and the Populist Party (see Donelly, Part I, p31). The assumption is that government-issued paper was more real than the stuff issued by banks.

This passage is taken from a letter of advice that Jefferson wrote to John Wayles Eppes, dated 24 June 1813. The war talk is significant, because the War of 1812 and how to pay for it was very much at the forefront of everybody's mind. The advice he gives about issuing paper in wartime and withdrawing it afterwards had been disastrous for the British economy only a handful of years later (see Owen, Part I, p28).

The main message of the letter is urging that the federal government issues its own paper currency when it has to, in order to supplant and replace the unsupported paper currency only issued by the banks – and he uses strong language. We are being 'cheated' by the banks, he writes. Governments should do it instead.

But perhaps the most interesting section of the letter is the part which deals with the length of loans. Pursuing them into the next generation is simply against natural justice, says Jefferson – giving a whole new edge to the argument about debt to Keynes' phrase that 'in the long run we are all dead'. There is a reflection here about modern criticisms of the idea that there is a 'moral hazard' in protecting people from their debts: Jefferson would say that there is also a moral hazard in protecting bankers from the consequences of unwise or usurious loans. It would be interesting to find out his views on today's Third World debt.

*   *   *

It is a wise rule and should be fundamental in a government disposed to cherish its credit, and at the same time to restrain the use of it within the limits of its faculties, 'never to borrow a dollar without laying a tax in the same instant for paying the interest annually, and the principal within a given term; and to consider that tax as pledged to the creditors on the public faith.'

On such a pledge as this, sacredly observed, a government may always command, on a *reasonable interest*, all the lendable money of their citizens, while the necessity of an equivalent tax is a salutary warning to them and their constituents against oppressions, bankruptcy, and its inevitable consequence, revolution. But the term of redemption must be moderate, and at any rate within the limits of their rightful powers.

But what limits, it will be asked, does this prescribe to their powers? What is to hinder them from creating a perpetual debt? The laws of nature, I answer. The earth belongs to the living, not to the dead. The will and the power of man expire with his life, by nature's law. Some societies give it an artificial continuance, for the encouragement of industry; some refuse it, as our aboriginal neighbours, whom we call barbarians.

The generations of men may be considered as bodies or corporations. Each generation has the usufruct of the earth during the period of its continuance. When it ceases to exist, the usufruct passes on to the succeeding generation, free and unincumbered, and so on, successively, from one generation to another forever. We may consider each generation as a distinct nation, with a right, by the will of its majority, to bind themselves, but none to bind the succeeding generation, more than the inhabitants of another country.

Or the case may be likened to the ordinary one of a tenant for life, who may hypothecate the land for his debts, during the continuance of his usufruct; but at his death, the reversioner (who is also for life only) receives it exonerated from all burthen. The period of a generation, or the term of its life, is determined by the laws of mortality, which, varying a little only in different climates, offer a general average, to be found by observation...

At nineteen years then from the date of a contract, the majority of the contractors are dead, and their contract with them. Let this general theory be applied to a particular case. Suppose the annual births of the State of New York to be twenty-three thousand nine hundred and ninety-four, the whole number of its inhabitants, according to Buffon, will be six hundred and seventeen thousand seven hundred and three, of all ages. Of these there would constantly be two hundred and sixty-nine thousand two hundred and eighty-six minors, and three hundred and forty-eight thousand four hundred and seventeen adults, of which last, one hundred and seventy-four thousand two hundred and nine will be a majority.

Suppose that majority, on the first day of the year 1794, had borrowed a sum of money equal to the fee-simple value of the State, and to have consumed it in eating, drinking and making merry in their day; or, if you please, in quarrelling and fighting with their unoffending neighbours. Within eighteen years and eight months, one half of the adult citizens were dead. Till then, being the majority, they might rightfully levy the interest of their debt annually on themselves and their fellow-revellers, or fellow-champions. But at that period, say at this moment, a new majority have come into place, in their own right, and not under the rights, the conditions, or laws of their predecessors.

Are they bound to acknowledge the debt, to consider the preceding generation as having had a right to eat up the whole soil of their country, in the course of a life, to alienate it from them, (for it would be an alienation to the creditors,) and would they think themselves either legally or morally bound to give up their country and emigrate to another for subsistence? Every one will say no; that the soil is the gift of God to the living, as much as it had been to the deceased generation; and that the laws of nature impose no obligation on them to pay this debt. And although, like some other natural rights, this has not yet entered into any declaration of rights, it is no less a law, and ought to be acted on by honest governments.

It is, at the same time, a salutary curb on the spirit of war and indebtment, which, since the modern theory of the perpetuation of debt, has drenched the earth with blood, and crushed its inhabitants under burthens ever accumulating. Had this principle been declared in the British bill of rights, England would have been placed under the happy disability of waging eternal war, and of contracting her thousand millions of public debt. In seeking, then, for an ultimate term for the redemption of our debts, let us rally to this principle, and provide for their payment within the term of nineteen years at the farthest.

Our government has not, as yet, begun to act on the rule of loans and taxation going hand in hand. Had any loan taken place in my time, I should have strongly urged a redeeming tax. For the loan which has been made since the last session of Congress, we should now set the example of appropriating some particular tax, sufficient to pay the interest annually, and the principal within a fixed term, less than nineteen years.

And I hope yourself and your committee will render the immortal service of introducing this practice. Not that it is expected that Congress should formally declare such a principle. They wisely enough avoid deciding on abstract questions. But they may be induced to keep themselves within its limits.

I am sorry to see our loans begin at so exorbitant an interest. And yet, even at that you will soon be at the bottom of the loan-bag. We are an agricultural nation. Such an one employs its sparings in the purchase or improvement of land or stocks. The lendable money among them is chiefly that of orphans and wards in the hands of executors and guardians, and that which the farmer lays by till he has enough for the purchase in view. In such a nation there is one and one only resource for loans, sufficient to carry them through the expense of war; and that will always be sufficient, and in the power of an honest government, punctual in the preservation of its faith. The fund I mean, is *the mass of circulating coin.*

Every one knows, that although not literally, it is nearly true, that every paper dollar emitted banishes a silver one from the circulation. A nation, therefore, making its purchases and payments with bills fitted for circulation, thrusts an equal sum of coin out of circulation. This is equivalent to borrowing that sum, and yet the vendor receiving payment in a medium as effectual as coin for his purchases or payments, has no claim to interest. And so the nation may continue to issue its bills as far as its wants require, and the limits of the circulation will admit.

Those limits are understood to extend with us at present, to two hundred millions of dollars, a greater sum than would be necessary for any war. But this, the only resource which the government could command with certainty, the States have unfortunately fooled away, nay corruptly alienated to swindlers and shavers, under the cover of private banks.

Say, too, as an additional evil, that the disposal funds of individuals, to this great amount, have thus been withdrawn from improvement and useful enterprise, and employed in the useless, usurious and demoralizing practices of bank directors and their accomplices. In the war of 1755, our State availed itself of this fund by issuing a paper money, bottomed on a specific tax for its redemption, and, to insure its credit, bearing an interest of five per cent.

Within a very short time, not a bill of this emission was to be found in circulation. It was locked up in the chests of executors, guardians, widows, farmers, &c. We then issued bills bottomed on a redeeming tax, but bearing no interest. These were readily received, and never depreciated a single farthing. In the revolutionary war, the old Congress and the States issued bills without interest, and without tax. They occupied the channels of circulation very freely, till those channels were overflowed by an excess beyond all the calls of circulation. But although we have so improvidently suffered the field of circulating medium to be filched from us by private individuals, yet I think we may recover it in part, and even in the whole, if the States will cooperate with us.

If treasury bills are emitted on a tax appropriated for their redemption in fifteen years, and (to insure preference in the first moments of competition) bearing an interest of six per cent, there is no one who would not take them in preference to the bank paper now afloat, on a principle of patriotism as well as interest; and they would be withdrawn from circulation into private hoards to a considerable amount. Their credit once established, others might be emitted, bottomed also on a tax, but not bearing interest; and if ever their credit faltered, open public loans, on which these bills alone should be received as specie.

These, operating as a sinking fund, would reduce the quantity in circulation, so as to maintain that in an equilibrium with specie. It is not easy to estimate the obstacles which, in the beginning, we should encounter in ousting the banks from their possession of the circulation; but a steady and judicious alternation of emissions and loans, would reduce them in time. But while this is going on, another measure should be pressed, to recover ultimately our right to the circulation. The States should be applied to, to transfer the right of issuing circulating paper to Congress exclusively, *in perpetuum*, if possible, but during the war at least, with a saving of charter rights.

I believe that every State west and South of Connecticut river, except Delaware, would immediately do it; and the others would follow in time. Congress would, of course, begin by obliging unchartered banks to wind up their affairs within a short time, and the others as their charters expired, forbidding the subsequent circulation of their paper. This they would supply with their own, bottomed, every emission, on an adequate tax, and bearing or not bearing interest, as the state of the public pulse should indicate.

Even in the non-complying States, these bills would make their way, and supplant the unfunded paper of their banks, by their solidity, by the universality of their currency, and by their receivability for customs and taxes. It would be in their power, too, to curtail those banks to the amount of their actual specie, by gathering up their paper, and running it constantly on them. The national paper might thus take place even in the non-complying States.

In this way, I am not without a hope, that this great, this sole resource for loans in an agricultural country, might yet be recovered for the use of the nation during war; and, if obtained *in perpetuum*, it would always be sufficient to carry us through any war; provided, that in the interval between war and war, all the outstanding paper should be called in, coin be permitted to flow in again, and to hold the field of circulation until another war should require its yielding place again to the national medium.

But it will be asked, are we to have no banks? Are merchants and others to be deprived of the resource of short accommodations, found so convenient? I answer, let us have banks; but let them be such as are alone to be found in any country on earth, except Great Britain. There is not a bank of discount on the continent of Europe, (at least there was not one when I was there,) which offers anything but cash in exchange for discounted bills.

No one has a natural right to the trade of a money lender, but he who has the money to lend. Let those then among us, who have a monied capital, and who prefer employing it in loans rather than otherwise, set up banks, and give cash or national bills for the notes they discount. Perhaps, to encourage them, a larger interest than is legal in the other cases might be allowed them, on the condition of their lending for short periods only.

It is from Great Britain we copy the idea of giving paper in exchange for discounted bills; and while we have derived from that country some good principles of government and legislation, we unfortunately run into the most servile imitation of all her practices, ruinous as they prove to her, and with the gulph yawning before us into which these very practices are precipitating her. The unlimited emission of bank paper has banished all her specie, and is now, by a depreciation acknowledged by her own statesmen, carrying her rapidly to bankruptcy, as it did France, as it did us, and will do us again, and every country permitting paper to be circulated, other than that by public authority, rigorously limited to the just measure for circulation.

Private fortunes, in the present state of our circulation, are at the mercy of those self-created money lenders, and are prostrated by the floods of nominal money with which their avarice deluges us. He who lent his money to the public or to an individual, before the institution of the United States Bank, twenty years ago, when wheat was well sold at a dollar the bushel, and receives now his nominal sum when it sells at two dollars, is cheated of half his fortune; and by whom? By the banks, which, since that, have thrown into circulation ten dollars of their nominal money where was one at that time.

CHARLES MACKAY

TULIPMANIA (1841)

The tulipmania in the Netherlands in the 1630s was one of the first manias and bubbles of the modern world. It has become a familiar pattern since – wild price rises, speculation, people borrowing money on the basis of their paper gains to invest some more, followed by miserable collapse that extends way beyond those who had got so over-excited. It's a classic part of the argument against too much money. It was also no coincidence that the first bubble of this kind happened in the Netherlands, which was by some way the most innovative and sophisticated financial nation throughout the 17th century.

Even so, the tulipmania was a forgotten event until it was written up in 1841 by Charles MacKay (1814–1889) in his book *Memoirs of Extraordinary Popular Delusions and the Madness of Crowds*. MacKay was a journalist, poet and highly successful song-writer, and an editor of *The Illustrated London News*.

MacKay had his own reasons for collecting together examples of the financial insanities of crowds, because at the time Britain was showing early signs of hurtling into a whole new one, fed by the rapidly rising value of railway stocks. Like the internet stocks boom of the 1990s, the railway stocks boom of the 1840s came to a shuddering halt as their value collapsed amid increasing examples of profiteering and corruption, outlined by Dickens in his novel *Little Dorrit*.

Even so, MacKay's classic account of the 'madness of crowds' remains a key text for anyone who feels a little bearish when the claims fly – as they do in every generation – that this time it's all going to be different.

✳   ✳   ✳

The demand for tulips of a rare species increased so much in the year 1636, that regular marts for their sale were established on the Stock Exchanges of Amsterdam, in Rotterdam, Harlaem, Leyden, Alkmar, Hoorn, and other towns. Symptoms of gambling now became, for the first time, apparent. The stock-jobbers, ever on the alert for a new speculation dealt largely in tulips, making use of all the means they so well know how to employ to cause fluctuations in prices.

At first, as in all these gambling mania, confidence was at its height, and every body gained. The tulip-jobbers speculated in the rise and fall of the tulip stocks, and made large profits by buying when prices fell, and selling out when they rose. Many individuals grew suddenly rich.

A golden bait hung temptingly out before the people, and one after the other, they rushed to the tulip-marts, like flies around a honey-pot. Every one imagined that the passion for tulips would last for ever, and that the wealthy from every part of the world would send to Holland, and pay whatever prices were asked for them. The riches of Europe would be concentrated on the shores of the Zuyder Zee, and poverty banished from the favoured clime of Holland.

Nobles, citizens, farmers, mechanics, seamen, footmen, maid-servants, even chimney-sweeps and old clotheswomen, dabbled in tulips. People of all grades converted their property into cash, and invested it in flowers. Houses and lands were offered for sale at ruinously low prices, or assigned in payment of bargains made at the tulip-mart. Foreigners became smitten with the same frenzy, and money poured into Holland from all directions. The prices of the necessities of life rose again by degrees: houses and lands, horses and carriages, and luxuries of every sort, rose in value with them, and for some months Holland seemed the very antichamber of Plutus.

The operations of the trade became so extensive and so intricate, that it was found necessary to draw up a code of laws for the guidance of the dealers. Notaries and clerks were also appointed, who devoted themselves exclusively to the interest of the trade. The designation of public notary was hardly known in some towns, that of tulip-notary usurping its place. In the smaller towns, where there was no exchange, the principal tavern was usually selected as a 'show-place', where high and low traded in tulips, and confirmed their bargains over sumptuous entertainments. These dinners were sometimes attended by two or three hundred persons, and large vases of tulips, in full bloom, were placed at regular intervals upon the tables and sideboards for the gratification during the repast.

At last, however, the more prudent began to see that this folly could not last for ever. Rich people no longer bought the flowers to keep them in their gardens, but to sell them again at cent per cent profit. It was seen that somebody most lose fearfully in the end. As this conviction spread, prices fell, and never rose again. Confidence was destroyed, and a universal panic seized upon the dealers.

A had agreed to purchase ten *Semper Augustines* from *B*, at four thousand florins each, at six weeks after the signing of the contract. *B* was ready with the flowers at the appointed time; but the price had fallen to three or four hundred florins, and *A* refused either to pay the difference or receive the tulips. Defaulters were announced day after day in all the towns of Holland. Hundreds who, a few months previously, had begun to doubt that there was such a thing as poverty in the land suddenly found themselves the possessors of a few bulbs, which nobody would buy, even though they offered them at one quarter of the sums they had paid for them.

The cry of distress resounded every where, and each man accused his neighbour. The few who had contrived to enrich themselves hid their wealth from the knowledge of their fellow-citizens, and invested it in the English or other funds. Many who, for a brief season, had emerged from the humbler walks of life, were cast back into their original obscurity. Substantial merchants were reduced almost to beggary, and many a representative of a noble line saw the fortunes of his house ruined beyond redemption.

WASHINGTON IRVING

A TIME OF UNEXAMPLED PROSPERITY (1855)

After an abrupt change in US economic policy (see Jackson, Part IV, p115), America soon began a cycle of land speculations of its own, followed by the worst depression that the country had experienced, starting in 1837. The writer Washington Irving (1783–1859) – creator among other things of *Rip Van Winkle* – tried to explain the problem by writing about the Great Mississippi Bubble of 1719 (see Law, Part V, p142).

Irving set out the bizarre paradoxes of those periods of too much money – the banks will lend anyone almost anything, but after the bubble has been burst, when loans are really important, they will hardly lend a thing. He also makes clear what Defoe and the others merely hinted at, by using a double meaning to the word 'inflation'. Inflation happens, of course, when there is too much money, but Irving also refers to the way that inflationary language creates the trouble in the first place. For Irving, it is words, not money, that are at fault here.

But he does pinpoint the basic truth that Galbraith (p66) and others have noted so many times since. At the height of the bubble, people believe – as Irving Fisher (see Part VI, p238) put it later – that shares 'have reached a permanently high plateau'. That widespread belief gets repeated until it insulates people from realizing the crash that is about to happen to them. The same idea was repeated immediately before the Wall Street Crash, and again during the recent internet-stocks boom.

* * *

Every now and then the world is visited by one of those delusive seasons, when 'the credit system' as it is called, expands to full luxuriance: everybody trusts everybody; a bad debt is a thing unheard of; the broad way to certain and sudden wealth lies plain and open; and men are tempted to dash forward boldly, from the facility of borrowing.

Promissory notes, interchanged between scheming individuals, are liberally discounted at the banks, which become so many mints to coin words into cash; and as the supply of words is inexhaustible, it may readily be supposed what a vast amount of promissory capital is soon in circulation. Everyone now talks in thousands; nothing is heard but gigantic operations in trade; great purchases and sales of real property, and immense sums made at every transfer. All, to be sure, as yet exists in promise; but the believer in promises calculates the aggregate as solid capital, and falls back in amazement at the amount of public wealth, the 'unexampled state of public prosperity!'

Now is the time for speculative and dreaming or designing men. They relate their dreams and projects to the ignorant and credulous, dazzle them with golden visions, and set them maddening after shadows. The example of one stimulates another; speculation rises on speculation; bubble rises on bubble; everyone helps with his breath to swell the windy superstructure, and admires and wonders at the magnitude of the inflation he has contributed to produce.

Speculation is the romance of trade, and casts contempt upon all its sober realities. It renders the stock-jobber a magician, and the Exchange a region of enchantment. It elevates the merchant into a kind of knight errant, or rather a commercial Quixote. The slow but sure gains of snug percentage become despicable in his eyes: no 'operation' is thought worthy of attention, that does not double or treble the investment. No business is worth following, that does not promise an immediate fortune. As he sits musing over his ledger, with pen behind his ear, he is like La Mancha's hero in his study, dreaming over his books of chivalry. His dusty counting-house fades before his eyes, or changes into a Spanish mine; he gropes after diamonds, or dives after pearls. The subterranean garden of Aladdin is nothing to the realms of wealth that break upon the imagination.

Could this delusion last, the life of a merchant would indeed be a golden dream; but it is as short as it is brilliant.

THE GREAT CRASH (1954)

The great liberal economist John Kenneth Galbraith (1908–) wrote his classic account of the Stock Market crash of 1929, which ushered in the Great Depression, during a mini stock market boom in the mid-1950s. He also did so after giving evidence to the US Congress on the same subject, just – by coincidence – as the market suffered a mini-crash. As a result of this juxtaposition of events, he was accused by one senator of being a communist – a worrying moment in American history to face that kind of accusation.

The book, *The Great Crash 1929*, was written within living memory of the events he described, but at a time of unprecedented and rather smug prosperity. As he writes here, many of the reforms brought in after 1929 were now in place. But he warns of the continuing need for 'guardians of sound pessimism'. Because one day, another generation would delude themselves that some new innovation had pushed stock prices permanently high, and we would all be awash with speculative over-abundance.

How right he was, not just once but a handful of times. And by the time the internet bubble was upon us, many of the 1929 reforms had been swept away by US Congress, and the same pattern seemed in some ways to be repeating itself – newspaper columnists talking up the boom, market analysts employed by banks talking up their own bank's IPOs delusion, hype and finally bust. Though luckily not on the scale of 1929.

Charles Mitchell, the head of National City Bank, described by Galbraith as defying the Federal Reserve, was one of the cheer-leaders of the 1920s boom, and after his arrest, one of its fall-guys. The signs are that the internet boom will have its very own Mitchells too.

*   *   *

The military historian when he has finished this chronicle is excused. He is not required to consider the chance for a renewal of war with the Indians, the Mexicans, or the Confederacy. Nor will anyone press him to say how such acrimony can be prevented. But economics is taken more seriously.

The economic historian, as a result, is invariably asked whether the misfortunes he describes will afflict us again and how they may be prevented.

The task of this book, as suggested on an early page, is only to tell what happened in 1929. It is not to tell whether or when the misfortunes of 1929 will recur. One of the pregnant lessons of that year will by now be plain: it is that very specific and personal misfortune awaits those who presume to believe that the future is revealed to them. Yet, without undue risk, it may be possible to gain from our view of this useful year some insights into the future. We can distinguish, in particular, between misfortunes that could happen again and others which events, many of them in the aftermath of 1929, have at least made improbable. And we can perhaps see a little of the form and magnitude of the remaining peril.

At first glance the least probable of the misadventures of the late twenties would seem to be another wild boom in the stock market with its inevitable collapse. The memory of that autumn, although now much dimmed, is not yet gone. As those days of disenchantment drew to a close, tens of thousands of Americans shook their heads and muttered, 'Never again'. In every considerable community there are yet a few survivors, aged but still chastened, who are still muttering and still shaking their heads. The New Era had no such guardians of sound pessimism.

Also, there are the new government measures and controls. The powers of the Federal Reserve Board — now styled the Board of Governors, the Federal Reserve System — have been strengthened both in relation to the individual reserve banks and the member banks. Mitchell's defiance of March 1929 is now unthinkable. What was then an act of arrogant but not abnormal individualism would now be regarded as idiotic. The New York Federal Reserve Bank retains a measure of moral authority and autonomy, but not enough to resist a strong Washington policy. Now also there is a power to set margin requirements. If necessary, the speculator can be made to post the full price of the stock he buys. While this may not completely discourage him, it does mean that when the market falls there can be no outsurge of margin calls to force further sales and insure that the liquidation will go through continuing spasms. Finally, the Securities and Exchange Commission is, one hopes, effective to large-scale market manipulation, and it also keeps rein on the devices and salesmanship by which new speculators are recruited.

Yet, in some respects, the chances for a recurrence of a speculative orgy are rather good. No one can doubt that the American people remain susceptible to the speculative mood — to the conviction that enterprise can be attended by unlimited rewards which they, individually, were meant to share. A rising market can still bring the reality of riches. This, in turn, can draw more and more people to participate. The government preventatives and controls are ready. In the hands of a determined government their efficacy cannot be doubted.

There are, however, a hundred reasons why a government will determine not to use them. In our democracy an election is in the offing even on the day of an election. The avoidance of depression and prevention of unemployment have become for the politician the most critical of all questions of public policy. Action to break up a boom must always be weighed against the chance that it will cause unemployment at a politically inopportune moment. Booms, it must be noted, are not stopped until after they have started. And after they have started the action will always look, as it did to the frightened men in the Federal Reserve Board in February 1929, like a decision in favour of immediate as against ultimate death. As we have seen, the immediate death not only had a disadvantage of being immediate but of identifying the executioner.

The market will not go on a speculative rampage without some rationalization. But during the next boom some newly rediscovered virtuosity of the free enterprise system will be cited. It will be pointed out that people are justified in paying the present prices – indeed, almost any price – to have an equity position in the system. Among the first to accept these rationalizations will be some of those responsible for invoking the controls. They will say firmly that controls are not needed. The newspapers, some of them, will agree and speak harshly of those who think action might be in order. They will be called men of little faith.

RALPH BORSODI

THE TROUBLE WITH
KEYNESIANISM (1974)

It's strange to realize – in these days when radicals rail against the so-called Washington consensus, squeezing the money supply of the impoverished countries on earth and making the fight against inflation their highest ambition – that a generation ago, radicals saw these things differently. The tail end of the Keynesian era seemed to them sometimes like a giant theft of the wealth of ordinary people by those in power, who seemed powerless to tackle rampant inflation. It was all right for those wealthy enough to hedge against inflation, but for anyone on welfare or government pensions, or anyone trying to work independently or employ themselves, it could be nightmarish as the value of their money eroded away.

We are encouraged to believe that Keynesian economics, in the shape of Roosevelt's New Deal, was welcomed by radicals everywhere as an effective counter to the Depression, but there was a critique right from the beginning from a decentralist perspective. For people like Ralph Borsodi (1888–1977), the New Deal and Keynes represented an unacceptable shift of power to the centre, and they both had to be fought.

There is nothing very rare about passages criticizing inflation and its effects on ordinary people, but this one displays such beautiful invective, using such controlled anger, that it still makes good reading today. It was also written by one of the key figures in the development of the alternative economics movement.

Borsodi was a pioneer in the development of the green movement, starting with his influential book *This Ugly Civilization* in 1929, which pre-dates similar books in the UK by half a decade. His *Flight from the City* four years later led to the foundation of the Dayton Project, the School of Living and a string of eco-villages and communes in the decades that followed, founded along the principals he set out.

This passage is taken from *Inflation and the Coming Keynesian Catastrophe*, actually published 12 years after his death, because it is also a description of the innovative non-inflationary currency he created (see Part VI, p202). It develops material that originally appeared in his 1948 pamphlet *Inflation is Coming!* – the only one of his books that became a best-seller, though copies now seem to be extraordinarily scarce. That in turn developed ideas he originally introduced at a talk in New York City to the prestigious Aldine Club in 1943, which makes him one of the very first to predict post-war inflation.

Strangely enough, for someone who so despised the legacy of Keynes, Borsodi finds himself echoing a remark by Keynes himself that when investment comes from the by-product of a casino 'that job is likely to be ill done'. It is remarkably like Borsodi's sentiment here. Maybe they weren't quite so far apart after all.

*   *   *

Among the cynics of today there is a saying: 'Statistics do not lie, but statisticians do.' In the preparation of the chart describing the history of the dollar, I discovered that what used to merely irritate me was in fact a means of misrepresentation, of concealing the truth. Of – to use a short and ugly word – lying. I have always been irritated by the frequency and the variety of the 'base years' used in statistical tables and charts. When I wanted to prepare a single graphic chart to show what had happened to the dollar since it came officially into existence, I was faced with four sets of base numbers. The only available data consisted of four sets of base numbers. The only available data consisted of four sets of Wholesale Price Indexes with four different base years: 1910–1914=100; 1926=100; 1947=100, and 1957–1959=100. To convert them into a single table was a tedious, tricky and irritating job.

The current issue of the Survey of Current Business uses still another base year to show the movement of prices, 1967=100. Why all these changes? To mystify? Why do statisticians and economists change these base years for the indexes which purport to show the cost of living and the purchasing power of the dollar? Why do they change them more and more frequently since inflation has become a part of the American way of life?

The fact is, their changes make it easier to misrepresent the facts, to avoid the truth, to lie in the meanest way – by telling a half truth. The truth about the matter is that if the increase in wholesale prices which was shown as 115 on a 1967 basis had been shown on a 1926 base, the figure which would have to be used would have had to be around three times as much, 445 – a figure so startling as to focus attention upon the real magnitude of the inflation with which the Country is cursed.

The base year I am using in my charts is 1793 – the year the dollar came legally into existence. The chart makes a graphic presentation of the fact that since Keynesianism took over, Washington has been murdering the dollar.

No wonder there is an undercurrent of unease in Washington. Unconsciously Washington knows that we are sitting on a time-bomb and that the moment something happens so that confidence in the dollar is threatened, something like 1929 will repeat itself. They talked about a 'New Era' before the Great Depression. They are not calling the present period a New Era today. But the psychological climate is the same — everybody has been conditioned to feel that the laws now regulating money and banking make a repetition of anything like 1929 impossible.

I wonder. The nature of technology changes; we now use atomic bombs instead of bows-and-arrows. But the nature of the human animal does not — or changes so slowly that for all practical purposes it does not change at all.

That is another 'lie' to which I think it worth calling attention — an inadvertent rather than a deliberate lie. This is the lie represented by the use of the word inflation. The word suggests something getting bigger — when a balloon is inflated, it becomes bigger. But they are not inflating the dollar in Washington, they are degrading and debasing it. They are increasing the quantity, but they are debasing its quality. . . .

The United States Treasury Department produces detriments and not goods by issuing money and inflating the quantity of it with the assistance of the Federal Reserve Board and all its member banks throughout the country.

It alternatively expands and contracts the supply not in accordance with the needs of the economy but in accordance with the needs of Wall Street at worst. So intimate is the tie between Washington and Wall Street that it is difficult to decide to whom to assign the major responsibility for the debasement and murdering of the dollar. But that these two centres do bear the major responsibility is incontestable: Wall Street by printing insecurities and the Treasury Department in Washington by printing dollars. Wall Street issues pseudo-securities and Washington pseudo-money. Similar centres exist in all the large industrial nations of the world. England, with the appearance of the Industrial Revolution, pioneered in pseudo-production. Japan is the latest present-day industrial nation to join in the game of pseudo-production. No doubt others will arise until the last of the free economies disappears, and the verdict of the Inquest of History upon what Lincoln called 'the last great hope of mankind' will be death by monetary suicide.

I will throughout this study stress the fact that neither Wall Street nor Washington should have any part in or control over the issuance of money. To make clear what I mean when I speak of Wall Street and Washington, it is necessary to distinguish between what they in theory are supposed to be and what they in fact are.

Wall Street, in theory, is the centre of the financial system which provides properly and effectively for the capital needs of the nation. But Wall Street is in fact a speculation centre organized and operated for the purpose of enabling a self-selected minority of men of boundless greed to become millionaires and billionaires. Whatever Wall Street does to provide for the capital needs of the nation is incidental to, and misshaped and distorted by, what it in fact is.

Washington, in theory, is the establishment which governs the nation for the purpose of providing for the protection and for the welfare of the people it governs. Washington in fact is an establishment misshaped and distorted for the purpose of enabling men of boundless ambition to gratify their desire to exercise power and to exploit it as long as they can.

In theory the functions which the two perform are entirely different. In practice, however, both the men of greed and the men of power have found that they can gratify their desires far more effectively if they work together. In practice, Wall Street and Washington operate as if they were Siamese twins. And this is the way they are both operating in dealing with Keynesianism.

PAUL GLOVER

HOMETOWN MONEY (1992)

The Reagan years in the USA coincided with a massive expansion of the national debt which now backs the value of the dollar, until it reached over $65,000 per US household. The economic implications of unrepayable debt on that scale are not clear, especially now that the USA has become the world's largest debtor nation. Since President Nixon cut the last vestiges of the dollar's link to gold in 1971, debt – and the belief that the US government will pay – has underpinned its value. A similar system underpins the value of all 'fiat' currencies.

Of course, this may not be a very reliable backing, and that is the argument here by Paul Glover (1947–), contrasting the reliability of the dollar with the reliability of the local currency he invented in Ithaca in upstate New York, which is backed by the work and belief of local people.

Like many of the money 'heretics' in this book, Glover became interested in currencies not through economics, but through technology – in this case energy technology. His radical energy plans for Los Angeles and then his own home town of Ithaca made him realize the extent to which money can seep out of a local economy, to utilities, to big chains and to the government. His Ithaca *hours*, a printed currency, stay circulating locally, and they have been an enormous success.

Though sheer force of personality, he and his colleagues have inspired belief in his printed notes to such an extent that they are now accepted by more than 300 businesses in the town, backed by the local chamber of commerce and accepted at some of the local banks. The result has been a thriving series of farmers' markets, support for local farmers and a healthy small business sector.

Hours have a value of $10 each, and there are various denominations issued in colourful notes made of bizarre kinds of paper. They are not demurrage currency (see p233), in fact they carry neither positive nor negative interest. Glover got the idea listening to Bob Swann and Susan Witt (see Part VI, p211) on the radio in 1991. The idea has been copied in about 70 other towns across North America, with varying degrees of success.

The currency is issued to advertisers in the bimonthly *Ithaca Money* newspaper, as well as given in interest-free loans or grants to worthy local causes. *Ithaca Money* also promotes the power of the currency in a series of trenchant editorials by Glover, of which this was the first. It appeared under the headline 'Strength of Ithaca Hour grows while value of dollar declines' in January 1992.

Hours are, of course, a way of providing more money in a local economy. But they are based on a critique, set out here, that says the dollar has become unreliable.

*   *   *

The number of businesses and people accepting Ithaca HOURS has nearly tripled in our first three months of operation, from 90 to 230. These participants provide 400 different products and services, and make 100 different requests. The Ithaca HOUR is backed by real goods and skills, while the US dollar is backed by government waste, bank failure and debt.

Worst of all, though, the dollar is declining because America's natural resource base shrinks. The natural wealth that fed American factories and filled our stores has been dumped into landfills. Most of the USA's prime fuels, metals, forests and fields have been largely used up, requiring us to import more food, oil and industrial ores.

About 80 per cent of original US oil reserves are gone, and oil imports cause half the trade deficit. Nearly all steelmaking and aluminum depends on imported manganese and bauxite. Nearly all the basics of industry, like chromium and nickel are imported. Nearly all uranium and even one third our natural gas is imported.

Most coal is now stripmined, and these raw cuts have begun devouring good cropland. The best soil has already been ruined, especially by corporate farms. The US Midwest, our nation's breadbasket, is drying up as the underground water is pumped out.

At the same time, many US corporations globalize, becoming no longer American. They use American resources and labour to enrich themselves, then send jobs overseas. New York state lost 200,000 jobs last year.

This destruction and dependency signals conversion of the United States into a Third World nation. There are fewer US jobs per person and fewer hours per job, paid with weaker dollars. One seventh of us are impoverished, one tenth use food stamps. The Tompkins County paycheck, for trades workers, has eight per cent less spending power today than in 1980.

Although this process is happening worldwide and all nations are at risk, we may see surprising changes. Russia has fabulous wealth in metals, forest, oil and natural gas, and so might become one of the world's great entrepreneurial powers. And we may see Japan's sun set, when aggressive nations change the rules of commerce, seizing Japan's assets.

None of the above are good changes. To avoid cycles of gluttony, war and collapse, all nations could develop environmentally-efficient locally-controlled economies.

When you use Ithaca HOURS you are part of a healthy transition. Our Action Ideas column shows other US communities making similar changes.

Business-as-usual: Elements of an Unhealthy Economy:

1. Bland overpackaged chemically-damaged food of inferior nutritional value, whose harvest depends on destruction of soil and harsh use of domestic and foreign labour.

2. Deteriorating, poorly-insulated housing at high rents, luxury housing sprawling across agricultural land or displacing low-income mid-city residents.

3. Poorly-made imported clothing, sewn by virtual slave labour.

4. Energy-wasteful household goods designed to be thrown away.

5. Dependence on automobiles and token funding for bus, rail and bikeway systems.

6. Carcinogenic air and water, especially damaging to children and elderly, from industrial waste, pesticides and automobiles. World heat shock from combustion. Destruction of ozone layer.

7. Worst health care protection in the industrialized world. Most cancers caused by pollution of air and water.

8. State-imposed schooling which teaches obedience rather than thinking.

9. Use of TV channels for commercial propaganda rather than free exchange of ideas.

10. Ill-paid jobs which increase the waste of forests, metals, soil, water and air, and/or which endanger world peace and worker safety. Loss of jobs overseas and increase of poorly-paid service jobs.

11. Military power so huge and corrupt that most of our nation's wealth is lost supporting war preparation and inspiring fear in half the world.

12. Federal policy which rewards dangerous and wasteful dependence on imported petroleum and uranium while cutting subsidies for solar and wind power, transit and railroads.

Democrats and Republicans both promote false beliefs about our economy:

- Government must allow corporations to pollute, to keep jobs here. However, there are businesses which produce clean goods without polluting.

- America must produce, sell and buy huge quantities of useless playthings to keep people employed. But local production and purchase with net export is sufficient to keep money moving.
- Business must create goods of low quality so that they must be soon replaced so that profits and jobs are renewed. Yet, the more careful crafting and manufacture of durable goods will employ far more people more profitably.
- Workers are too dumb to run businesses. On the contrary, wherever cooperative shop-floor management has been tried, productivity and profits have risen.
- GNP measures economic strength. Instead, GNP measures contraction of the economy, by depletion of essential raw materials.

DEBT-BASED MONEY SUPPLY (1997)

In some ways, this passage ought to belong in the next section, with others arguing that basic corruption is the problem at the heart of the system. But the Earl of Caithness (1948–) is also arguing that the creation of money by banks, with interest attached, has led to a massive expansion of the money supply – over 2000 per cent in a quarter of a century in the UK. He is also arguing that it's unsustainable, because it will lead to higher interest rates and therefore to more division in society.

The Earl – a former Paymaster General and junior minister under Margaret Thatcher in the 1980s – gave the speech in the British House of Lords on 5 March 1997, in the dying days of the last Conservative government under John Major. It seems at first sight to be a conventional speech, but then bemoans the way that currencies were cut adrift from reality in 1971 – the year that President Nixon finally cut all links between the dollar and gold – and then launches a heretical attack on the banks, as you only could do in the old-style House of Lords.

The speech was collected together and published by the right-wing Monday Club, which has traditionally been suspicious of the way that banks create money.

*　*　*

Looking at it from a conventional viewpoint, the economy is in good shape and the government have done better than most of their counterparts in Europe. We have moved out of recession and on the surface the economy is stronger and people are more confident. There is much that I could say about that. I think the government have done a very good job.

However, it is also a good time to stand back, to reassess whether our economy is soundly based. I would contest that it is not, not for the reason to which the noble Lord, Lord Eatwell, alluded, which is that it is the government's fault, but our whole monetary system is utterly dishonest, as it is debt-based. 'Dishonest' is a strong word, but a system by which its very actions causes the value of money to decrease is dishonest and has within it its own seeds of destruction. We did not vote for it. It grew upon us gradually but markedly since 1971 when the commodity-based system was abandoned.

Let us look at what has happened since then. The money supply in 1971 was just under £31 billion. At the end of the third quarter of last year, it was about £665 billion. In 25 years it has grown by a staggering 2145 per cent. Where has the money come from? Interestingly, the government have only minted a further £20 billion in that time. It is the banks, the building societies and our commercial lenders who have created the balance of £614 billion. If this rate of growth is projected over the next 25 years, the money supply in 2022 will be over £14,000 billion.

When the money supply increases, as it is doing, the previously existing money is debased accordingly. Therefore, either wages or salaries must also increase to maintain parity or those who earn wages and salaries will find that they no longer participate in the national economy to the same extent as they did previously. This exacerbates the growing fragmentation of our society, which cannot go on for ever. I am not advocating high wages but I am advocating less debasement and better control of the money supply.

When inflation does happen, it will feed through to all parts of the economy. The result, sadly, will be that the government have to use the only tool they know – an increase in interest rates. That has happened fairly recently, but it is not the first time that it has happened. We saw it in the 1970s and again in the 1980s. It is a consequence of our debt-based monetary system that it leads inevitably to business and economic cycles.

Conventional wisdom tells us that in order to create new jobs and boost the economy, interest rates have to be reduced. That has happened. People are encouraged to borrow to invest and spend. That has happened. As the continuing flow of new money finds its way into the economy, inflation will follow and up will go interest charges again to reduce the level of borrowing. In order to pay the increasing levels of interest, borrowers will once more have to reduce expenditure in other areas of economic activity. The cycle will continue, but the next time, as before, we will all start deeper in debt and with a burden harder to carry.

Personal debt has already increased by nearly 3000 per cent since 1971. How much more can we take? I hope for the sake of our economy, without which we cannot finance what we want to see – a good health service and a good social security system among other things – we will question this conventional wisdom.

We all want our business to succeed, but under the existing system the irony is that the better our banks, building societies and lending institutions do, the more debt is created. The noble Lord, Lord Kingsdown, said that there is little that can be done about debt. No, I do not believe that. There is a different way: it is an equity-based system and one in which those businesses can play a responsible role.

The next government must grasp the nettle, accept their responsibility for controlling the money supply and change from our debt-based monetary system. My Lords, will they? If they do not, our monetary system will break us and the sorry legacy we are already leaving our children will be a disaster.

GEORGE SOROS

THE LOOMING CRISIS (1995)

'Unrestrained competition without regard to the common good can endanger the market mechanism. . . With this attitude I cannot see the global system surviving.' That was how the best known hedge-fund manager in the world, George Soros (1930–), introduced his sceptical attack on the speculative international markets. This passage marked the beginning of his shift from global investor to philosophical guru. It began in an interview in German by the journalist Krisztina Koenen, which was expanded by Soros into a book-length interview in 1995, including his famous statement that he could imagine the system collapsing more easily than he could imagine it surviving in its current state.

Soros was born in Budapest but came to the UK when he was 17 and studied at the London School of Economics, where he came under the influence of the Open Society philosophy of Karl Popper – which has inspired him and his philanthropic Open Society Institute ever since. He reached financial megastardom in 1992 when his highly successful Quantum Fund bet US$10 billion that the pound would fall – forcing Britain out of the European Monetary System and tempting the British government into spending a third of their gold reserves in a vain attempt to prop it up. He made US$2 billion overnight.

He was writing here just after the Mexican currency crisis and his predictions came close to coming true three years later, when he lost US$2 billion during the Russian financial crisis. This led in turn to widespread speculative collapse across the Far East – which included patients in hospital being thrown out onto the street in Indonesia at bayonet point as their currency went through the floor – for which he was unfairly blamed by the prime minister of Malaysia. When he bet too early on the collapse of internet stocks, he retired from active financial management.

What he says about the world financial system, and how it is built on instability, deserves to be listened to, and not just because he predicted the currency crises correctly. The financial system is now driven by speculation, after all. Over US$2 trillion goes through the world markets every day, and over 95 per cent of it is speculation – enough to overwhelm the combined reserves of the world's central banks in just a matter of hours. It is probably the most urgent financial issue of the 21st century.

❊   ❊   ❊

Do you see a real crisis looming?

Yes. It is similar to the crisis in the international political system in the sense that it doesn't affect us directly and therefore we are not conscious of it. It is affecting people in Latin American and in the other so-called emerging markets. As I have said before, the crash in emerging markets is the worst since 1929. As long as it is confined to them, the international financial system is not really in danger. But if and when it has a negative fallout in the industrial countries, you could have a breakdown not only in the financial system but also in the international trading system.

That sounds alarmist

Deliberately so. As I have already mentioned, the Mexican crisis is bound to lead to a radical shift in the balance of trade between Mexico and the United States. If that coincides with a slowdown in the United States economy, there will be a political outcry that may lead to the election of a protectionist president in 1996. The similarity with the aftermath of the 1929 crash would be too close for comfort.

You are predicting a breakdown in free trade

I am not predicting it, but I can envisage it. The danger is that people are not aware of the danger. Everybody talks about the global financial markets as if they were irreversible. But that is a misconception. It involves a false analogy with a technological innovation like the internal combustion engine. Once the automobile was invented, it spread like wildfire. It may be improved, it may even be superseded by a superior invention, but it cannot be abolished. Not so with a financial innovation It differs from a technological invention in the same way that social science differs from natural science.

We came close to having a global financial market based on the gold standard toward the end of the nineteenth century, but the system broke down and by the end of World War II, when the Bretton Woods system was established, there was practically no private international capital movements. People don't remember it, but the Bretton Woods system was specifically designed to create institutions that would allow international trade to be financed in the absence of private capital movements. As capital movements picked up, the Bretton Woods system of fixed exchange rates broke down. The international financial institutions drafted by Bretton Woods — the IMF and the World Bank — have successfully adapted themselves to the changing circumstances and they continue to play an important role. But they are inadequate to the task of maintaining stability in the system. Their resources are dwarfed by the magnitude of private capital movements and they have no regulatory powers. There is some cooperation among governments — the Bank for International Settlements in Basel has been the main instrument for international cooperation — but it is quite limited in scope. The trouble is that the need for greater international cooperation is not generally recognized. The prevailing wisdom about the way financial markets operate is false, and a global market based on false premises is unlikely to survive indefinitely. The collapse of the global marketplace would be a traumatic event with unimaginable consequences. Yet I find it easier to imagine than the continuation of the present regime.

THE TROUBLE WITH MONEY: IT'S CORRUPT

Those who swallow usury cannot rise except as one whom Satan has prostrate by his touch.

THE QUR'AN

The bank hath benefit on the interest on all monies which it creates out of nothing.

THE CHARTER OF THE BANK OF ENGLAND, 1698

Critics of the money system sometimes end up in much the same place, even though they start somewhere slightly different. Those who are horrified at the lack of money in the right places, end up calling for free money in various different forms. Those who are appalled at the consequences of too much money in the wrong places, demand money that is rooted in the real world. But there is another related class: those who believe that the way money is created is basically wrong.

It's a peculiar thing, but even though hundreds of thousands of economics PhDs are being churned out around the world at any one moment, the question of where money comes from in a modern economy has never been absolutely settled. It seems clear to most commentators that the vast majority of it is now created in the form of loans or mortgages by banks, limited only by their reserve requirements – and even those can be pretty flexible.

'The process by which banks create money is so simple that the mind is repelled,' wrote John Kenneth Galbraith in his book *Money: Whence It Came, Where It Went.* 'Where something so important is involved, a deeper mystery seems only decent.' That remains the mainstream view.

This is not an aspect of economics that is discussed much in the modern world. It is occasionally argued, as the former Chancellor of the Exchequer Reginald McKenna did in 1928 that, although 'the amount of money in existence varies only with the action of the banks in increasing and decreasing deposits and bank purchases', still every repayment destroys a deposit. But as Michael Rowbotham points out (see Part III, p108), that really isn't so. When you repay your bank loan, it stays on the books of the bank, as real as any other money, ready to be lent out again.

All of this would be almost beyond argument were it not that, just occasionally, the financial world denies it. Bizarrely, the following answer was given by the Treasury spokesman Lord McIntosh of Haringey in answer to a question from Lord Beaumont in 2001, about James Robertson's report on creating new money (see Part IV, p133):

> *Contrary to the report of the New Economics Foundation, banks are not provided with a hidden subsidy. Funds loaned out to customers must either be obtained from depositors or the sterling money markets, both of which usually require the payment of interest.*

Of course, banks do offset the risk of new loans by using the money markets, but this misleading answer implies that economies are steady states, increasing only when governments put a little more cash into circulation – which clearly isn't the case. But there is at least a debate emerging about this, for the first time for half a century or more, which should pressurize mainstream economists to spread more understanding of what is actually happening.

Most of the passages of this section imply a different explanation for the way money is made, believing – as most people recognize – that it is normally created out of nothing, by banks and with interest attached that has to be repaid as well. The literature on this subject goes back almost as far as money itself. The creation of money in this way, and the charging of interest, has been variously abhorred because it:

- flies in the face of religious rules;
- takes away the right of the sovereign or the government to create money;
- isn't natural;
- allows money to become a commodity in its own right; or
- creates a built-in debt that may never be able to be paid off.

It may be that the radicals are being unfair to the system of interest, which after all has provided us with the ability to create investment income for the future – not to mention old age pensions. It is the main reason we no longer have workhouses and old people starving on the streets of London. And as such, it is a kind of original sin, a sort of Faustian bargain we have made with the economic system. But the 'sin' is potentially serious because the interest allows money to become a commodity that can be bought and sold for its own sake, which is why by far the biggest proportion of money circulating in the world is speculative.

Even so, the most conventional economists might have to concede that interest is supposed to do so many things in a modern economy – providing discipline to the person borrowing money, providing feedback on a project's efficiency, providing a means to squeeze the money supply – that at the very least, it can't do all of them very well.

There are other passages here about other design faults in the money system – Jane Jacobs (see p100) arguing that it fails to give the right information feedback to cities, and Joel Kurtzman (see p105) arguing that the system has become an uncontrollable electronic casino. These are other, more subtle, forms of corruption – corruption through ignorance. But the allegation that the system is unnatural lies behind most of the criticisms back to Aristotle.

Is there such a thing as natural money? Yes, say the historians – because money was once a circulation medium based on real wealth: grain kept in a warehouse or cattle on a farm. As Silvio Gesell argued before the First World War (see Part I, p40), this kind of money naturally lost value – it rusted. Modern money does the reverse, says the argument, and sets up such unnatural expectations of a return on investment, that the planet is plundered in search of it.

What can be done about it will be covered in other sections. This section is about the economic 'heresy' of natural money, and how far away from it we have drifted.

ARISTOTLE

UNNATURAL WEALTH

(350 BC)

The philosopher Aristotle (384–322 BC) was a pupil and teacher at Plato's
Academy in Athens and went on to be one of the founders of Western philosophical thought – not just in Europe but influential also in the Islamic world.
Money is man-made, he explained: it 'has been introduced by convention as a kind
of substitute for need or demand... And that is why we call it *nomisma*, because
its value is derived, not from nature, but from law, and can be altered or abolished
at will.'

His strictures against usury were reflected in most of the main religions of the
world, so he wasn't the first. And in practice, different ages have interpreted usury
differently. Sometimes it means the charging of interest on loans (as in Islam);
sometimes it means the misuse of a powerful position to charge too much interest
(its usual use in modern society). So as moderns, we might condemn Coca-Cola
as usurious if their new vending machines charge more money the hotter the
temperature, but we don't necessarily condemn the banks.

Islam does condemn the banks, and a thriving Islamic sector of financial services
has grown up in recent years that charges fees and equity rather than interest. The
successful JAK bank in Scandinavia has also show that it's possible to do the same
outside the Islamic world.

There was a time that the Christian world also condemned the charging of
interest, following St Thomas Aquinas – who took it from Aristotle – and in the
Middle Ages, kings and princes tended to turn to Jews to provide them with the
loans they needed instead. This practice led eventually to the expulsion of Jews
from medieval England under Edward I in 1290.

The following passage is taken from Aristotle's *Politics*, translated by Benjamin
Jowett, Book I, Part 10.

*   *   *

Here are two sorts of wealth-getting, as I have said; one is a part of household management, the other is retail trade: the former necessary and honourable, while that which consists in exchange is justly censured; for it is unnatural, and a mode by which men gain from one another. The most hated sort, and with the greatest reason, is usury, which makes a gain out of money itself, and not from the natural object of it. For money was intended to be used in exchange, but not to increase at interest. And this term interest, which means the birth of money from money, is applied to the breeding of money because the offspring resembles the parent. Wherefore of all modes of getting wealth this is the most unnatural.

FRANCIS BACON

OF USURY (1601)

By the Reformation, the blanket condemnation of usury seemed less useful than it was before, and the new Protestant merchants found ways round the rules to borrow money. Usury was beginning to settle down to its modern Western meaning. Francis Bacon (1561–1626), the statesman and philosopher, is trying to make sense of this in this passage. 'Usury' is necessary, he argues, because people will not lend money otherwise. Even so, the list of 'discommodities' of usury he lists echo some of the issues today, especially the accusation that it concentrates wealth into a few hands. Bacon himself died hideously in debt, ironically enough, having been imprisoned for taking bribes.

He was also living in a period when the government had caused terrible economic hardship by practising its own brand of usury. Henry VIII recalled all the coins in England, melted them down and re-minted them with less silver. When his daughter, Elizabeth I, tried to reverse this process, the shortage of coins caused enormous distress.

One of the contemporary places you could borrow money on security, in Bacon's day, was the goldsmiths. You could deposit your gold with them and receive in return a promissory note, which could be circulated like money. Of course, it didn't take long for the goldsmiths to realize that more than one promissory note could be in circulation for any given batch of gold. In 1704, promissory notes were made legal tender. The modern system of finance had begun.

Bacon's proposal that there should be different parallel rates of interest is remarkably modern. As I write, there are debates inside crisis-hit Argentina about what relationship the different currencies that the country relies on – the dollar, the peso and the new *argentino* – should have. As Bacon so rightly saw, different interest rates suit different sectors of the economy. The answer may be different currencies (see Parts VI and VII).

＊　＊　＊

Many have made witty invectives against usury. They say that it is pity the devil should have God's part, which is the tithe, that the usurer is the greatest Sabbath-breaker, because his plough goeth every Sunday; that the usurer is the drone that Virgil speaketh of: *Ignavum fucos pecus a praesepibus arcent*; that the usurer breaketh the first law that was made for mankind after the fall, which was, *in sudore vultûs tui comedes panem tuum*; not, *in sudore vultûs alieni*; that usurers should have orange-tawny bonnets, because they do Judaize; that it is against nature for money to beget money, and the like. I say this only, that usury is a *concessum propter duritiem cordis*: for since there must be borrowing and lending, and men are so hard of heart as they will not lend freely, usury must be permitted. Some others have made suspicious and cunning propositions of banks, discovery of men's estates, and other inventions; but few have spoken of usury usefully. It is good to set before us the incommodities and commodities of usury, that the good may be either weighed out or culled out; and warily to provide that, while we make forth to that which is betterd, we meet not with that which is worse.

The discommodities of usury are, first, that it makes fewer merchants; for were it not for this lazy trade of usury, money would not lie still but would in great part be employed upon merchandising, which is the *vena porta* of wealth in a state: the second, that it makes poor merchants; for as a farmer cannot husband his ground so well if he sit at a great rent, so the merchant cannot drive his trade so well if he sit at great usury: the third is incident to the other two; and that is, the decay of customs of kings or states, which ebb or flow with merchandising: the fourth, that it bringeth the treasure of a realm or state into a few hands; for the usurer being at certainties, and others at uncertainties, at the end of the game most of the money will be in the box; and ever a state flourisheth when wealth is more equally spread: the fifth, that it beats down the price of land; for the employment of money is chiefly either merchandising or purchasing, and usury waylays both: the sixth, that it doth dull and damp all industries, improvements, and new inventions, wherein money would be stirring if it were not for this slug: the last, that it is the canker and ruin of many men's estates, which in process of time breeds a public poverty.

On the other side, the commodities of usury are, first, that howsoever usury in some respect hindereth merchandising, yet in some other it advanceth it; for it is certain that the greatest part of trade is driven by young merchants upon borrowing at interest; so as if the usurer either call in or keep back his money, there will ensue presently a great stand of trade: the second is, that were it not for this easy borrowing upon interest, men's necessities would draw upon them a most sudden undoing, in that they would be forced to sell their means (be it lands or goods), far under foot; and so, whereas usury doth but gnaw upon them, bad markets would swallow them quite up. As for mortgaging or pawning, it will little mend the matter: for either men will not take pawns without use, or if they do, they will look precisely for the forfeiture.

I remember a cruel moneyed man in the country that would say, The devil take this usury, it keeps us from forfeitures of mortgages and bonds. The third and last is, that it is a vanity to conceive that there would be ordinary borrowing without profit; and it is impossible to conceive the number of inconveniences that will ensue, if borrowing be cramped: therefore to speak of the abolishing of usury is idle; all states have ever had it in one kind or rate or other; so as that opinion must be sent to Utopia.

To speak now of the reformation and reglement of usury, how the discommodities of it may be best avoided and the commodities retained. It appears, by the balance of commodities and discommodities of usury, two things are to be reconciled; the one that the tooth of usury be grinded that it bite not too much; the other that there be left open a means to invite moneyed men to lend to the merchants, for the continuing and quickening of trade. This cannot be done except you introduce two several sorts of usury, a less and a greater; for if you reduce usury to one low rate, it will ease the common borrower, but the merchant will be to seek for money: and it is to be noted that the trade of merchandise being the most lucrative, may bear usury at a good rate: other contracts not so.

To serve both intentions, the way would be briefly thus: that there be two rates of usury; the one free and general for all; the other under licence only to certain persons, and in certain places of merchandising. First therefore, let usury in general be reduced to five in the hundred, and let that rate be proclaimed to be free and current; and let the state shut itself out to take many penalty for the same; this will preserve borrowing from any general stop or dryness; this will ease infinite borrowers in the country; this will in good part raise the price of land, because land purchased at sixteen years' purchase will yield six in the hundred and somewhat more, whereas this rate of interest yields but five; this by like reason will encourage and edge industrious and profitable improvements, because many will rather venture in that kind than take five in the hundred, especially having been used to greater profit.

Secondly, let there be certain persons licensed to lend to known merchants upon usury at a higher rate, and let it be with the cautions following: let the rate be, even with the merchant himself, somewhat more easy than that he used formerly to pay; for by that means all borrowers shall have some ease by this reformation, be he merchant or whosoever; let it be no bank or common stock, but every man be master of his own money; not that I altogether mislike banks, but they will hardly be brooked in regard of certain suspicions.

JONATHAN SWIFT

DEBASING THE COINAGE

(1 7 2 4)

The difference between the face value of a coin and what it costs to produce it is the profit that governments traditionally make to pay for the whole business of coinage. This profit is known as seigniorage (see Part IV, p33), and it has an ancient and honourable lineage. These days, British coinage – only a tiny proportion of the money in circulation – simply stands for the face value. It's made of cupro-nickel, after all. But in days gone by, the coins were expected to relate in value to what they said they were worth, and hence were made out of silver or gold.

By reducing the silver content of coins, as Henry VIII did, the government could increase the number of coins in circulation and make more profit on them in seigniorage – but that would also create inflation and make it hard to buy goods from abroad. By privatizing the right to create coins – as Jonathan Swift (1667–1745) is complaining about here – they give the seigniorage to some agent in the private sector, and lose control over the metal content of the coins.

And, to take the argument on – as some money heretics did in the 20th century – by allowing the banks to create money in the form of loans, the government has handed over the considerable rights of seigniorage to them.

The author of *Gulliver's Travels* was one of the great satirists and pamphleteers of his day, and ever since. This passage is taken from his *Letter to the Tradesmen, Shop-Keepers, Farmers, and Common-People in General of Ireland*, and dates from the days after his political 'exile' as Dean of Dublin, when his rage at injustice was undiminished.

✳   ✳   ✳

The fact is thus: It having been many years since COPPER HALFPENCE OR FARTHINGS were last coined in this kingdom, they have been for some time very scarce, and many counterfeits passed about under the name of *raps*, several applications were made to England, that we might have the liberty to coin new ones, as in former times we did; but they did not succeed.

At last one Mr Wood, a mean ordinary man, a hardware dealer, procured a patent under His Majesty's broad seal to coin four score and ten thousand pounds in copper for this kingdom, which patent however did not oblige any one here to take them, unless they pleased. Now you must know, that the halfpence and farthings in England pass for very little more than they are worth. And if you should beat them to pieces, and sell them to the brazier you would not lose above a penny in a shilling. But Mr Wood made his halfpence of such base metal, and so much smaller than the English ones, that the brazier would not give you above a penny of good money for a shilling of his; so that his sum of four score and ten thousand pounds in good gold and silver, must be given for trash that will not be worth above eight or nine thousand pounds real value.

But this is not the worst, for Mr Wood when he pleases may by stealth send over another and another four score and ten thousand pounds, and buy all our goods for eleven parts in twelve, under the value. For example, if a hatter sells a dozen of hats for five shillings a-piece, which amounts to three pounds, and receives the payment in Mr Wood's coin, he really receives only the value of five shillings.

For suppose you go to an alehouse with that base money, and the landlord gives you a quart for four of these halfpence, what must the victualler do? His brewer will not be paid in that coin, or if the brewer should be such a fool, the farmers will not take it from them for their bere, because they are bound by their leases to pay their rents in good and lawful money of England, which this is not, nor of Ireland neither, and the 'squire their landlord will never be so bewitched to take such trash for his land, so that it must certainly stop somewhere or other, and wherever it stops it is the same thing, and we are all undone.

ABRAHAM LINCOLN

MONETARY POLICY (1865)

This passage, written a matter of weeks before the end of the American Civil War, is one of the most important and one of the most forgotten pieces of writing by Abraham Lincoln (1809–1865).

If he had managed to avoid the assassin's bullet a few weeks later, and his policy had been put into effect, it might have changed the way money is created every-where – and would certainly have been better placed in Part V – 'Future Money'. But he didn't and it wasn't, and it's main use since has been as implied criticism of the way money is created now. Hence its appearance here.

The outbreak of the Civil War led to economic upheaval as the banks called in their loans. American bank notes were then also privately issued – and every shop had to have a massive tome called a Counterfeit Detector next to the till to tell which ones to accept. But Lincoln refused to accept the terms offered by the banks for more currency at this critically unstable moment, and went ahead and printed his own, debt-free.

These became known as 'greenbacks' (see Part I, p31), and US$300,000 of them were issued during the war – much to the disapproval of economists ever since. Their eventual withdrawal under Lincoln's successors caused the economic difficulties that led to the Greenback Party and then the Populists, and made the second half of the 19th century in the USA the great age of monetary debate.

Reading Lincoln's policy now 140 years later, it is striking how tough it is. His intention is to protect people from what he calls 'vicious currency', so that 'money will cease to be the master and become the servant of humanity'. The wages of men are more important than the wages of money, he says – and that idea has made this passage a rallying cry for everyone since who wants governments to fund their own borrowing requirements with their own interest-free money, rather than borrowing it from the banks.

Conspiracy theorists ever since have regarded this passage – taken from Senate document No 23: National Economy and the Banking System of the United States – as the real reason for Lincoln's death. Of course we will never know.

✳   ✳   ✳

Money is the creature of law and the creation of the original issue of money should be maintained as an exclusive monopoly of National Government. Money possesses no value to the State other than that given to it by circulation. Capital has its proper place and is entitled to every protection. The wages of men should be recognized in the structure of and in the social order as more important than the wages of money. No duty is more imperative on the Government than the duty it owes the people to furnish them with a sound and uniform currency, and of regulating the circulation of the medium of exchange so that labour will be protected from a vicious currency, and commerce will be facilitated by cheap and safe exchanges. The available supply of gold and silver being wholly inadequate to permit the issuance of coins of intrinsic value or paper currency convertible into coin in the volume required to serve the needs of the people, some other basis for the issue of currency must be developed, and some means other than that of convertibility into coin must be developed to prevent undue fluctuations in the value of paper currency or any other substitute for money of intrinsic value that may come into use.

The monetary needs of increasing numbers of people advancing toward higher standards of living can and should be met by the Government. Such needs can be served by the issue of national currency and credit through the operation of a national banking system. The circulation of a medium of exchange issued and backed by the Government can be properly regulated and redundancy of issue avoided by withdrawing from circulation such amounts as may be necessary by taxation, redeposit, and otherwise.

Government has the power to regulate the currency and credit of the Nation. Government should stand behind its currency and credit and the bank deposits of the Nation. No individual should suffer a loss of money through depreciated or inflated currency or bank bankruptcy. Government possessing the power to create and issue currency and credit as money and enjoying the right to withdraw both currency and credit from circulation by taxation and otherwise, need not and should not borrow capital at interest as the means of financing governmental work and public enterprise.

The Government should create, issue, and circulate all the currency and credit needed to satisfy the spending power of the Government and the buying power of consumers. The privilege of creating and issuing money is not only the supreme prerogative of Government, but it is the Government's greatest creative opportunity. By adoption of these principles, the long-felt want for a uniform medium will be satisfied. The taxpayers will be saved immense sums of interest, discounts, and exchanges. The financing of all public enterprise, the maintenance of stable government and ordered progress, and the conduct of the Treasury will become matters of practical administration. The people can and will be furnished with a currency as safe as their own Government. Money will cease to be master and become servant of humanity. Democracy will rise superior to the money power.

FREDERICK SODDY

ARCH-ENEMY OF ECONOMIC FREEDOM (1943)

It's hard what to make of Sir Frederick Soddy (1877–1956), the Nobel prize-winning chemist and discoverer of isotopes, in his forays into economics. From the Great Depression, Soddy became increasingly enraged by the 'unscientific' way that money is created in society. He wasn't an easy man at the best of times, and as the years went by he got angrier and angrier about it – in the end attempting to take the Bank of England to court.

The former assistant to the pioneer nuclear phycisist Ernest Rutherford, Soddy would disconcert his academic colleagues by talking economics in physics lectures. He failed to win equal recognition in economics, but it is said for example that he persuaded the young Milton Friedman that something had to be done about monetary instability. The future Labour Party leader Hugh Gaitskell praised him for his 'extremely respectable monetary policy'.

Soddy and Douglas found themselves making a similar criticism of the way banks create money, and Soddy battled to distinguish between what he said were two different kinds of money: cheque money (created by banks) and crown money (notes and coins created by the government). Soddy's idea was to divide banks into two separate institutions: one a warehouse for depositing money and the other an investment trust that would sell shares to provide capital to borrow for new projects.

While other heretics looked for ways that banks could be compensated for his massive change in the way they earn their money, Soddy just wanted them prosecuted for making what he called 'fictitious loans' not backed by money in the bank.

This passage is taken from the pamphlet *The Arch-Enemy of Economic Freedom: What banking is, what first it was and again should be*, which Soddy published himself at the height of the Second World War in 1943. It was intended originally as a counterblast against Sir Reginald McKenna, the chairman of Midland Bank, for his defence of banking – but was slightly toned down because McKenna died while it was being written.

✳   ✳   ✳

Science achieves her triumphs by the patient unravelling of natural laws and by working with them, not setting out to defy and trick them. All her achievements are now being perverted by the money magicians, out to get something for nothing. Banking is become the supreme example of the folly of the belief in the power of the human mind and will to ignore and override fact. Already it has cost the world a thousand times as much human misery, frustration and waste of life as all the criminal classes put together. It is now nothing but a discredited and discreditable technique, for evading originally the laws against counterfeiting, by which bankers *make forced levies upon the community* by the creation of money on which they charge interest ever after.

Gradually as they grew fat with their alchemy, and now completely, they have suppressed genuine national money altogether, save the relatively trifling sums of pewter-silver alloy and bronze coinage still issued by the Royal Mint, which before this War totalled about £80 millions and is now £106 millions. They not only impose a tax of £75 millions per annum, or thereabouts, on the mere *existence* of money, but, by holding up the flow of wealth to ransom, have usurped supreme power over the State, and are now the effective rulers of the world. This hold-up of the flow of wealth is the prime cause of war.

The most sinister feature of this substitution is rarely apprehended in its true significance. All money is now a debt owed by the banks to the owners and owed to the banks by the banks' debtors. *The consequence is that it can never be repaid.* On the contrary, it must ever increase with every increase in the population and in the power of science and invention to increase the production of wealth. To anyone in his right mind, the very idea is crazy, though now so firmly rooted as to be taken by the victims as part of the natural order of things, that agriculture and industry upon which all life and all prosperity depend, of necessity can only operate as debtors to the banks, since they themselves are the creators of the wealth by which debts are repaid.

One has only to imagine what would happen if the creators of wealth succeeded in getting out of the bankers' debt to understand why it is impossible. The total money, coins apart, would vanish, and the whole economic life of the community would come to a stop. For the best part of a century at least, the bankers have known that in this way, simply by reducing their fictitious loans, they could bring down the proudest and wealthiest nations of the earth at their will. On a grand scale they did so between the two World Wars by carefully synchronized and purely artificial so-called 'economic blizzards', in this country and in the United States, which lost us the last 'Peace', and caused the present war.

It is the weapon that has reduced the ostensible internal political government to a sham and renders the nations naked and exposed to external monetary domination, universal, unsuspected and supreme. This is the price the world has paid for regarding science as a cow to be milked rather than a goddess to be worshipped.

JANE JACOBS

CITIES AND THE WEALTH OF NATIONS (1984)

Jane Jacobs (1916–) became famous in the 1960s thanks to her trenchant views about town planning in her book *The Death and Life of the Great American Cities*. And her fascination with why cities succeed or fail led her to take a sideways look at the economics of cities as well. Her central idea was that cities succeed or fail by their ability to innovate and replace imports with their own products.

Urged on by her involvement with Bob Swann and Susan Witt (see Part VI, p211), Jacobs saw currencies as information systems – giving feedback to national economies, allowing them to vary the value of their currencies according to whether their products were in demand. But – and here she veered away from accepted understandings of such matters – she argued that nations were far too big to give accurate feedback. If the real economic unit was the city, then national currencies would confuse the crucial economic messages that individual cities needed to receive via their currencies.

This is how she explained the problem in her book *Cities and the Wealth of Nations*, published by Random House, New York (1984) and Penguin/Pelican, London (1986). Like Douglas (see Part I, p43) and Glover (see Part II, p73), she brings the eye of an engineer to the money problem – but comes up with a different diagnosis. The problem isn't so much the charging of interest that makes money fail so many people so hopelessly, it's the failure of the information it feeds back. In this way, Jacobs comes up with the basic insight of 'new economics' that nations are not the only unit for currencies. She appears to favour the break-up of nations into 'families of sovereignties', but admits she can't see how this might come about – reaching the unnecessarily defeatist conclusion that 'we have no choice but to live with our economically deadly predicament as best we can.' We shall see.

* * *

National currencies, then, are potent feedback but impotent at triggering appropriate corrections. To picture how such a thing can be, imagine a group of people who are all properly equipped with diaphragms and lungs, but share only one single brainstem breathing centre. In this goofy arrangement, through breathing they would receive consolidated feedback on the carbon dioxide level of the whole group, without discriminating among the individuals producing it. Everybody's diaphragm would thus be triggered to contract at the same time.

But suppose some of these people were sleeping, while others were playing tennis. Suppose some were reading about feedback controls, while others were chopping wood. Some would have to halt what they were doing and subside into a lower common denominator of activity. Worse yet, suppose some were swimming and diving, and for some reason, such as the breaking of the surf, had no control over the timing of these submersions. Imagine what would happen to them. In such an arrangement, feedback control would be working perfectly on its own terms, but the results would be devastating because of a flaw designed right into the system.

I have had to propose a preposterous situation because systems as structurally flawed as this don't exist in nature; they wouldn't last. Nor do they exist in the machines we deliberately design to incorporate mechanical, chemical or electronic feedback controls; machines this badly conceived wouldn't work. Nations, from this point of view, don't work either, yet do exist. Nations are flawed in this way, because they are not discrete economic units, although intellectually we pretend that they are and compile statistics about them based on that goofy premise. Nations include, among other things in their economic grab bags, differing city economies that need different corrections at given times, and yet all share a currency that gives all of them the same information at a given time. The consolidated information is bad specific information for them even with respect to their foreign trade, and it is no information at all with respect to their trade with one another, as opposed to their international trade. Yet this wretched feedback is powerful stuff.

Because currency feedback, at bottom, all has to do with imports and exports and the balance or lack of balance between them, the appropriate responding mechanisms for such information are cities and their regions. Cities are the specific economic units that can replace imports with their own production, and the specific units that cast up streams of new kinds of exports. It is pointless to suppose that amorphous, undifferentiated statistical collections of a nation's economies perform those functions, because they don't.

Ideally, at a time when a city's exports are doing well, it needs to receive as wide a range and as great a volume of earned imports as it can, especially from other cities, because those funds of earned imports are the grist the city must have for its vital process of import-replacing. Conversely, at a time when its exports are in decline, imports should ideally become expensive because to escape decline from diminishing export work a city desperately needs to replace wide ranges of its imports with local production. It also needs maximum stimulation for tentative new types of export work it may soon be capable of casting up.

In other words, with falling exports a city needs a declining currency working like an automatic tariff and an automatic export subsidy — but only for as long as they are necessary. Once its exports are doing well, it needs a rising currency to earn the maximum variety and quantity of imports it can. Individual city currencies indeed serve as elegant feedback controls because they trigger specifically appropriate corrections to specific responding mechanisms.

This is a built-in design advantage that many cities of the past had but which almost none have now. Singapore and Hong Kong, which are oddities today, have their own currencies and so they possess this built-in advantage. They have no need of tariffs or export subsidies. Their currencies serve those functions when needed, but only as long as needed. Detroit, on the other hand, has no such advantage. When its export work first began to decline it got no feedback, so Detroit merely declined, uncorrected.

MARGRIT KENNEDY

THE DANGERS OF INTEREST

(1 9 8 8)

The following passage belongs in that category of economic writing you might describe as eschatalogical. It identifies the problem of money – and rather like Soddy does (see p97), the problem of human aggression too – firmly in the 'original sin' of interest. But it argues that interest charged in the way we do is hopelessly unsustainable because it is mathematically impossible.

Like many of the passages in this book, it isn't written by an economist. Margrit Kennedy (1939–) is an architect by training, and she became interested in economic issues through her work on eco-villages and the future of cities. Her book *Interest and Inflation-free Money* has been translated all over the world, and was read hungrily by a generation of environmentalists looking to explain the world's unsustainability in the economic system – and it has been very influential. It was a book that she co-wrote with her husband Declan.

It is also rather a frightening passage, as these writings tend to be. The answer to it may be that, in practice, the money system may tend towards that extreme point. Yet we reached the year 1990 with the poor of the earth owing a very great deal, but without actually owing 8190 balls of gold each equivalent to the mass of the earth that she feared – or anything near it. Charging interest may inject instability into the system, but something saves us from that extremity. Margrit Kennedy would no doubt reply that, although something has saved us so far, there is no guarantee that it will continue to do so.

※   ※   ※

Based on interest and compound interest, our money doubles at regular intervals, that is it follows an exponential growth pattern. This explains why we are in trouble with our monetary system today. *Interest, in fact, acts like cancer in our social structure.* Even at one per cent compound interest, we have an exponential growth curve, with a doubling time of 72 years.

Through our bodies we have only experienced the physical growth pattern of nature which stops at an optimal size. Therefore, it is difficult for human beings to understand the full impact of the exponential growth pattern in the *physical* realm.

This phenomenon can best be demonstrated by the famous story of the Persian emperor who was so enchanted with a new chess game that he wanted to fulfil any wish the inventor of the game had. This clever mathematician decided to ask for one seed of grain on the first square of the chess board, doubling the amounts on each of the following squares. The emperor, at first happy about such modesty, was soon to discover that the total yield of his entire empire would not be sufficient to fulfil the 'modest' wish. The amount needed on the 64th square of the chess board equals 440 times the yield of grain of the entire planet.

A similar analogy, directly related to our topic, is that one penny invested at the birth of Jesus Christ at four per cent interest would have bought in 1750 one ball of gold equal to the weight of the earth. In 1990, however, it would buy 8190 balls of gold. At five per cent interest, it would have bought one ball of gold by the year 1466. By 1990, it would buy 2200 billion balls of gold equal to the weight of the earth. The example shows the enormous difference one per cent makes. *It also proves that the continual payment of interest and compound interest is arithmetically, as well as practically, impossible.* The economic necessity and the mathematical impossibility create a contradiction which – in order to be resolved – has led to innumerable feuds, wars and revolutions in the past.

JOEL KURTZMAN

THE DEATH OF MONEY

(1 9 9 3)

It wasn't exactly corruption, but it clearly was outside our control. It was clear after the 1987 crash on the world stock markets that the whole money system had changed. It was driven as never before by the speculation in London, New York and Tokyo — especially in the late 1980s with the growth of junk bonds, earning the notorious junk bond financier Michael Milken a reputed US$1.5 million a day.

What's more, the way that money had transformed itself into electronic blips on computer screens, governed often by other computers which would sell automatically when the market reached certain levels, had created a wildly uncertain system. Worse, it was one where its main users — the speculators — benefited from its sheer volatility.

This wasn't exactly a new thought, but it was a book by journalist Joel Kurtzman called *The Death of Money* — seven years after the 1987 crash and two years after Black Wednesday that plummeted the pound out of the European Monetary System — that made the world fully aware of the change and the potential peril it represented. What he revealed was a new electronic money system based on speculation, where changes in supply and demand had little to do with the wild fluctuations that send shivers through the market every day, and where — today — around 97 per cent of the US$2 trillion that shoots through the markets has nothing to do with trade or services. This is how he introduced the problem.

*　*　*

Money has been transmogrified. It is no longer a *thing*, an object you can dig up at a beach or search for behind the cushions of a sofa; it is a *system*. Money is a network that comprises hundreds of thousands of computers of every type, wired together in places as lofty as the Federal Reserve — which settles accounts between banks every night that are worth trillions of dollars — and as mundane as the thousands of gas pumps around the world outfitted to take credit and debit cards. The network of money includes all the world's markets – stock, bond, futures, currency, interest rate, options, and so on. It is connected to the huge number-crunching super-computers at Morgan Stanley & Company and the computers of individual investors using the Equalizer programme to buy stocks through Charles Schwab & Company. The network is juxtaposed by computers that chart investment risk using the Nobel Prize-winning formulas developed by Harry Markowitz and Merton Miller of the University of Chicago, on the one hand, and the quasi-mystical technical formulas developed by Robert Prector, of the *Elliot Wave Theorist*, on the other.

In the new world of money, even the largest banks no longer need vaults. Instead, they store their money on disk drives and computer tapes, and they protect those funds not by hiring brawny guards but by employing brainy PhD mathematicians and software specialists to write secret codes.

The new network of money is much more volatile than the five-thousand-year-old monetary system it replaced. Interest rates, stock prices, currency prices, bond prices – all fluctuate as never before. In the last decade alone, the dollar has lost more than half its value against the world's other major currencies; American interest rates have fallen by 50 per cent; world stock prices have more than doubled (they have collapsed then risen in Japan); world real estate prices rose to all-time highs before deflating; and oil went from almost US$40 a barrel to $12 a barrel before settling in at the current rate. In each of these case, changes in supply and demand – the two bedrock tenants of economics – had little to do with the price changes.

For people in business, the ups and downs of the global markets are the economic equivalent of Yugoslavia. And in that kind of economy, where conditions mutate moment to moment, the time frames of investors and the planning horizons of executives have – of necessity – been compressed.

The death of money has also splintered the world into two economies. The smaller of the two economies I call the 'real economy'. That is where products are made, trade is conducted, research is carried out and services are rendered. The real economy is where the factory workers toil, doctors tend the sick, and teachers teach, and where roads, bridges, harbours, airports, and railways systems are built. Tragically, in the United States, it is also the impoverished part of the economy, starved for investment, backward and in disrepair.

The other economy, the 'financial economy', is somewhere between twenty and fifty times larger than the real economy. It is not the economy of trade but of speculation. Its commerce is in financial instruments. Mostly, it is concerned with the exchange of equities, such as stocks, and securities, such as bonds and other forms of debt. The latest and largest type of debt that the financial economy trades, from a technical standpoint, is money.

Unlike the real economy, the financial economy has been undergoing something of an investment boom for more than two decades. And while its ultra-high-tech infrastructure straddles the globe and moves several trillion dollars a day between the major and minor 'nodes' on the network, it is largely unregulated.

MICHAEL ROWBOTHAM

THE GRIP OF DEATH (1998)

If any one person has been responsible for reigniting the debate about how we create money, it is Michael Rowbotham. His book *The Grip of Death, A study of modern money, debt slavery and destructive economics*, from which this passage was taken, wasn't published by one of the big publishers – yet it has had an enormous influence, and has got people discussing the design of money for the first time in half a century. The book is a sparkling piece of detailed research and logic, arguing that banks should be forced to have 100 per cent reserve requirements (see Fisher, Part VI, p192) – but its most exciting sections are closely argued dissections of the current financial situation, and the burgeoning cost of debt in all our lives. He describes how the money supply has increased since 1963 from £14 billion to £680 billion in 1997, the year before the publication of the book. By this time, outstanding debt in the country stood at £780 billion, considerably more than all the money in circulation.

It's a frightening thought that all the money in the UK is insufficient to pay off our debts. It's also an echo of previous writers (see Soddy, p97, for example) who warned that it is impossible for us now as a society to find our way out of debt, because that is the only mechanism we have available for creating money.

The so-called 'Grip of Death' is actually the original meaning of the word 'mortgage', and Rowbotham's heaviest invective is reserved for the way in which we rely on mortgages to provide us with more than half the money in circulation. He explains in this passage that the price of houses has more to do with what people are allowed to borrow than with anything else. The logical and terrifying result – though he doesn't say it here – are the 'grandparent mortgages' in Japan, used to buy Tokyo's frighteningly expensive property, and finally paid off by the generation after next. Even in Britain, we can see what Rowbotham calls the 'unrelenting transfer of housing equity to financial institutions, via mortgages'.

* * *

History does much to obscure the extension of ownership by the financial system, particularly in the case of housing. Up to the beginning of this century, a large proportion of the population rented their homes. During the past 60 years, 'home-owning' has been seen as a sign of the increasing prosperity of the individual; a mark of the redistribution of wealth, in which the landlord owning several properties has gradually given way to more widespread property ownership. But this historic trend has simply served to obscure the unrelenting transfer of housing equity to financial institutions, via mortgages.

In 1900, almost all houses were owned outright, even if it was wealthy landlords who owned most of them. Indeed, perhaps less than five per cent of the housing stock was mortgaged. If there had been a genuine transfer from the rich to the poor, we would own our homes today with no more than the five per cent total mortgage debt that existed in 1900. A century of home building and home buying has disguised the major transfer of property, which has not been from the rich to the poor, but a substantial transfer of all forms of wealth to the financial system.

If we go back to the middle ages, and the origins of mortgages, we get a number of warnings concerning the power of mortgages. The historical land lawyer Maitland describes mortgages as 'one long *suppressio veri* and *suggestio falsi*'. Such suppression of the truth and false suggestion would certainly apply to today's mortgage, in which house purchase and money creation is dressed up as 'borrowing', and where there is covert reliance upon mortgages to supply 60 per cent of the money stock.

There is a further warning. In its medieval origins, the word mortgage means literally *'death-pledge'* or *'death grip'*. Then, mortgages were never a method of buying a property; they were a method of raising money on property you already owned if you had fallen on hard times; a last resort in times of dire financial need. Even so, mortgages were regarded with great suspicion, since it was generally goldsmiths employing usury not dissimilar from modern banking methods who supplied the money, hoping at the least for a large profit, and possibly the chance of ending up with the property. But a method of buying was categorically not what mortgages were. . .

Although it is possible for one person to pay off his or her mortgages, it is absolutely impossible for the community as a whole to buy its houses outright, since mortgages are heavily relied upon for money creation. Thus, for the nation as a whole . . . the death grip is locked onto our houses. Nor is this a stable situation, but a deteriorating one, with ever more dwellings subject to mortgage and ever more money raised against housing. . .

If we go back just another 30 years (from 1960) to the inter-war period, the comparison with today's housing debt is even more stark. In the 1930s, it was reckoned that buying a house cost the equivalent of about twice a man's salary for one year. This was an accepted rule of thumb. Houses were cheaper relative to income, and buyers commonly held 20–30 per cent of the price of the house as savings, to put down as a deposit. The great majority of mortgages were for 15 or at most 20 years, took about 8 per cent of the average annual income and were frequently paid off in advance of the full term. . .

The short life span of mortgages was not because the person moved on, transferring his mortgage to another property, as is now the case, but because the mortgage was generally settled early. Compare this with today, when mortgage terms are becoming ever longer, initial deposits ever smaller, repayments average about 20 per cent of annual income and re-mortgaging is becoming ever more widespread. By 1960, prices had risen relative to incomes to the point where a house cost 2.9 times the average annual wage. During the housing boom in the 1980s, house prices rose to four times the average annual income.

It is often suggested that house prices are set by a process of supply and demand, with home-buyers competing the price of houses upwards. But this is not the full story, and omits the impact of past debt. The prices of houses are heavily influenced by the costs of building new houses. . . Commercial debt is a major factor in raising costs and consistently elevating prices above what people can afford. The other major factor contributing to the progressive growth of mortgages is that, under a debt-based financial system, the ability of people to save and the amount of their disposable income both suffer progressive decline. Thus, deposits put down by first-time buyers become smaller whilst the high level of commercial debt, impacting through the construction industry, drives the price of new houses higher and higher. Deposits for first-time buyers have steadily declined from the pre-war level of approximately 25 per cent of the price of houses, to the point where the average deposit is tiny, and 100 per cent mortgages are now commonplace. Ultimately, the price of houses reflects not what people can afford to pay, but *what they can be persuaded to borrow*.

Of course, we appear to 'do well' out of house buying, and are impressed by the apparently escalating value of our property. But we only obtain this value if we sell up and move out of housing. Meanwhile, the *next* generation faces an even greater task in getting on the ladder of buying a house. With the increase in mortgages for each generation, even less equity is left to subsequent generations, which makes their mortgages even higher still. Which means that even less is passed down to the next generation, and so on. Raising large sums of money through house mortgages helps us to 'buy' these houses now, and provides the rest of the economy with sufficient money to function. But under this arrangement, we do not own these houses and will own less and less of them as time goes by.

If one reflects upon it, a situation in which over half the population carry housing debts averaging more than 50 per cent of the value of their house, and where over 37 per cent of the value of the housing stock is mortgaged, is just plain ridiculous. It is made all the more ridiculous by the fact that many of these houses have had previous owners who *also* had a mortgage. The unreality of the position is emphasised when it is considered that mortgages are a statement of financial poverty; a statement which completely belies our obvious modern wealth.

We have lived for so long in an economy dominated by the scarcity of money that the absurdity of the situation easily escapes us. These houses we live in and on which we pay such massive sums – they have *been* paid for in real terms. In terms of all the raw materials; in terms of the blood, sweat and tears of labour; the manufacturing, the transporting, the bricklaying, the decorating and plumbing and all the grovel and grind of work, and the sacrifice of time – they are already paid for. They were paid for on the day they were completed. No physical debt exists when a house is completed. No physical debt exists when a house has been built. What exists is an asset. There they stand. They are ours, or at least, they should be. It seems beyond dispute that the money for their purchase should *also* exist, and most people assume it does. They assume that when they borrow from a building society, they are literally borrowing money, not having to assume a lifetime's debt simply because no principle for the supply of money currently exists, other than via the issue of loans.

It is difficult to get a perspective on these matters when the behaviour of the economy and our judgement of what we might expect of money, prices and incomes has even distorted for so long by debt finance, and the unwarranted scarcity of money which it generates. It is interesting to consider what might be a legitimate level of mortgage indebtedness.

If there is any real economic justification for a degree of debt on housing via mortgages, this should be as a reflection of the rate at which houses have to be replaced. If you like, this is a real debt to the inevitability of time, and the fact that the housing stock must gradually be rebuilt at least at the rate at which it is deteriorating. If the average house lasts for 50 years, a figure commonly used for the depreciation of capital goods, then one would expect the overall mortgage indebtedness of the nation to be 2 per cent. This would reflect the need to replace the housing stock over a cycle of 50 years, and the aggregated mortgage of two per cent would be a financial reflection of that overall economic obligation. Obviously, some people would have a higher mortgage, and some people would have none, as is the situation now. But the current extent for 37 per cent of the total value of the housing stock under mortgage is clearly absurd, and implies that the private housing stock needs to be replaced every three years!

It is so difficult to get this point across without appearing unrealistic, but the fact is that these huge mortgages are a wholly illegitimate debt; they are part of the debt-money supply. These houses are ours — they belong to the nation, were built by ourselves and the generations that preceded us. They have *been* built; they have *been* paid for in real terms, and the money for their purchase should exist. There is absolutely no moral, ethical or economic reason for their ownership by the financial system, and for disbarring the majority of people from outright ownership of a dwelling place.

PART IV INTRODUCTION
DEMOCRATIC MONEY

I am qualified to tell the public that, in my view, it is entirely mistaken if it believes that the monetary system of this country is normally managed by 'recognized monetary experts' working in accordance with the most scientific and up to date methods known to modern economists.

VINCENT VICKERS, DIRECTOR OF THE BANK OF ENGLAND, WRITING
A PREFACE TO A BOOK BY ROBERT EISLER

If our nation can issue a dollar bond, it can issue a dollar bill.

THOMAS EDISON, 1921

In July 1914, the Chancellor of the Exchequer – then David Lloyd George – and the Governor of the Bank of England stared at the figures for bank reserves and realized there was a good chance of a banking panic. They extended the bank holiday, suspended gold payments and – rather like Lincoln had done in the American Civil War – they issued their own money.

The new 'Treasury notes', all £3.2 million of them, were signed by Sir John Bradbury and became known as 'bradburys'. But under pressure from the Bank of England, they were withdrawn from circulation as quickly as possible and most of the First World War was financed in the usual way, by borrowing from the banks and, via War Bonds, ordinary punters.

Until the First World War, prices in the UK had remained pretty steady since Napoleonic times, but by the end of the war the economy was in the grip of serious inflation. The 'bradburys' got some of the blame, though – since the National Debt was eight times higher in 1918 than it had been in 1914 – they probably had a comparatively small effect. Still, for those who came after who believed that the function of money creation should be restored to the people's representatives, 'bradburys' have always been suffused with a fond glow.

This was, in the end, the central tenet of Social Credit – but not just Social Credit – that the state and only the state should create money. This section tracks that tradition, and we can see it emerging in weaker forms of the argument – that at least some money for capital projects should be created interest-free in this way – as well as in the full-scale clampdown on banks.

I have to admit to being a sceptic about giving governments a monopoly of money creation. The records of governments in the Middle Ages were pretty appalling when it came to debasing the coinage, and however much modern governments might believe they know how much money needs to be in circulation, their capacity for self-delusion is proved weekly. The failure of the Keynesian Revolution, and the era of 'stagflation', would have to give anyone pause who wants to hand over the delicate operation of creating money lock, stock and barrel to central banks.

To be fair, the proposal put forward by modern advocates distinguishes between the *government* issuing money and professionally independent agencies of the state – along the lines of law courts in democratic societies, or the monetary committee of the Bank of England – which would be entrusted with the task of issuing money.

There are those who would also question whether it is possible to prevent banks creating money now, especially as – with credit cards – they may have handed over that right to individual customers, though that example is disputed by Joseph Huber and James Robertson in his recent pamphlet *Creating New Money* (see p133). I am more attracted by the idea of making the power to create mediums of exchange much broader, encouraging commercial and community enterprises to issue their own means of payment at their own risk, and subject to safeguards (see Parts VI and VII).

Either way, there are powerful arguments that the financial system has now escaped democratic control to such an extent that it is endangering itself. When decisions are taken not by central banks, and not even by the IMF or World Bank but by a handful of hedge funds – the main actors in the currency crises at the end of the 20th century – you have to wonder how to claw some of it back. It also seems likely that the current system depends on massive hidden subsidies to financial institutions to create official money, controlled by central banks by the use of interest rates, in a secretive, ambiguous system that is almost completely removed from public scrutiny. That is the context for the passages in this section.

There is also the argument about the future of public sector capital projects. If they are funded by the public–private partnerships, borrowing money from banks, or if they are funded by bond issues, the interest and fees can add enormously to the cost of the projects – and make many urgently needed items of infrastructure from railways to hospitals unaffordable. You can't help feeling there must be a better way.

ANDREW JACKSON

THE BANK VETO (1832)

It is said that American politics fractured between those who looked to Jefferson (see Part II, p55) as inspiration, and those – more corporate types – who looked towards the first US Treasury secretary Alexander Hamilton. If so, then the president most on the Jeffersonian side, who sided most with small shop-keepers and farmers – and who most disliked the banks – was probably the saddle-maker's assistant turned general, Andrew Jackson (1767–1845).

Having been saddled with somebody else's debts early in life, Jackson disapproved of all banks on principal, and asked why, he would cite the South Sea Bubble, then more than a century before. They were, he said, 'more formidable and dangerous than the naval and military power of an enemy'. On 10 July 1832, he acted on this disapproval by using his veto against renewing the charter to the Second Bank of the United States, which he accused of being a monopoly to make a few people rich.

The Second Bank of the United States was chartered by Congress in 1816 to issue banknotes, make loans and tackle the mess that was created by the demise of the First Bank of the United States in 1811. The charter was to last 20 years. It was a private institution, with the government owning a fifth of the original stock. Having refused to renew its licence, and got himself re-elected with an overwhelming majority as a result, Jackson set about killing it off, leaving money creation in the form of loans and notes mainly in the hands of the small local banks – some of them pretty dodgy. True to his roots, he later ordered all payments for land to be made in gold and silver.

This is dangerous territory because the mere existence of a central bank has been fodder for American conspiracy theorists ever since, for whom Jackson is a rare hero standing up against the power of the banks. For them the assassinations of Kennedy and Lincoln, and the attempted assassination of Jackson, all related to their attitude to bankers and money creation. Again, we shall never know.

* * *

A bank of the United States is in many respects convenient for the Government and useful to the people. Entertaining this opinion, and deeply impressed with the belief that some of the powers and privileges possessed by the existing bank are unauthorized by the Constitution, subversive of the rights of the States, and dangerous to the liberties of the people, I felt it my duty at an early period of my Administration to call the attention of Congress to the practicability of organizing an institution combining all its advantages and obviating these objections. I sincerely regret that in the act before me I can perceive none of those modifications of the bank charter which are necessary, in my opinion, to make it compatible with justice, with sound policy, or with the Constitution of our country.

The present corporate body, denominated the president, directors, and company of the Bank of the United States, will have existed at the time this act is intended to take effect twenty years. It enjoys an exclusive privilege of banking under the authority of the General Government, a monopoly of its favour and support, and, as a necessary consequence, almost a monopoly of the foreign and domestic exchange. The powers, privileges, and favours bestowed upon it in the original character, by increasing the value of the stock far above its par value, operated as a gratuity of many millions to the stockholders. . .

It is not our own citizens only who are to receive the bounty of our Government. More than eight millions of the stock of this bank are held by foreigners. By this act the American Republic proposes virtually to make them a present of some millions of dollars. For these gratuities to foreigners and to some of our own opulent citizens the act secures no equivalent whatever. . . It is not conceivable how the present stockholders can have any claim to the special favour of the Government. The present corporation has enjoyed its monopoly during the period stipulated in the original contract. If we must have such a corporation, why should not the Government sell out the whole stock and thus secure to the people the full market value of the privileges granted? Why should not Congress create and sell twenty-eight millions of stock, incorporating the purchasers with all the powers and privileges secured in this act and putting the premium upon the sales into the Treasury?. . . There are no necessary evils in government. Its evils exist only in its abuses. If it would confine itself to equal protection, and, as Heaven does its rains, shower its favours alike on the high and the low, the rich and the poor, it would be an unqualified blessing. In the act before me there seems to be a wide and unnecessary departure from these just principles.

Nor is our Government to be maintained or our Union preserved by invasions of the rights and powers of the several States. In thus attempting to make our General Government strong we make it weak. Its true strength consists in leaving individuals and States as much as possible to themselves – in making itself felt, not in its power, but in its beneficence; not in its control, but in its protection; not in binding the States more closely to the centre, but leaving each to move unobstructed in its proper orbit.

Experience should teach us wisdom. Most of the difficulties our Government now encounters and most of the dangers which impend over our Union have sprung from an abandonment of the legitimate objects of Government by our national legislation, and the adoption of such principles as are embodied in this act. Many of our rich men have not been content with equal protection and equal benefits, but have besought us to make them richer by act of Congress. By attempting to gratify their desires we have in the results of our legislation arrayed section against section, interest against interest, and man against man, in a fearful commotion which threatens to shake the foundations of our Union.

It is time to pause in our career to review our principles, and if possible revive that devoted patriotism and spirit of compromise which distinguished the sages of the Revolution and the fathers of our Union. If we can not at once, in justice to interests vested under improvident legislation, make our Government what it ought to be, we can at least take a stand against all new grants of monopolies and exclusive privileges, against any prostitution of our Government to the advancement of the few at the expense of the many, and in favour of compromise and gradual reform in our code of laws and system of political economy.

C H DOUGLAS

ECONOMIC DEMOCRACY

(1 9 1 9)

One of the peculiarities of Social Credit was that its originator, Major Douglas (see p43), wrote very little about what should be done to counteract the problems he had identified – and what he did write is sometimes pretty obscure. But this passage, in his book *Economic Democracy* – serialized in the magazine *The New Age* in 1919 – does outline the basic premise that was to be built on by his followers over the next two decades.

Here are all the basics of the idea: the state shouldn't be in the business of borrowing, it should be creating money – and the bottom line: by lending money, the bankers 'usurp the functions of the state'. Other elements of Social Credit are outlined here as well: the idea of distributing purchasing power directly to the population – later known as the National Dividend – and the idea of a 'Just Price'.

Social Credit has been gaining in popularity again recently, though I have my doubts whether this amount of state control over the economy is either achievable or desirable. When governments start setting prices, it's a difficult business, as we all witnessed in the 1970s. The phrase 'jaw-boning' came from that phase of the Second World War in the USA when the government set price limits with no legal controls to enforce them. Later writings (see Aberhart, p124) emphasize the National Dividend rather more than the Just Price.

Even so, there are some questions raised by Social Credit which demand to be answered. Douglas gave evidence to the Macmillan Committee of 1928, which ignored him, and that line of least resistance has been followed by mainstream economics ever since. But the economic historian Frances Hutchinson recently revealed, in an interview with the leading economist James Meade, that Meade had based his ideas on Douglas – and he believed that Keynes may have done so too.

So what are we to do, Douglas asked back in 1919? We need to 'level up' purchasing power. Neither increasing wages or taxing profits is going to help – because there just isn't enough money in general circulation. This was his alternative.

*   *   *

There is no doubt whatever that the first step towards dealing with the problem is the recognition of the fact that what is commonly called credit by the banker is administered by him primarily for the purpose of private profit, whereas it is most definitely communal property. In its essence it is the estimated value of the only real capital – it is the estimate of the *potential* capacity under a given set of conditions, including plant etc, of a Society to do work. The banking system has been allowed to become the administrator of this credit and its financial derivatives with the result that the creative energy of mankind has been subjected to fetters which have no relation whatever to the real demands of existence, and the allocation of tasks has been placed in unsuitable hands.

Now it cannot be too clearly emphasised *that real credit is a measure of the reserve of energy belonging to a commodity and in consequence drafts on this reserve should be accounted for by a financial system which reflects that fact.*

If this be borne in mind, together with the conception of 'Production' as a conversion, absorbing energy, it will be seen that the individual should receive something representing the diminution of the communal credit-capital in respect of each unit of converted material.

It remains to consider how these abstract propositions can be given concrete form. . . To put the matter another way: For every shell made and afterwards fired and destroyed, for every aeroplane built and crashed, for all the stores lost, stolen or spoilt, the Capitalist has an entry in his books which he calls wealth, and on which he proposes to draw interest at five per cent, whereas that entry represents loss not gain, debt not credit, to the community, and, consequently, is only realizable by regarding the interest of the Capitalist as directly opposite to that of the community. *Now, it must be perfectly obvious to anyone who seriously considers the matter that the State should lend, not borrow, and that in this respect, as in others, the Capitalist usurps the function of the State.*

But, however the matter be considered, the National debt as it stands is simply a statement that an indefinite amount of goods and services (indefinite because of the variable purchasing power of money) are to be rendered in the future to the holders of the loan, that is, it is clearly a distributing agent.

Now, instead of the levy on capital, which is widely discussed, let it be recognized that credit is a communal, not a bankers' possession; let the loan be redistributed by the same methods suggested in respect of a capital levy so that no holding of over £1000 is permitted; to the end that, say, 8,000,000 heads of families are credited with £50 per annum of additional purchasing power.

And further, let all production be costed on a uniform system open to inspection, the factory cost being easily ascertained by making all payments through a credit agency; the manner of procedure to this end is described hereafter. Let all payments for materials and plant be made through the Credit Agency and let plant increases be a running addition to the existing National debt, and let the yearly increase in the debt be equally distributed after proper depreciation. Let the selling price of the product be adjusted in reference to the effective demand by means of a depreciation rate fixed on the principle described subsequently, and let all manufacturing and agriculture be done, with broad limits, to a programme. Payment for industrial service rendered should be made somewhat on the following lines:

Let it be assumed that a given production centre has a curve of efficiency varying with output, which is a correct statement for a given process worked at normal intensity. The centre would be rated as responsible for a programme over a given time such that this efficiency would be a maximum when considered with reference to, say, a standard six-hour day. On this rating it is clear that the amount of money available for distribution in respect of labour and staff charges can be estimated by methods familiar to every manufacturer.

Now let this sum be allocated in any suitable proportion between the various grades of effort involved in the undertaking, and let a considerable bonus together with a recognized claim to promotion be assured to any individual who by the suggestion of improved methods or otherwise, can for the specified programme, reduce the hours worked by the factory or department in which he is engaged.

Now, consider the effect of these measures: Firstly, there is an immediate fall in prices which is cumulative, and, consequently, a rise in the purchasing power of money. Secondly, there is a widening of effective demand for all kinds by the wider basis of financial distribution. There is a sufficient incentive to produce, but there is communal control of undesirable production through the agency of credit; and there is incentive to efficiency. There is the mechanism by which the most suitable technical ability would be employed where it would be most useful, while the separation of a sufficient portion of the machinery of economic distribution from the processes of production would restore individual initiative, and, under proper conditions, minimize the effects of bureaucracy.

MUSCLE SHOALS AND THE END OF WAR (1921)

Between the First and Second World Wars, the great experts on dam-building and flood prevention were the US Army Corps of Engineers. It was they who developed the study of cost–benefit analysis and they who decided where the latest flood technology would be built. The peculiar entry of the two greatest American industrialists of the age, Henry Ford (1863–1947) and Thomas Alva Edison (1847–1931) into the debate came over the question of how the Muscle Shoals hydroelectric scheme on the Tennessee River should be financed.

Once again, it's fascinating to see how often it is engineers who are at the forefront of demands for a better system for creating money, and both men were engineers by profession – in fact Ford was the chief engineer at the Edison Illumination Company before going on to build motor cars.

During their interview on the subject, which stretched across two days in the *New York Times*, Ford and Edison suggested that the money should be created interest-free by the government, rather than borrowed from the banks, and withdrawn from circulation when it was paid off. 'Gold is a relic of Julius Caesar, and interest is an invention of Satan,' said Edison. 'It is the control of money that is the root of all evil.'

The idea that dependence on gold lay at the heart of the causes of war was also central to their thinking – which was, after all, being described just three years after the Armistice in 1918. But it was also a clue to the darker side to all this: Ford had recently started publishing a weekly paper called the *Dearborn Independent*, which concluded – as so often – that the international conspiracy of bankers he believed in throughout his life was also a Jewish conspiracy. He later removed all anti-Semitic material from the paper and apologized for upsetting the Jewish community, but this kind of rhetoric probably undermined the democratic legitimacy of this kind of financial innovation.

This passage is taken from the interview with Henry Ford about Muscle Shoals in Florence, Alabama, published in the *New York Times* on 4 December 1921, and quoted in *The Social Crediter*, vol 77, no 3, May/June1998.

* * *

'That's just where the Muscle Shoals comes in,' said Mr Ford: 'see what a spectacle we have. Army engineers say it will take $40,000,000 to complete that big dam. But Congress is economical just now and not in a mood to raise the money by taxation. The customary alternative is thirty-year bonds at four per cent. The United States, the greatest Government in the world, wishing $40,000,000 to complete a great public benefit is forced to go to the money sellers to buy its own money. At the end of thirty years the Government not only has to pay back the $40,000,000 but it has to pay 120 per cent interest, literally, has to pay $88,000,000 for the use of $40,000,000 for thirty years. . . Think of it. Could anything be more childish, more unbusinesslike!

'Now, I see a way by which our Government can get this great work completed without paying a nickel to the money sellers. It is as sound as granite, and there is but one thing hard about it. It is so simple and easy that, maybe, home folks can't see it.

'The Government needs $40,000,000. That is 2,000,000 twenty-dollar bills. The Government issue those bills and with them pay every expense connected with the completion of the dam. The dam completed we can set the whole works running, and in a shorter time than you would suppose, the entire $40,000,000 issued can be retired out of the earnings of the plant.'

'But suppose the contractor would be unwilling to accept that kind of currency in payment?' he was asked.

'There is not that kind of suppose in the situation at all,' said Mr Ford, smiling. 'He would take Government bonds in payment wouldn't he? Certainly! Here,' said the manufacturer, pulling a twenty-dollar bill from his pocket, 'he wouldn't hesitate about taking that kind of money would he? Of course not. Well, what is there behind a bond or this bill that makes it acceptable? Simply this, the good faith and credit of the American people, and twenty-dollar bills issued by the Government to complete this great public improvement would have just as much of the good faith and credit of the American people behind them as any bond or other American currency ever issued. You see it is just a question of faith in the American people.'

'But your plan would upset the money system of the world and might work incalculable harm,' he was told.

'Not necessarily. . . We need not abolish anything. . . whenever the Government needs money for a great public improvement, instead of thinking of bonds with heavy interest charges, think of redeemable non-interest bearing currency. . . Do you appreciate that 80 cents of every dollar raised by taxation is spent in the payment of interest? The national debt is nothing more nor less than the nation's interest liability pile. Every public improvement this country makes means an increase to the national debt. Here is a way to get the improvements without increasing the debt. The interest load is breaking down our whole financial system. We've got to stop somewhere. . .'

'Under the new currency system a certain amount of energy exerted for one hour would be equal to one dollar. It is simply a case of thinking and calculating in terms different than those laid down to us by the international banking group to which we have grown so accustomed that we think there is no other desirable standard. We should chance our minds on that question. The only difference between the currency plan and the bond plan is that there is no interest to be paid and the Wall Street money merchants, who do nothing to build the dam and deserve nothing, will get nothing.'

'But how is all this going to stop war?'

'Simply because if tried here at Muscle Shoals this plan will prove so. . . successful that the American people will never again consent to the issuance of an interest-bearing bond for a national improvement. When the Government needs money it will raise it by issuing currency against its imperishable natural wealth. Other countries seeing our success will undoubtedly do likewise. The function of the money seller will have disappeared.'

WILLIAM ABERHART

SOCIAL CREDIT MANUAL

(1 9 3 5)

Of all the countries where the Social Credit movement managed to lever an enthusiastic following, it was in Canada where they came closest to putting the ideas into practice. This came about largely through the efforts of the headmaster and broadcaster William Aberhart (1878–1943), who became interested in the ideas in the early 1930s, formed the Social Credit Party of Alberta and found himself swept to power in the 1935 elections. The party stayed in power until 1971.

There was a similar electoral breakthrough in British Columbia in 1952, but by then the original ideas had received a series of setbacks – and the movement had transmuted into something much more conservative.

The party had promised Alberta electors a national dividend of $25 a month, which never happened, but they did manage to issue a stamp scrip (see Fisher, p238) to boost the amount of currency in circulation. As many as 359,000 Canadian dollar certificates were issued before the scheme was abandoned in 1937.

Most of their other Social Credit measures were struck down one by one by Canada's Supreme Court – including their attempt to control local banks and their notorious Accurate News and Information Act 1937, an attempt to restrict freedom of the press. The Social Credit government in British Columbia managed to declare itself debt-free in 1959, but did so using the tried-and-tested methods of squeezing the budget.

Aberhart himself died unexpectedly in the middle of the war, but his followers carried on winning seats in the Canadian and New Zealand parliaments right through to the 1970s. This passage is taken from his original election material from 1935, and is a genuine attempt to describe Social Credit solutions for a mass audience.

✳   ✳   ✳

The Three Factors of the System Explained

The Basic System of Dividends and the Encouragement of Individual Enterprise

The State shall be viewed by its citizens as a gigantic joint-stock company with the resources of the province behind its credit. The bona fide citizens are each and all shareholders entitled to basic dividends sufficient to provide the bare necessarities of food, clothing and shelter for each individual and his family. The qualifications of citizenship shall be clearly defined and rigidly enforced. No citizen shall be allowed to barter away or otherwise dispose of his basic dividend beyond the extent of the then current month, and thereby become a vagabond or tramp with no fixed place of abode or sustenance. Basic dividends should be $25 a month for every bona fide citizen, male or female, twenty-one years or more. Children of bona fide citizens sixteen years old will receive $10 a month. Those, seventeen and eighteen years old will receive $10 a month. Those, nineteen, $15, and those, twenty, $20.00 a month. (These figures are merely suggested for illustration purposes.) This basic dividend rate may be changed at the end of any period to suit the standard of living then prevalent. Those dividends are not to be given on the basis of so much work done, but as a bare support of citizenship, loyalty to the State and the best interests of the country. Salaries or wages for work done will be paid as now, but in credit, not money. Any who are handicapped physically or mentally should be given bonus dividend protection. Individual enterprise must be encouraged in every way possible.

The Price Control Under Social Credit

Periodically a commission of our best experts from every sphere of life will be assembled for the purpose of deciding upon a fair and just price for all goods and services used in the Province. This price must give the producer, importer, or distributor, a fair commission on turnover, and, at the same time, must not exploit the purchasing power of the consumer. Excessive profits will thus be eliminated. To help make consumption balance and control production a compensating price will be declared from time to time. This compensating price will be fixed according to the following formula:

$$\text{Market Price} = \frac{\text{Total Consumption}}{\text{Total Production}} \times \text{Just Price}$$

The difference between the Just Price and the compensating price will be made up to the retailer or consumer much in the same way that the basic dividends are issued and recovered.

The Provision for Continuous Circulation of Credit (Not Money)

Credit is the life blood of the State or community. Under no circumstances must it be allowed to stop its flow. All basic dividend credit and all salaries or wages or incomes from whatever source, must be expended by the end of the year following the receipt of the same. To encourage individual enterprise and to enable the individuals to provide more adequately for the future, surplus credit may be used to purchase Government Bonds, maturing at a later date, for himself or for another. All producers will be allowed temporary, supervised credit to enable them to serve the citizenship in the best possible way. Direction should be given from time to time as to the products most needed. In order that credit may be adequate to provide and distribute goods, the state must be prepared to issue credit without interest to bona fide producers and distributors. This will prevent hoarding for the same of making high interest.

B F SKINNER

LABOUR CREDITS (1948)

When Pavlov first conditioned his drooling dogs using a bell, it was just a short step to thinking about money as a tool for conditioning the population to work. And when the leading psychologist Burrhus Frederic Skinner (1904–1990) wrote his utopian vision of a peaceful behaviourist community – called *Walden Two* – he put a credit system at the heart of it.

As you will see in the passage below, Skinner imagined that the labour–credit system wouldn't involve real money – in the sense of notes or coins – but credits which had to be earned at the rate of about four hours a day to pay your dues to society, after which everything was free.

The credit system is tweaked in *Walden Two*, to encourage people to do the jobs nobody else wants to do. It's a behaviourist economy, but with its vision of price control and useful work, not completely different to Social Credit – which is why the passage is included here, rather than in the next part with the other utopian visions.

There are still real-life *Walden Two*-style communities around the world, modelled on Skinner's novel, though the most famous of these – Twin Oaks in Virginia – abandoned Skinner's behaviourist vision early on. Behaviourism belonged to the 1940s and 50s, and fitted oddly with the spirit of the age in the following decades, yet *Walden Two* was the first of a series of communal visions that inspired the hippy generation to go off and find new ways of living. Some of these were science fiction, like Robert Heinlein's novel *Stranger in a Strange Land;* some were downright anarchic, but together they launched a new generation prepared to redesign the world from scratch – and that included money (see, for example, Hodroff, Part VII, p249).

✻　✻　✻

W e're grateful for your kindness,' I said to Frazier, 'not only in asking us to visit Walden Two but in giving us so much of your time. I'm afraid it's something of an imposition.'

'On the contrary,' said Frazier. 'I'm fully paid for talking with you. Two labour-credits are allowed each day for taking charge of guests of Walden Two. I can only use one of them, but it's a bargain even so, because I'm more than fairly paid by your company.'

'Labour-credits?' I said.

'I'm sorry. I had forgotten. Labour-credits are a sort of money. But they're not coins or bills – just entries in a ledger. All goods and services are free, as you saw in the dining room this evening. Each of us pays for what he uses with twelve hundred labour-credits each year – say, four credits for each workday. We change the value according to the needs of the community. At two hours of work per credit – an eight-hour day – we could operate at a handsome profit. We're satisfied to keep just a shade beyond breaking even. The profit system is bad even when the worker gets the profits, because the strain of overwork isn't relieved by even a large reward. All we ask is to make expenses, with a slight margin of safety; we adjust the value of the labour-credit accordingly. At present it's about one hour of work per credit.'

'Your members work only four hours a day?' I said. There was an overtone of outraged virtue in my voice, as if I had asked if they were all adulterous.

'On the average,' Frazier replied casually. In spite of our obvious interest he went on at once to another point. 'A credit system also makes it possible to evaluate a job in terms of the willingness of the members to undertake it. After all, a man isn't doing more or less than his share because of the time he puts in; it's what he's doing that counts. So we simply assign different credit values to different kinds of work, and adjust them from time to time on the basis of demand. Bellamy suggested the principle in *Looking Backwards* [see Bellamy, p148].'

'An unpleasant job like cleaning sewers has a high value, I suppose,' I said.

'Exactly. Somewhere around one and a half credits per hour. The sewer man works a little over two hours a day. Pleasanter jobs have lower values – say point seven or point eight. That means five hours a day, or even more. Working in the flower gardens has a very low value – point one. No one makes a living at it, but many people like to spend a little time that way, and we give them credit. In the long run, when the values have been adjusted, all kinds of work are equally desirable. If they weren't, there would be demand for the more desirable, and the credit value would be changed. Once in a while we manipulate a preference, if some job seems to be avoided without cause.'

'I suppose you put phonographs in your dormitories which repeat "I like to work in sewers. Sewers are lots of fun,"' said Castle.

'No, Walden Two isn't that kind of brave new world,' said Frazier. 'We don't *propagandize*. That's a basic principle. I don't deny that it would be possible. We could make the heaviest work appear most honourable and desirable. Something of the sort has always been done by well-organized governments – to facilitate the recruiting of armies, for example. But not here. You may say that we propagandize *all* labour, if you like, but I see no objection to that. If we can make work pleasanter by proper training, why shouldn't we? But I digress.'

'What about the knowledge and skill required in many jobs?' said Castle. 'Doesn't that interfere with free bidding? Certainly you can't allow just anyone to work as a doctor.'

'No, of course not. The principle has to be modified where long training is needed. Still, the preferences of the community as a whole determine the final value. If our doctors were conspicuously overworked *according to our standards*, it would be hard to get young people to choose that profession. We must see to it that there are enough doctors to bring the average schedule within range of the Walden Two standard.'

'What if nobody wanted to be a doctor?' I said.

'Our trouble is the other way round.'

'I thought as much,' said Castle. 'Too many of your young members will want to go into interesting lines in spite of the work load. What do you do then?'

'Let them know how many places will be available, and let them decide. We're glad to have more than enough doctors, of course, and could always find some sort of work for them, but we can't offer more of a strictly medical practice than our disgustingly good health affords.'

'Then you don't offer complete personal freedom, do you?' said Castle, with ill-concealed excitement. 'You haven't really resolved the conflict between a *laissez-faire* and a planned society.'

'I think we have. Yes. . .'

EMPOWERING LOCAL GOVERNMENT (1999)

Just when it might have seemed that all vestiges of Social Credit had disappeared from respectable discourse, a draft bill was put before the US Congress that proposed a very limited version of Douglas' ideas – to make interest-free money, created by the central bank, available for capital projects at local level.

The State and Local Government Economic Empowerment Act (known as SLGEEA or, more officially HR 1452) was introduced by the Republican congressman Ray LaHood, a representative from Illinois, on 15 April 1999. It remains on the table.

Actually, the story of SLGEEA started in 1989 with the foundation of Sovereignty, a US campaign specifically for a change in the law along these lines. Sovereignty is now part of the grassroots citizen campaigning organization, the Impact Network. When the bill was finally introduced, it had the support of over 3300 local authorities and four states. The vast majority of those, like Ray LaHood, were from the American Midwest, the home – you may remember – of the Greenback Party and the Populist Party a century before.

Under the bill's provisions, the Federal Reserve would be asked by Congress to create US$72 billion each year for five years and deposit it in the government's account. The government would then use these deposits for loans to state and local governments for the exclusive purpose of building and repairing their respective infrastructures.

Conventional economics suggests that this kind of money-printing activity would dangerously increase inflation, but the originators of the bill don't agree. 'The Federal Reserve banking system increased the US money supply by $1.5 trillion in the three years 1997–1999 and inflation has stayed at 1.5 to 1.7 per cent during the same period,' said Sovereignty chairman Ken Bohnsack. 'These facts explode the myth once and for all that the creation of money. . . is automatically inflationary.' He also points out that each dollar created increases the production of goods and services.

The loan would be available to each state and local government for projects and for a maximum of 30 years. And just as Ford and Edison suggested back in 1921 (see p12), the money would be 'extinguished from the money supply' once it was repaid. It also meant the projects could avoid fees to consultants, banks or bond dealers, which – as we know from projects like London Underground's proposed public–private partnership – can cost anything up to a third of the total cost.

It's a fascinating, heretical but very practical proposal, which doesn't add to the National Debt and provides real independence to local government. I'm looking forward to somebody adopting it in the UK.

A Bill

To create United States money in the form of non-interest bearing credit in accordance with the 1st and 5th clauses of section 8 of Article I of the Constitution of the United States, to provide for non-interest bearing loans of the money so created to State and local governments solely for the purpose of funding capital projects.

Be it enacted by the Senate and House of Representatives of the United States of America in Congress assembled:

Section 1. Short Title

This Act may be cited as the 'State and Local Government Economic Empowerment Act'.

Section 2. Findings

The Congress hereby finds the following:

1 As of the date of the enactment of this Act, money is principally created in the domestic economy by banks through the process known as 'deposit expansion' under which credit is extended by banks to customers in exchange for the assumption of an obligation by each customer to repay the amount of any such credit with interest.
2 The creation of money through the extension of credit and creation of debt, a traditional banking function, preceded the establishment by the Congress of, first, the national banking system and, subsequently, the Federal Reserve System.
3 The constitutional authority to create and regulate money does not limit the Federal Government to creating money through the production of

coins or currency or the process of debt creation but, except for a brief period during the administration of President Lincoln, the Federal Government has not exercised such authority more broadly.

4 The creation of money by the banks in conjunction with the Federal Reserve banks does not limit the constitutional authority of the Congress to create Government credit funds in the form of non-interest bearing credit to fund a legislatively approved programme or prevent the Congress from creating such funds.

5 The creation of non-interest-bearing government credit funds in measured or limited increments for the purpose of funding capital and environmental projects in the public interest

a) will allow projects to be built for one-half to one-third the normal cost; and

b) will allow more necessary projects to be built at a lower cost to the taxpayers and at the same time build additional wealth in the communities where such projects are located.

JAMES ROBERTSON AND
JOSEPH HUBER

RESTORING SEIGNIORAGE

(2 0 0 0)

Creating money is 'the government's greatest creative opportunity,' said Abraham
Lincoln (see Part III, p94) in 1865, and the idea that the state could and should
issue its own money has surfaced every few years in new ways. If the argument ran
out of steam in the 1940s, it has been emerging increasingly again at the turn of
the millennium. One of the most authoritative sources so far has been a collab-
oration between James Robertson and Professor Joseph Huber (1948–), who
published this passage in a joint pamphlet for the New Economics Foundation in
2000. Robertson went public with his ideas at an alternative Mansion House
Speech, the same day as the official speech by the Chancellor of the Exchequer at
the Mansion House where he set out the state of the economy.

The thesis owes a great deal to Huber, a pioneer of green banking and ethical
investment, and professor of economic and environmental sociology at Martin
Luther University in Halle. Huber's ideas owe more to the German tradition of
alternative thinking than to Social Credit – in fact he had not heard of Douglas
until his 1999 paper *Plain Money* was circulated more widely.

The pamphlet introduced the idea of 'seigniorage reform'. Seigniorage is the
profit that governments made putting money into circulation – traditionally it was
the difference between the cost of minting a coin and its face value. The creation
of electronic money by banks is a much more profitable business, which might be
characterized as the loan minus the risk. Robertson and Huber argue that this
'seigniorage' – a hidden subsidy of around £21 billion a year in the UK alone, they
said – belongs to the people. A state agency would issue it debt-free, relieving the
people of some of their tax burden and of the interest component in their
transactions.

Their prescription would mean that – just as Douglas (see p118) and Soddy
(see Part III, p97) suggested – banks should be prevented from creating money,
and allowed to lend only the deposits they had received, and all money in

circulation should be spent into existence by governments. Whether it is possible or desirable in the modern day to give the state a monopoly of official currency – and I'm not sure it is – this is a radical proposal, and probably a good deal more practical than mainstream Social Credit. It would also help central banks evolve into democratic agencies and banks into unsubsidized competitive businesses.

∗   ∗   ∗

New non-cash money will be issued and put into circulation in the following way: The first step will be for the central bank simply to write it into a current account which it manages for its governments (or, in the case of the European Central Bank, the current accounts which it manages for its governments). Instead of the commercial banks printing the new money into their customers' accounts, the central banks will be entering it into the accounts of their governments. A central bank will probably make these payments to its governments at regular two- or four-week intervals, not necessarily at constant amounts. Most importantly, it will make them as debt-free payments – outright grants – not as interest-bearing loans.

For example, in the UK, USA, Japan and other countries, the national central banks will make these payments into accounts which they manage for the Treasury or Finance Ministry of their respective national governments. In the Eurozone, the European Central Bank (ECB) will make the payments into accounts which it manages for the national governments of members states. The ECB could distribute the total between member states in proportion to their national population, or in proportion to their national Gross Domestic Product (GDP), or according to a mixture of the two – this third possibility reflecting the formula that governs the proportions in which the share capital of the ECB is held by each national central bank. The basis for distribution will be decided by member states and the ECB as part of their decision to create new money debt-free as public revenue.

The second step will be for governments to spend the new money into circulation, just as they spend other public revenue – on public expenditure programmes such as education, defence, servicing the national debt, etc.

Issuing new non-cash money will thus have become a source of public revenue, as issuing cash already is. This will enable governments to increase public spending, or to reduce taxation or government borrowing, or both in combination. As can be seen, the amounts will be significant – of the order of £48bn in the UK, $114bn in the USA, more than €160bn in the euro area, and more than ¥17 trillion in Japan. These figures amount to 5–15 per cent of annual tax revenues in the major OECD countries.

Decisions about how to use this revenue will be for governments to take, according to their political principles. Left-of-centre governments will tend to prefer increases in public spending, whereas right-of-centre governments will tend to prefer tax reductions. Owing to the great increase in public spending, taxation and borrowing over the past century and a half, the creative opportunities offered by seigniorage reform today may not seem quite so dramatic as they did to Abraham Lincoln. But governments of all persuasions will welcome it.

PART V INTRODUCTION
FUTURE MONEY

For in every country of the world, I believe, the avarice and injustice of princes and sovereign states abusing the confidence of their subjects, have by degrees diminished the real quality of the metal, which had been originally contained in their coins.

ADAM SMITH, QUOTED BY F A HAYEK IN HIS PAMPHLET
THE DE-NATIONALIZATION OF MONEY

Money is coined liberty.

FYODOR DOSTOEVSKY

The money historian Glyn Davies says that the history of money is also the story of the slow loss of control by governments over money. With each new innovation, from paper money to e-cash, the power over money slips out of the hands of the state just a little bit further. And perhaps that's not surprising: money may have been the cause of countless wars and disasters of human greed, but it has also been the great equalizer. It recognizes no religious scruple and no aristocracy — and in the end sweeps both away. In that sense, the development of money has been about spreading the wings of human liberty from church and state.

But of course that isn't the end of the story either. Monetary developments have also often led down the most bizarre blind alleys, as the Promethean money innovators struggle to control the fire they have created. The Chinese gave up paper currency before it spread to the West because it caused hyperinflation (see Marco Polo, p139); John Law escaped with his life from Paris after his innovations turned French society upside down (see p142). Even so, there are recognizable dreams that recur over and over again through this part.

There's the dream of disconnecting money from state control, repeated in different ways through economists like Hayek (see p157) or crypto-graphers like Chaum (see p164) — though as John Law and Marco Polo found out, paper money requires a strong legal context to give it value. There's the dream that money could disappear completely, repeated in different ways through utopians like William Morris (see p153) and economists like Fischer Black (see p155).

There's also the mirror-image dream that money might be developed in more targeted ways to improve society, repeated in rather frightening forms by novelists like Edward Bellamy (see p148) and psychologists like B F Skinner (see Part IV, p127) – and in more practical ways by the creativity guru Edward de Bono (see p168).

And through many of these passages, the same theme emerges of money and information slowly collapsing together, with writers like Birch and McEvoy (see p171) dreaming of a whole range of competing currencies for different aspects of life, which to some extent we can already see around us. Even back in 1867, the British colony of Singapore made a whole series of currencies legal tender, including those of Hong Kong, Mexico, Bolivia and Peru, adding the yen and the US dollar to the approved list later. Anyone who has visited the duty free shop in Moscow airport over the past decade will have experienced something similar because they could pay in any one of 20 or so currencies at the same till. Information technology makes this kind of world possible, when it would have been just too complex before.

Whether this trend will continue, or whether we see an extension of legal controls – as some reformers are now demanding (see Part IV) – remains to be seen. But I'd lay a pretty strong bet that, even if society responds to economic chaos by strengthening democratic controls over money creation, the underlying historic drive is going to contine: money will carry on fragmenting, and becoming more like information, and becoming at the same time more targeted.

Paper Money (circa 1299)

Marco Polo (1254–1324) may have made the whole thing up, as some scholars say, basing his travelogue on the anecdotes of merchants he ran into as he wandered around the Middle East. But this is nonetheless the earliest surviving description of paper money – a futuristic concept for the medieval mind if ever there was one. The whole point of medieval money was that the actual coins were supposed to be worth what they said they were worth, and here was paper which claimed to be worth something – just because the Grand Khan said it was.

It is also extraordinary how much Kublai Khan's paper money was created in such a similar way to the way paper currency is created these days. Ritual, as the anthropologist Mary Douglas argued, is very similar to money – and in Marco Polo's description, it is a ritual involving royal seals that conjures up the necessary belief that this paper money really does have buying power.

But of course it isn't quite the same. The next passage goes on to reveal that this is still more revolutionary than it looks at first sight. What backs the paper issue? Fear of the Grand Khan – and he was pretty fearful. This is a prime example of Aristotle's claim that money gets its value through the law.

But here's another difference. What happens when Marco Polo's paper currency notes wear out? You can replace them if you pay them a percentage. This was, in other words, to some extent a negative interest currency – as envisaged by Silvio Gesell (see Part I, p40). If you didn't hurry up and spend it, the rats could eat the notes or they would tear and you could end up paying 3 per cent of the face value to get a new bundle. In other words, Kublai Khan's currency was designed to encourage circulation rather than saving.

Marco Polo was writing about a trip with his Venetian merchant father and uncle way out East starting in 1271, which ended with him setting out on diplomatic missions for Kublai Khan and spending three years as governor of a Chinese city. Whether it was true or not, the description of the currency clearly came from someone who had seen it for themselves. China began to abandon paper currency around the year 1455 because it tended to cause inflation, and it didn't reappear until its first tentative and – to the people first presented with it – highly suspicious flowerings in Scotland and Massachusetts in the 1690s.

* * *

In this city of Kanbalu is the mint of the Grand Khan, who may truly be said to possess the secret of the alchemists, as he has the art of producing money by the following process. He causes the bark to be stripped from those mulberry-trees the leaves of which are used for feeding silk worms, and takes from it that thick inner rind which lies between the coarser bark and the wood of the tree.

This being steeped, and afterwards pounded in a mortar, until reduced to a pulp, is made into paper, resembling (in substance) that which is manufactured from cotton, but quite black. When ready for use, he has it cut into pieces of money of different sizes, nearly square but somewhat longer than they are wide. Of these, the smaller pass for a dernier tournois, the next size for a Venetian silver groat; others for two, five, and ten groats; others for one, two three, and as far as ten besants of gold.

The coinage of this paper money is authenticated with as much form and ceremony as if it were actually of pure gold or silver; for to each note a number of officers, specially appointed, not only subscribe their names, but affix their signets also; and when this has been regularly done by the whole of them, the principal officer, deputed by his majesty, having dipped into vermillion the royal seal committed to his custody, stamps with it the piece of paper, so that the form of the seal tinged with the vermillion remains impressed upon it, by which it receives full authenticity as current money, and the act of counterfeiting it is punished as a capital offence.

When thus coined in large quantities, this paper currency is circulated in every part of the Grand Khan's dominions; nor dares any person, at the peril of his life, refuse to accept it in payment. All his subjects receive it without hesitation, because, wherever their business may call them, they can dispose of it again in the purchase of merchandise they may have occasion for; such as pearls, jewels, gold or silver. With it, in short, every article may be procured.

Several times in the course of the year, large caravans of merchants arrive, with such articles as have just been mentioned, together with gold tissues, which they lay before the Grand Khan. He thereupon calls together twelve experienced and skilful persons, selected for this purpose, who he commands to examine the articles with great care, and to fix the value at which they should be purchased. Upon the sum at which they have been conscientiously appraised he allows a reasonable profit, and immediately pays for them with this paper; to which the owners can have no objection, because, as has been observed, it answers the purpose of their own disbursements; and even though they should be inhabitants of a country where this kind of money is not current, they invest the amount in other articles of merchandise suited to their own markets.

When any persons happen to be possessed of paper money, which from long use has become damaged, they carry it to the mint, where, upon payment of only three per cent, they may receive fresh notes in exchange.

JOHN LAW

THE PAPER CURRENCY PROPOSAL (1705)

For about a century after 1540, Europe went through a period known as the 'Price Revolution'. Never having suffered much from inflation before, the influx of gold from the Americas caused prices to rise about six times over. By the end of the 17th century, with the massive increase in trade, there was a serious shortage of coinage – given that all of it needed to be made from precious metals. There is, after all, only about enough gold ever discovered in the world to fill about two modest semi-detached homes. It wasn't enough to run a world economy, and the stage was set for the arrival of paper money.

The first banknotes in Europe should not have filled anyone with confidence. Their progenitor, Johan Palmstruch – founder of Stockholm Banco in 1656 – nearly suffered the death penalty for causing wild inflation in Sweden. But if anyone could be said to be the father of paper money, and with it the information economy, it was probably the great Scottish gambler and banker John Law (1671–1729).

Maybe it helped enforce the paper currency that Law was working under the jurisdiction of a pre-revolutionary absolute monarchy, rather as Marco Polo found with the Great Khan (see p139). But Law was a much more modern figure than that implies, on the run from England after a duelling murder conviction, when he brought his ideas for a backed paper currency to the French court.

His scheme for paper money, backed by coins, made Law briefly the richest man in Europe when it was finally accepted in 1716. He added to that wealth by setting up the Mississippi Company, creating the first stock market boom, followed soon afterwards by the first stock market bust when Law had to escape Paris with his life, leaving the French aristocracy and economy in ruins.

Law was years ahead of his time, and he was no simple adventurer. He had thought long and hard about his proposals. This passage is taken from his book *Money and Trade considered: with a proposal for supplying the nation with money*, which was first published in Edinburgh in 1705 – so bear in mind that the nation he wants to supply with money is rather ambiguous since Scotland and England are still separate. This is how he proposes a new currency, backed by the value of land.

* * *

THE PROPOSAL WITH REASONS FOR IT

To supply the nation with money, it is humbly propos'd, that 40 commisioners be appointed by parliament, answerable to parliament for their administration, and the administration of the officers under them: the nomination of the officers being left to the commissioners.

That the commissioners have power to coin notes: which notes to be receiv'd in payments, where offer'd.

That a committee of parliament be appointed to inspect the management, and that none of the commissioners be members.

That the commission and committee meet twice a year at Whitsunday and Martinmas; their meetings, to being 10 days before, and to continue 10 days after each terms.

There are three ways humbly offer'd to the parliament, for giving out these notes; they in their wisdom may determine which will be the most safe.

1 To authorize the commission to lend notes on land security, the debt not exceeding one half, or two-thirds of the value: and at the ordinary interest.
2 To give out the full price of land, as it is valued, 20 years purchase more or less, according to what it would have given in silver-money, the commission entering into possession of such lands, by wadset granted to the commission of assignees; and redeemable betwixt and the expiring of a term of years.
3 To give the full price of land upon sale made of such lands, and disponed to the commission or assignees irredeemably.

That any person shall have such bonds, wadsets or estates assigned or dispon'd to them, upon paying in the value to the commission.

That the commission don't receive other money than these notes.

That no person who has contracted for these notes, shall be obliged to receive silver or metal money.

That the commission have not power to coin more than 50,000 *lib* at a time, and that no more be coin'd so long as there is 25,000 *lib* remaining in the office.

That for a year and a half the commission be limited to a certain sum, after that time to have power to coin what sums are demanded: unless restricted by ensuing parliaments.

That these who desire to have money from the commission, give in a note to the lawyers for the commission, a month before the term, of what sums they want, with the rights of the lands they offer in pledge: and that these who have note to pay in to the commission, give warning 10 days before the term.

That the state of the commission, the sum of the notes coin'd, the debt and credit, with the highest number of the different notes, be publish'd every term.

That any person who shall discover two notes of the same number, or of a higher number that these publish'd shall have a 100 *lib* reward.

That the under-officers be instructed with the sum of 20,000 *lib* to change notes with; and that they attend the whole year.

That any member of parliament may inspect the state of the commission.

That no notes be coined, money lent, or rights assigned by the commission, but at the terms of Whitsunday and Martinmas: and in presence of at least 20 commissioners, and one third of the committee.

That the revenue of the commission, over what pays the charges, and what part the parliament thinks needful to make good any losses which may happen to the commission, be applied by way of drawback, for encouraging the export, and manufacture of the nation.

That paper-money do not rise more than 10 per cent above silver-money; so that he who contracts to pay in paper, may know what he is to pay in case he cannot get paper money.

The parliament may enter into a resolve, that the next sessions of this or the next ensuing parliament, the state of the commission be taken into consideration, preferable to all other business: and if found hurtful to the country, the parliament may discharge any more notes to be given out, and order what notes are then out to be called in.

That after three months from the date of the act, Scots and foreign money be reduced to the English standard. The English crown to 60 pence, and the other money in proportion to its value of silver. The 40 pence to 38 pence, the new merk to 13, the old merk to its weight, the ducat-downs to 68 pence, dollars to their weight, guineas not to pass 22sh.

That after four months no Scots money, (except what shall be coined after the act), nor any foreign money except the English money, be received in any payments, or be sold as bullion but at the mint.

This paper-money will not fall in value as silver-money has fallen, or may fall: goods or money fall in value, if the increase in quantity, or if the demand lessens. By the commission giving out what sums are demanded, and taking back what sums are offered to be returned; this paper-money will keep its value, and there will always be as much money as there is occasion or imployment for, and no more.

WALTER BAGEHOT

A UNIVERSAL MONEY

(1 8 6 9)

The question of whether Britain should abandon the pound and embrace the euro seems to have stifled debate in the UK about whether there might be better ways of organizing the money system for a decade or more. And even then the question of whether the Queen's head should appear on the notes and coins seems to exercise people's minds more than some of the more important economic unknowns.

International currencies are really beyond the scope of this book, but this passage is an exception – partly because it prefigures so many 20th century debates, and partly because it introduces the idea that money and the nation state might not be inextricably linked after all. Even more important, it implies the idea that currencies can compete – not just in the money markets – but for the attention of individuals.

Walter Bagehot (1826–1877) was the great constitutional and economic writer who married the founder of *The Economist*, and became its editor until his death. This plea, not just for a European currency but for an international one, was first published in that magazine in 1869, but became more famous when it was reissued as a book called *A Universal Money*, more than a decade after his death in 1889.

The comments of Prime Minister Gladstone – doubting whether it would be possible for Britain to get rid of the penny – are closely followed for their influence, just as the comments of Prime Minister Blair on whether Britain can get rid of the pound are followed now. And Bagehot's plan is to merge the British and American currencies first, provide a currency for the new German nation along the same lines – and compete with the franc until the whole world was using what he calls the Teutonic money. It never happened. Nor did his suggestion of decimalizing on the basis of the penny rather than the pound, when – over a century later – Britain finally adopted a decimal currency.

*   *   *

The great difficulty in all changes of coin is with the smaller coins. This is the difficulty which has prevented, and is long likely to prevent, a decimalization of a coinage founded on the pound. Twenty years ago and more the florin was struck as a first step to that scheme, and to prepare men's minds. But we are not a bit nearer that scheme than we then were. Mr Gladstone told a deputation that he was by no means certain 'we could get rid of the penny', and there the plan stuck. The mass of the community could not be persuaded to change the petty coins they use and reckon in; and so many tolls and charges – some belonging to private people – are assessed in the smaller coins, that we should be immersed in a complexity of compensations. No doubt it *could* be done, and for a great object ought to be done, but there would be endless difficulty in persuading the people to do it.

On the contrary, if you retain the smaller coins all other changes are in comparison easy; you do not require to change the habits of the mass of mankind; you address yourself to the users of valuable coins, who are in some degree educated; you can translate exactly each old sum, however small, into the coinage you propose; everybody could pay exactly what they had contracted to pay; no man's income would be menaced, and no one's diminished.

Now, a system can certainly be devised which would keep English small money, and also the American small money. The plan of decimal coinage known as the 'farthing plan' does this. We should have to change the sovereign to 1,000 farthings, or £1 0s. 10d; now, this is almost exactly the half-eagle of five dollars. Taking the dollar at 4s. 2d., which by Act of Congress it is, the American cent is equal to an English halfpenny, and the cent therefore could be retained in the United States as a paying coin just as the halfpenny could be kept here. It would, therefore, be not only possible, it would for such a matter be even easy, to found a great *Anglo-Saxon* system of coins – a system of coins which would be common to both the great nations which speak the English language. And the two countries would not only obtain the advantage of uniformity – each of them would have a better coinage than it now has. America would have a high gold unit, and would reckon her vast debt and great taxation in units of suitable size; counting such large sums by dollars seems, and always must seem, like measuring their enormous territory by inches. England would have a decimal coinage and a decimal system of accounts, which now she has not, and which, as long as we keep the sovereign as our principal unit, she is not at all likely to have.

No doubt it would be long before the French and the other nations which have adopted their money would change, and adopt the Anglo-Saxon money.

But still the mercantile transactions of the English-speaking race are so much greater than those of any other race; a price current that an Anglo-Saxon can effectually deal with is a price current so much more important and so much more read than a price current which only the French and the copiers of French money can readily use that in the course of years it is very likely that the Anglo-Saxon money would become the *one* money. And even before then it might be and would be largely used as the principal money of *wholesale account*. Every great firm in the world would quote prices in that great spreading and so to say oceanic money, as well as in its own local money.

Besides it must not be forgotten that Germany will have a currency to choose; none of her many currencies are suitable to modern commerce; and she ought to have and will have, we may be sure, ere long one uniform coinage and one single money of account. It is very likely, considering her great intercourse with America and England, that she might choose to select the money which we put forward rather than that which France puts forward. In that case, there would be one Teutonic money and one *Latin* money; the latter mostly confined to the West of Europe; and the former circulating through the world. Such a monetary state would be an immense improvement on the present.

CREDIT CARDS (1888)

The trouble with utopian novels that are written primarily because the author wants to change the world is that they are often indescribably pompous and dull. They mainly consist of an incredulous narrator in conversation with an all-knowing man of the future, who has found solutions – miraculously very close to those proposed by the author – to human problems that seem intractable.

The book from which this passage is taken is one of those. Its author, Edward Bellamy (1850–1898) was an unsuccessful New England journalist when he wrote his novel *Looking Backward 1887–2000*, but it catapulted him suddenly to best-seller status. Highly moral, highly romantic about his experience in the American Civil War, Bellamy's hero wakes up having slept for 113 years and finds a martial world, run by an industrial army, all ruled by what certainly seems to me a particularly unpleasant brand of state control. He called his heady mix of state socialism and martial law, 'nationalism' – as well he might – and it was enthusiastically adopted by a strange amalgam of ex-military men, feminists, theosophists and Christian socialists. Bellamy left them to it after a while and became instead an organizer for the Populist Party (see Donnelly, Part I, p31). He died not long afterwards of tuberculosis at the age of just 48.

Looking Backward is hardly read these days, except for one reason. Within its pages, Bellamy predicted the credit card, but not quite as we understand it. He imagined that 'money' was put into circulation – the same amount per person – as a citizen's income, which was deposited on their credit card every year. It was, in some ways, an early version of Social Credit (see Douglas, p118).

The pressures of launching your own political party, and having to face the same kind of criticisms that the Social Credit movement did half a century later, probably explains the passage which I've put in bold – explaining how they would deal with people who spent more than they were allowed to. This was a new sentence, put into the second edition.

The whole idea of money is actually pretty ambiguous here, as the narrator says. On the one hand the idea of buying and selling between individuals has been abolished because it's distasteful; on the other hand, there is still this credit system deposited on people's cards. So money isn't abolished altogether, as some utopias have it (see Morris, p153). Even so, *Looking Backwards* was republished very quickly as an early 50 cent paperback and it was immensely influential on the new generation, who a few decades later became the prophets of industrial efficiency.

*   *   *

'You were surprised,' he said, 'at my saying that we got along without money or trade, but a moment's reflection will show that trade existed and money was needed in your day simply because the business of production was left in private bands, and that, consequently, these are superfluous now.'

'I do not at once see how that follows,' I replied.

'It is very simple,' said Dr Leete. 'When innumerable different and independent persons produced the various things needful to life and comfort, endless exchanges between individuals were requisite in order that they might supply themselves with what they desired. These exchanges constituted trade, and money was essential as their medium. But as soon as the nation became the sole producer of all sorts of commodities, there was no need of exchanges between individuals that they might get what they required. Everything was procurable from one source, and nothing could be procured anywhere else. A system of direct distribution from the national storehouses took the place of trade, and for this money was unnecessary.'

'How is this distribution managed?' I asked.

'On the simplest possible plan,' replied Dr Leete. 'A credit corresponding to his share of the annual product of the nation is given to every citizen on the public books at the beginning of each year, and a credit card issued him with which he procures at the public storehouses, found in every community, whatever he desires whenever he desires it. This arrangement, you will see, totally obviates the necessity for business transactions of any sort between individuals and consumers. Perhaps you would like to see what our credit cards are like.

'You observe,' he pursued as I was curiously examining the piece of pasteboard he gave me, 'that this card is issued for a certain number of dollars. We have kept the old word, but not the substance. The term, as we use it, answers to no real thing, but merely serves as an algebraical symbol for comparing the values of products with one another. For this purpose they are all priced in dollars and cents, just as in your day. The value of what I procure on this card is checked off by the clerk, who pricks out of these tiers of squares the price of what I order.'

'If you wanted to buy something of your neighbour, could you transfer part of your credit to him as consideration?' I inquired.

'In the first place,' replied Dr Leete, 'our neighbours have nothing to sell us, but in any event our credit would not be transferable, being strictly personal. Before the nation could even think of honouring any such transfer as you speak of, it would be bound to inquire into all the circumstances of the transaction, so a to be able to guarantee its absolute equity. It would have been reason enough, had there been no other, for abolishing money, that its possession was no indication of rightful title to it. In the hands of the man who had stolen it or murdered for it, it was as good as in those which had earned it by industry. People nowadays interchange gifts and favours out of friendship, but buying and selling is considered absolutely inconsistent with the mutual benevolence and disinterestedness which should prevail between citizens and the sense of community of interest which supports our social system. According to our ideas, buying and selling is essentially anti-social in all its tendencies. It is an education in self-seeking at the expense of other, and no society whose citizens are trained in such a school can possibly rise above a very low grade of civilization.'

'What if you have to spend more than your card in any one year?' I asked.

'The provision is so ample that we are more likely not to spend it all,' replied Dr Leete. 'But if extraordinary expenses should exhaust it, we can obtain a limited advance on the next year's credit, though this practice is not encouraged, and a heavy discount is charged to check it. **Of course if a man showed himself a reckless spendthrift he would receive his allowance monthly or weekly instead of yearly, or if necessary not be permitted to handle it all.**'

'If you don't spend your allowance, I suppose it accumulates?'

'That is also permitted to a certain extent when a special outlay is anticipated. But unless notice to the contrary is given, it is presumed that the citizen who does not fully expend his credit did not have occasion to do so, and the balance is turned into the general surplus.'

'Such a system does not encourage saving habits on the part of citizens,' I said.

'It is not intended to,' was the reply. 'The nation is rich, and does not wish the people to deprive themselves of a good thing. In your day, men were bound to lay up goods and money against coming failure of the means of support and for their children. This necessity made parsimony a virtue. But now it would have no such laudable object, and, having lost its utility, it has ceased to be regarded as a virtue. No man any more has any care for the morrow, either for himself or his children, for the nation guarantees the nurture, education, and comfortable maintenance of every citizen from the cradle to the grave.'

'That is a sweeping guarantee!' I said. 'What certainty can there be that the value of a man's labour will recompense the nation for its outlay on him? On the whole, society may be able to support all its members, but some must earn less than enough for their support, and others more; and that brings us back once more to the wages question, on which you have hitherto said nothing. It was at just this point, if you remember, that our talk ended last evening; and I say again, as I did then, that here I should suppose a national industrial system like yours would find its main difficulty. How, I ask once more can you adjust satisfactorily the comparative wages or remuneration of the multitude of avocations, so unlike and so incommensurable, which are necessary for the service of society? In our day the market rate determined the price of labour of all sorts, as well as of goods. The employer paid as little as he could, and the worker got as much. It was not a pretty system ethically, I admit; but it did, at least, furnish us a rough and ready formula for settling a question which must be settled in thousand times a day if the world was ever going to get forward. There seemed to us no other practicable way of doing it.'

'Yes,' replied Dr. Leete, 'it was the only practicable way under system which made the interests of every individual antagonistic to those of every other; but it would have been a pity if humanity could never have devised a better plan, for yours was simply the application to the mutual relations of men of the devil's maxim, "Your necessity is my opportunity". The reward of any service depended not upon its difficulty, danger, or hardship, for throughout the world it seems that the most perilous, severe, and repulsive labour was done by the worst paid classes; but solely upon the strait of those who needed the service.'

'All that is conceded,' I said. 'But, with all its defects, the plan of settling prices by the market rate was a practical plan; and I cannot conceive what satisfactory substitute you can have devised for it. The government being the only possible employer, there is of course no labour market or market rate. Wages of all sorts must be arbitrarily fixed by the government. I cannot imagine a more complex and delicate function than that must be, or one, however performed, more certain to breed universal dissatisfaction.'

'I beg your pardon,' replied Dr Leete, 'but I think you exaggerate the difficulty. Suppose a board of fairly sensible men were charged with settling the wages for all sorts of trades under a system which, like ours, guaranteed employment to all, while permitting the choice of avocations. Don't you see that, however unsatisfactory the first adjustment might be, the mistakes would soon correct themselves? The favoured trades would have too many volunteers, and those discriminated against would lack them till the errors were set right. But this is aside from the purpose, for, though this plan would, I fancy, be practicable enough, it is no part of our system.'

'How, then, do you regulate wages?' I once more asked.

Dr Leete did not reply till after several moments of meditative silence. 'I know, of course,' he finally said, 'enough of the old order of things to understand just what you mean by that question and yet the present order is so utterly different at this point that I am a little at loss how to answer you best. You ask me how we regulate wages; I can only reply that there is no idea in the modern social economy which at all corresponds with what was meant by wages in your day.'

'I suppose you mean that you have no money to pay wages in,' said I. 'But the credit given the worker at the government storehouse answers to his wages with us. How is the amount of the credit given respectively to the workers in different lines determined? By what title does the individual claim his particular share? What is the basis of allotment?'

'His title,' replied Dr Leete, 'is his humanity. The basis of his claim is the fact that he is a man.'

'The fact that he is a man!' I repeated, incredulously. 'Do you possibly mean that all have the same share?'

'Most assuredly.

The readers of this book never having practically known any other arrangement, or perhaps very carefully considered the historical accounts of former epochs in which a very different system prevailed, cannot be expected to appreciate the stupor of amazement into which Dr Leete's simple statement plunged me.

ABOLISHING MONEY (1891)

William Morris (1834–1896) the great visionary, poet, artist and wallpaper designer, had very pronounced views about politics and the ideal world, which formed the theology of the Arts and Crafts Movement that he founded. As an influential follower of John Ruskin (see Introduction, p13), he firmly believed that wealth meant more than just money. 'Wealth is what nature gives us,' he wrote.

He believed there was a difference between 'good' and 'bad' work – that factories and industry destroyed people and places, while simplicity and craftsmanship fulfilled them. His romantic medieval ideal assumed that the rift between arts and crafts could be healed if art became part of life. In his utopian story *News from Nowhere*, from which this passage is taken, he imagines waking up in the distant future after a revolution in 1952, to find that London's population had spread out and the dirty old city which he hated had been forested over.

Trafalgar Square was an orchard for apricots. Money was no longer used, leisure and work had become inextricable, and the Houses of Parliament had become a manure-store. The state socialists of the following generations rejected William Morris' vision, as he predicted they would, and *News from Nowhere* was much ridiculed. But he did actually predict a number of things correctly. People *do* look healthier and wear simpler clothes. They are no longer 'upholstered like an armchair,' as he put it. The 'great clearing of houses' *did* happen in the 1950s: unfortunately they were replaced by more slums which now urgently need the same treatment.

Salmon *have* returned to the Thames. Leisure and crafts *are* increasingly important. And the Countryside Commission *has* been working on plans to grow forests on the outskirts of major cities. People *are* moving out of cities to the country towns all over the Western world, just as Morris said they would – flocking into the villages 'like a wild beast on its prey'.

And, of course, cash *is* disappearing from use – though not in quite the way he suggests here, where he echoes Bellamy's (see p148) distaste at what he calls 'extinct commercial morality' that things have to be paid for. In every other way, Morris was appalled by Bellamy's book, and it inspired him to write his own alternative utopia. Here he is going shopping.

* * *

'Now for the pipe: that also you must let me choose for you; there are three pretty ones just come in.' She disappeared again, and came back with a big-bowled pipe in her hand, carved out of some hard wood very elaborately, and mounted in gold sprinkled with little gems. It was, in short, as pretty and gay as a toy as I had ever seen; something like the best kind of Japanese work, but better.'

'Dear me!' said I, when I set eyes on it, 'this is altogether too grand for me, or for anybody by the Emperor of the World. Besides, I shall lose it: I always lose my pipes.'

The child seemed rather dashed, and said, 'Don't you like it, neighbour?'

'O yes,' I said, ' of course I like it.'

'Well, then, take it,' said she, 'and don't trouble about losing it. What will it matter if you do. Somebody is sure to find it, and he will use it, and you can get another.'

I took it out of her hand to look at it, and while I did so, forgot my caution, and said, 'But however am I to pay for such a thing as this?'

Dick laid his hand on my shoulder as I spoke, and turning I met his eyes with a comical expression in them, which warned me against another exhibition of extinct commercial morality; so I reddened and held my tongue, while the girl simply looked at me with the deepest gravity, as if I were a foreigner blundering in my speech, for she clearly didn't understand me a bit.

'Thank you so very much,' I said at last, effusively, as I put the pipe in my pocket, not without a qualm of doubt as to whether I shouldn't find myself before a magistrate presently.

FISCHER BLACK

A WORLD WITHOUT MONEY

(1970)

There is a leap of nearly 80 years between this passage and the last one, and at first sight, there isn't much connection between them, except that they are both concerned with imaginary logical futures – Morris from the point of view of a campaigner and Fischer Black (1938–1995) as an academic economist. What does hold them together is that, in very different ways, they were also imagining a world without money, and doing so from a laissez-faire point of view.

Black narrowly missed out on the Nobel Prize for economics in 1997 – two years after his death – which went to his two colleagues for their work on pricing options – now the basis for the way the options market works. The academic article, written in 1970, from which this passage is taken – 'Banking and Interest rates in a World without Money: The effects of uncontrolled money' – imagines a world without central banks, or coinage, or governments creating money. It went unnoticed in the academic community for ten years, but then suddenly became the jumping-off point for a number of academics trying to imagine a world where money was issued privately.

It wasn't the first time anyone had written on the subject – especially when private currencies had been common in North America and Scotland in the 18th century. But he went further than that, back to first principles, imagining a series of very simple worlds without currency. The fifth of these was a world he called 'Checking accounts and bank money'.

What Black meant by a world with no money wasn't quite what it might seem to a non-economist. He was writing ahead of time about a world when money was simply information about debts – a world, in other words, without the kind of money we are used to. It was one where people have bank accounts, and the money is simply internal credits shifted around by the banks.

The problem with Black's imaginary world – and indeed a world without central banks or national currencies – is that there was no immediate mechanism for setting value. How did people agree without prices quoted, and what would the prices be quoted in? It was an important question, and 30 years of literature have followed to answer it.

*   *   *

To solve these problems, we allow the banks to participate in the payments mechanism in a unique way. Instead of remaining outstanding, individual notes will be used only temporarily in making payments, and will then be extinguished. Individuals will have bank accounts that will have positive balances for lenders and negative balances for borrowers. Banks will credit interest to accounts with positive balances and will debit interest to accounts with negative balances. The individual will write a note whenever he wants to make a payment. This note will be either in the form of a cheque or in the form of a credit card purchase receipt. His note will serve to credit the balance of the seller and to debit his balance. It will also credit the balance of the seller's bank with his bank. This system will be a convenient, safe, low-cost means of payment.

In none of these five worlds was there any clearly defined quantity of money. The world of private business and commodity money came closest to having a money supply, but even there, a commodity used as means of payment also has other uses. And it may not be clear when it is to be counted as part of the money supply, and when it is to be counted as involved in one of its other uses. Once we introduced financial markets, however, and intangible means of payment, the idea of 'quantity of money' loses its meaning.

In none of these five worlds is there any role for a central bank. And the only effect that the financial sector had on the real sector was that as we go to successively more efficient means of payment, we reduce the cost of making payments and release real resources for other uses. In none of these worlds was there any mechanism that would cause uncontrolled inflation in the absence of a central bank.

F A HAYEK

DENATIONALIZATION OF MONEY (1976)

Once Keynes was dead and Keynesian economics began to recede, the mantle of wisest man in the world fell to his great rival Friedrich August von Hayek (1899–1992), the Austrian emigré and free market enthusiast. It was Hayek who laid the foundations, with his 1948 book *The Road to Serfdom*, for the revolution wrought by Thatcher and Reagan a generation later.

When he gave a lecture to the free market Institute of Economic Affairs in London in 1976, towards the end of his life, entitled 'Choice in Currency' – and followed it up with a pamphlet on *The Denationalization of Money – the Argument Refined: An analysis of the theory and practice of concurrent currencies* – most people thought he was just playing around academically. But reading the opening passage a quarter of a century later, it is clear he was actually intending to be very practical. He was putting forward a scheme to tackle rampant inflation, the 1970s bugbear, and an alternative to the euro, then in its very earliest dream phase.

We can see that now because so much of what he predicted came to pass. An early decision by the Thatcher government only three years later led to the abolition of exchange controls around the world, and the competing currencies he predicted – with the traders of Wall Street and the City of London acting as puritanical free market 'policemen' against governments that spend more than they feel they should – are with us now. We also have the result he wanted to achieve: national governments are now nearly powerless to raise public spending.

This has certainly slain inflation, but it has left us with other frightening consequences. Those policing money flows, the foreign exchange markets, now make up over 97 per cent of the daily monetary exchanges around the world. The speculative tail is wagging the free-trade dog. The combined central bank reserves of the world could resist a wholehearted onslaught by traders and hedge funds for less than 12 hours. It's at least as frightening as inflation ever was.

But Hayek's vision went further. He saw no reasons why the currencies traded should just be national. He imagined that for some small countries, their own small currencies would be replaced by bigger ones – and since Argentina and other countries pinned their currencies to the dollar, Hayek was right about that too.

He only hints at it here, but if anyone can issue a currency, why should they all be national? That's why Hayek's essay is now Exhibit A in the free market case for extending the idea of competing currencies further.

* * *

THE CONCRETE PROPOSAL FOR THE NEAR FUTURE, AND THE OCCASION FOR THE EXAMINATION OF A MUCH MORE FAR-REACHING SCHEME IS THAT:

The countries of the Common Market, preferably with the neutral countries of Europe (and possibly later the countries of North America) mutually bind themselves by formal treaty not to place any obstacles in the way of the free dealing throughout their territories in one another's currencies (including gold coins) or of a similar free exercise of the banking business by any institution legally established in any of their territories.

This would mean in the first instance the abolition of any kind of exchange control or regulation of the movement of money between these countries, as well as the full freedom to use any of the currencies for contracts and accounting. Further, it would mean the opportunity for any bank located in these countries to open branches in any other on the same terms as established banks.

Free Trade in Money

The purpose of this scheme is to impose upon existing monetary and financial agencies a very much needed discipline by making it impossible for any of them, or for any length of time, to issue a kind of money substantially less reliable and useful than the money of any other. As soon as the public became familiar with the new possibilities, any deviations from the straight path of providing an honest money would at once lead to the rapid displacement of the offending currency by others. And the individual countries, being deprived of the various dodges by which they are now able temporarily to conceal the efforts of their actions by 'protecting' their currency, would be constrained to keep the value of their currencies tolerably stable.

Proposal more Practicable than Utopian European Currency

This seems to me both preferable and more practicable than the utopian scheme of introducing a new European currency, which would ultimately only have the effect of more deeply entrenching the source and root of all monetary evil, the government monopoly of the issue and control of money. It would seem that, if the countries were not prepared to adopt the more limited proposal advanced here, they would be even less willing to accept a common European currency. The idea of depriving government altogether of its age-old prerogative of monopolizing money is still too unfamiliar and even alarming to most people to have any chance of being adopted in the near future. But people might learn to see the advantages if, at first at least, the currencies of the governments were allowed to compete for the favour of the public. . .

Free Trade in Banking

The suggested extension of the free trade in money to free trade in banking is an absolutely essential part of the scheme if it is to achieve what is intended. First, bank deposits subject to cheque, and thus a sort of privately issued money, are today of course a part, and in most countries much the largest part, of the aggregate amount of generally accepted media of exchange. Secondly the expansion and contraction of the separate national superstructures of bank credit are at present the chief excuse for national management of the basic money.

On the effects of the adoption of the proposal all I will add at this point is that it is of course intended to prevent national monetary and financial authorities from doing many things politically impossible to avoid so long as they have the power to do them. These are without exception harmful and against the long-run interest of the country doing them but politically inevitable as a temporary escape from acute difficulties. They include measures by which governments can most easily and quickly remove the causes of discontent of particular groups or sections but bound in the long run to disorganize and ultimately to destroy the market order.

Preventing Government from Concealing Depreciation

The main advantage of the proposed scheme, in other words, is that it would prevent governments from 'protecting' the currencies they issue against the harmful consequences of their own measures, and therefore prevent them from further employing these harmful tools. They would become unable to conceal the depreciation of the money they issue, to prevent an outflow of money, capital, and other resources as a result of making their home use unfavourable, or to control prices – all measures which would, of course, tend to destroy the Common Market. The scheme would indeed seem to satisfy all requirements of a common market better than a common currency without the need to establish a supra-national authority.

The scheme would, to all intents and purposes, amount to a displacement of the national circulations only if the national monetary authorities misbehaved. Even then they could still ward off a complete displacement of the national currency by rapidly changing their ways. It is possible that in some very small countries with a good deal of international trade and tourism, the currency of one of the bigger countries might come to predominate, but, assuming a sensible policy, there is no reason why most of the existing currencies should not continue to be used for a long time. (It would, of course, be important that the parties did not enter into a tacit agreement not to supply so good a money that the citizens of the other nations would prefer it! And the presumption of guilt would of course always have to lie against the government whose money the public did not like!)

DAVID CHAUM

THE BEGINNINGS OF DIGITAL MONEY (1992)

'The sacred distinction between money and just payments systems is fading,' said David Chaum at the height of the excitement about his new company DigiCash. Chaum was a cryptographer at the University of California at Berkeley when he invented a method of blurring the distinction a little bit further, creating an electronic payments system that was absolutely private.

The 1990s were the great age of electronic money development, but it was slow-going because of the difficulty negotiating common standards between the various players, and battles with government security specialists over the future of codes on the internet. The British contender Mondex, eventually owned by Mastercard, got round the problem by actually putting the electronic money on the card – downloadable by telephone – but, with some exceptions, the public greeted it without enthusiasm.

Chaum's DigiCash was founded in 1990, but by 1998 had filed for bankruptcy and put its patents for an absolutely private internet currency up for sale. The patents are now owned by the Seattle-based eCash Technologies, but Chaum's idea is also being adapted for electronic voting. On the internet, cash, votes, data and tokens all merge into pretty much the same thing.

This passage is taken from his 1992 *Scientific American* article 'Achieving Electronic Privacy', which first launched the DigiCash idea to a popular market.

* * *

The growing amounts of information that different organizations collect about a person can be linked because all of them use the same key (in the USA the social security number) to identify the individual in question. This identifier-based approach perforce trades off security against individual liberties. The more information that organizations have (whether the intent is to protect them from fraud or simply to target marketing efforts), the less privacy and control people retain.

Over the past eight years, my colleagues and I at CWI (the Dutch nationally funded Centre for Mathematics and Computer Science in Amsterdam) have developed a new approach, based on fundamental theoretical and practical advances in cryptography, that makes this trade-off unnecessary. Transactions employing these techniques avoid the possibility of fraud while maintaining the privacy of those who use them.

In our system, people would in effect give a different (but definitively verifiable) pseudonym to every organization they do business with and so make dossiers impossible. They could pay for goods in untraceable electronic cash or present digital credentials that serve the function of a banking passbook, driver's licence or voter registration card without revealing their identity. At the same time, organizations would benefit from increased security and lower record-keeping costs. . .

To see how digital signatures can provide all manner of unforgeable credentials and other services, consider how they might be used to provide an electronic replacement for cash. The First Digital Bank would offer electronic bank notes: messages signed using a particular private key. All messages bearing one key might be worth a dollar, all those bearing a different key five dollars, and so on for whatever denominations were needed. These electronic bank notes could be authenticated using the corresponding public key, which the bank has made a matter of record. First Digital would also make public a key to authenticate electronic documents sent from the bank to its customers.

To withdraw a dollar from the bank, Alice generates a note number (each note bears a different number, akin to the serial number on a bill); she chooses a 100-digit number at random so that the chance anyone else would generate the same one is negligible. She signs the number with the private key corresponding to her 'digital pseudonym' (the public key that she has previously established for use with her account). The bank verifies Alice's signature and removes it from the note number, signs the note number with its worth-one-dollar signature and debits her account. It then returns the signed note along with a digitally signed withdrawal receipt for Alice's records.

In practice, the creation, signing and transfer of note numbers would be carried out by Alice's card computer. The power of the cryptographic protocols, however, lies in the fact that they are secure regardless of physical medium: the same transactions could be carried out using only pencil and paper.

When Alice wants to pay for a purchase at Bob's shop, she connects her 'smart' card with his card reader and transfers one of the signed note numbers the bank has given her. After verifying the bank's digital signature, Bob transmits the note to the bank, much as a merchant verifies a credit card transaction today. The bank reverifies its signature, checks the note against a list of those already spent and credits Bob's account. It then transmits a 'deposit slip', once again unforgeably signed with the appropriate key. Bob hands the merchandise to Alice along with his own digitally signed receipt, completing the transaction.

This system provides security for all three parties. The signatures at each stage prevent any one from cheating either of the others: the shop cannot deny that it received payment, the bank cannot deny that it issued the notes or that it accepted them from the shop for deposit, and the customer can neither deny withdrawing the notes from her account nor spend them twice.

This system is secure, but it has no privacy. If the bank keeps track of note numbers, it can link each shop's deposit to the corresponding withdrawal and so determine precisely where and when Alice (or any other account holder) spends her money. The resulting dossier is far more intrusive than those now being compiled. Furthermore, records based on digital signatures are more vulnerable to abuse than conventional files. Not only are they self-authenticating (even if they are copied, the information they contain can be verified by anyone), but they also permit a person who has a particular kind of information to prove its existence without either giving the information away or revealing its source. For example, someone might be able to prove incontrovertibly that Bob had telephoned Alice on 12 separate occasions without having to reveal the time and place of any of the calls.

I have developed an extension of digital signatures, called blind signatures, that can restore privacy. Before sending a note number to the bank for signing, Alice in essence multiplies it by a random factor. Consequently, the bank knows nothing about what it is signing except that it carries Alice's digital signature. After receiving the blinded note signed by the bank, Alice divides out the blinding factor and uses the note as before.

The blinded note numbers are 'unconditionally untraceable' that is, even if the shop and the bank collude, they cannot determine who spent which notes. Because the bank has no idea of the blinding factor, it has no way of linking the note numbers that Bob deposits with Alice's withdrawals. Whereas the security of digital signatures is dependent on the difficulty of particular computations, the anonymity of blinded notes is limited only by the unpredictability of Alice's random numbers. If she wishes, however, Alice can reveal these numbers and permit the notes to be stopped or traced.

Blinded electronic bank notes protect an individual's privacy, but because each note is simply a number, it can be copied easily. To prevent double spending, each note must be checked on-line against a central list when it is spent. Such a verification procedure might be acceptable when large amounts of money are at stake, but it is far too expensive to use when someone is just buying a newspaper. To solve this problem, my colleagues Amos Fiat and Moni Naor and I have proposed a method for generating blinded notes that requires the payer to answer a random numeric query about each note when making a payment. Spending such a note once does not compromise unconditional untraceability, but spending it twice reveals enough information to make the payer's account easily traceable. In fact, it can yield a digitally signed confession that cannot be forged even by the bank.

Cards capable of such anonymous payments already exist. Indeed, DigiCash, a company with which I am associated, has installed equipment in two office buildings in Amsterdam that permits copiers, fax machines, cafeteria cash registers and even coffee vending machines to accept digital 'bank notes'. We have also demonstrated a system for automatic toll collection in which automobiles carry a card that responds to radioed requests for payment even as they are travelling at highway speeds.

LAWRENCE WHITE

THE TRANSITION PROBLEM

(1994)

Of all the current crop of monetary thinkers in mainstream economics, none has been quite so assiduous in debating the idea of private currencies – or 'free banking' as the idea is more respectably known – than Lawrence H White, now Hayek Professor of Economic History at the University of Missouri. For most of his career he has been writing away on the subject – monographs, histories and learned articles. And after a spell at Queen's University, Belfast, he wrote a ground-breaking history of free banking in Britain.

It was, after all, Scottish banks which were allowed to issue their own cash in the 18th century. So were the so-called 'country banks' in England – those some distance from London. In books like *The Theory of Monetary Institutions*, he has put these ideas into a conceptual framework, and through free-market think-tanks like the Institute for Economic Affairs in the UK and the Cato Institute in the USA, he has constantly tried to move the debate forward towards a new generation of free banking and competing currencies.

This passage is taken from his 1984 article 'Competitive Payments Systems and the Unit of Account' (*American Economic Review, LXXIV*), where he tries to answer some of the questions raised by Black (see p155) and others – and in particular the problem of how people would value things if there was no widely accepted standard of value, like the one we usually have provided by central banks. And how we could practically get to a world of free banking from the one we are in.

It may be, after the atrocities of 11 September 2001, that the more ambitious free market ideas will be that much less popular for a while – the world is realizing, after all, that they do need governments in some form or another. But even if that is so, the idea of competing private currencies – maybe issued by institutions other than banks as well – does still offer a potential way out of the stranglehold of central banks over the money supply.

* * *

A thorny question thus arises for those who would denationalize the American currency industry: How to make the transition away from the dollar standard? The dollar must initially be linked to any new standard, so that an unbiased competition among alternative new standards hardly seems possible. The route to a predetermined new commodity standard is straight-forward: Have the Treasury lay in a stock of the commodity, establish convertibility of dollars into the commodity, withdraw Federal Reserve notes and token Treasury coins from circulation via conversion, and open the market to private issuers of coin and convertible bank notes.

The route to a system of competing private inconvertible currencies is less clear. One way might be to do to the Federal Reserve note what Roosevelt did to gold: Have banks issue their own dollar-convertible hand-to-hand currency (these would be just like traveller's cheques without the signatory bother and refundability) and coins, then suspend convertibility of these and other bank-issued near-monies (Chequing- and savings-account deposits, savings certificates, and so on) into Federal Reserve notes and confiscate the Federal Reserve notes in private hands. In any case some resolution would have to be found to an important problem that troubled American free-banking advocates in the 1830s, that of discovering a means by which the federal government could avoid favouritism among privately issued currencies in its own fiscal dealings.

Were the first route taken and a new metallic or commodity standard initially adopted, it is no more likely that privately issued inconvertible currencies could gain a footing than it is that they can gain a footing against the fiat dollar. While the commodity serving as the new standard would have been chosen outside the market, as it were, competition from other com-modities would not be foreclosed. It is not implausible to postulate that another metallic standard might eventually supplant the metallic standard initially chosen. Full-bodied coins of different metals might well circulate in parallel, it being convenient for portability reasons to mint coins of lower purchasing power from less precious metals.

It might then be possible for different banks to market notes convertible into the different metals, whose exchange-values would float against one another. Out of that situation the market process might converge on notes convertible into a single metal as the general medium of exchange; the metal need not be the one into which the old Federal Reserve notes were converted. It is also conceivable that parallel standards would persist.

Were the second route taken and inconvertible currencies initially adopted, it is similarly unlikely that commodity-convertible currency would gain a footing against them. Since an issuer offering convertibility would not be able to pay interest on currency and deposits quite as high as that paid by competitive issuers of inconvertible money – he has to hold commodity reserves where they hold only earnings assets – he would have to attract customers on the basis of superior purchasing-power reliability. His notes would fluctuate in value, however, with the relative price of the commodity to which they were claims. Until that commodity became the monetary standard, it would not enjoy the stable demand facing a monetary commodity. Nor could the issuer vary supply at will so as to offset the impact of demand changes on price. His notes would therefore probably not be reliable for purchasing-power stability. . .

Bank-issued private currencies would float against one another unless convertibility into some common medium, or purchasing-power stabilization in terms of some common commodity basket, were adopted. A pegged exchange rate system among rival issuers would clearly be in no issuer's self-interest under inconvertibility. A bank pledged to trade its rival's inconvertible notes at par could be forced to accumulate them ad infinitum by a more expansive rival, and in any event would have to hold costly reserves.

A joint-float arrangement might nonetheless emerge via an invisible hand or market process of the following sort. Each issuing bank would most likely find that it did better business by accepting the notes of other issuers at market value (rather than refusing them) from customers making deposits or repaying loans. A pair of issuers might then discover that both did better business by accepting one another's notes at a fixed parity, thereby sparing their mutual customers calculational difficulty and exchange risk. The issuing banks might later join them.

These issuers would at the same time have to enter into a mutual clearing arrangement for settlement of accumulated balances of one another's liabilities. Each member bank would have to pledge to honour its liabilities at a rate fixed in terms of some common medium, so as to obviate the forced-accumulation problem. Adverse clearing balances would be liquidated by transfer of the clearing medium, loss of which would automatically signal to the relatively expansive issuer the need for restraint. In this day and age, it is not obvious that gold would be chosen as the principal clearing medium. Treasury bills, or some other low risk earning asset that virtually all banks held to begin with, would likely be used.

EDWARD DE BONO

THE IBM DOLLAR (1994)

The Centre for the Study of Financial Innovation was set up in London in 1993, and the following passage is taken from one of their first pamphlets, written by the innovator and inventor of 'lateral thinking', Edward de Bono (1933–).

His idea was that companies should issue their own currencies, which could be redeemed at a later date for their products – and that a secondary market in them would reduce the risk of holding them. The proposal opened up the possibility of a range of other currencies which could avoid inflation by being tightly targeted on geographical areas or specific sectors, like housing.

The pamphlet was widely influential, just as the development of the internet was opening up the idea of private electronic currencies. But in some ways it wasn't new. He was proposing what, in a simple way, any money-off coupon, luncheon voucher, or phone card is. But his ideas built on those of Hayek (see p157), raising the possibility of people using corporate currencies, backed by shares, as new stores of value.

He mentions that 'company currencies' – which could only be spent back in the company store – got a bad record in the 18th and 19th centuries. In fact, they were made illegal in the UK under a series of laws known as the Truck Acts, which were eventually disposed of by the Thatcher government in the 1980s. This is how he introduces the idea of an 'IBM dollar'.

✳   ✳   ✳

The IBM dollar is only one example of possible target currencies. The scheme could be of value to any large organization selling quasi-commodity products. Motor cars might fall into this bracket. Indeed the GM [General Motors] credit card, with its cumulative discount feature, is a step in this direction.

Companies like British Airways or Sainsbury's could issue their own currencies, and could benefit from the float until these currencies were used. This could be done in a number of innovative ways. Where an identifiable and easily comparable item is sold, like a first class transatlantic air passage, the currency could be valued against that product. For instance, a hundred units could purchase such a flight at any future date. This would provide a hedge against inflation.

On a much larger scale, it might even be possible to think about a *housing currency* which could be used to finance building projects.

Of equal interest is the possibility, albeit less clearly defined at present, of using target currencies in smaller communities to finance the start up of local businesses which would be selling into that community.

A kind of target currency exists in the form of the US Food Stamp programme which caters very successfully for 26 million Americans. There is now even a food stamps credit card.

The Central Provident Fund in Singapore is a further example. The Singapore government takes a percentage of wages, matched by employers, which is put into a fund which will be paid out to the employee at a certain date or upon retirement. Meanwhile the employee can borrow against this fund for certain specific purposes: housing, health, education and the stock market. (The inclusion of the last item is one explanation for the boom in the Singapore stock market.)

Historically, target currencies acquired a bad reputation when they were used to force employees to spend their wages back in the company store. *But that particular experience should not prejudice our willingness to explore the potential of this concept.* After all capital itself is only a time-shift phenomenon whereby predicted sales are used to finance the production of the product with profit as the reward for assessing the risk.

Computers now make it possible to run a system with multiple target currencies. In such a system, an employee might be rich in 'housing currency' but poor in 'luxury currency.' Wages might be split between different currencies – though the consumer would be able to trade between different types of currency, exercising his or her choice.

The consumer is already able to exercise choice in many ways. For instance, in spite of the recent GATT [General Agreement on Tariffs and Trade] agreement on agriculture there is a looming trans-Atlantic trade battle because Europe is reluctant to admit US steroid-fed beef. The matter will probably be resolved by eventually allowing in the beef – but insisting that it be labelled as 'steroid-fed beef'. The consumer, aided by proper health information, may then prefer to avoid buying such beef. Unless governments insist on fooling the consumer, this kind of non-tariff barrier is bound to multiply.

The target currencies that people select would be merely another manifestation of consumer choice. The only difference is that the choice can be time-shifted backwards from the moment of purchase. For example, bulk negotiations may mean that workers are partly paid in a target currency which has a much higher value at Sainsbury's than normal currency. That is a free choice on the part of the consumer. It now becomes possible to distribute the benefits of competitive bulk buying in a personal manner.

The notion of multiple target currencies opens up a new way of thinking in economics. Volatility and fluctuation could be much reduced. It could become considerably easier to stimulate individual sectors of the economy without immediately running into inflation. The present obsession with free markets and deregulation sometimes obscures the inherent dangers in fungible 'soup' systems where everything can flow in any direction. Multiple parallel systems, with permeable membranes between them, give very stable systems – as in the human body. This is a whole field which needs, and will get, attention.

DAVID BIRCH AND
NEIL MCEVOY

DOWNLOADSAMONEY (1996)

Just as money reformers were discussing the future of private electronic currencies, it was becoming clear that – if you broadened your definition of money – some of these were already in circulation. Big barter companies like Atwood Richards and Active International were using electronic barter currencies called *trade dollars* or *trade pounds*. Middle-sized companies like Bartercard, which arrived in the UK from Australia in 1999, were even encouraging clients to donate surplus trade pounds to charities run by the Metropolitan Police.

Then there were the loyalty currencies, like frequent flyer points or *air miles*. The insight that these were increasingly acting like corporate currencies was introduced in the article 'Downloadsamoney', from which this passage is taken, by two leading luminaries from the leading British electronic money consultancy, Consult Hyperion – David Birch (1959–) and Neil McEvoy (1957–). It appeared first in 1996 in the magazine run by what was then the trendy 'New Labour' think-tank Demos, and it was widely quoted.

By that stage, at least one airline was using frequent flyer points to pay for major global contracts like public relations. Loyalty currencies have merged together, just as predicted here, but they have managed to resist becoming the currencies that Birch and McEvoy suggested by refusing to let holders trade them with each other. But since competing loyalty-points systems will win by being more widely spendable, it may just be a matter of time before they do. At that stage, they may quickly develop into alternative payment systems – there are already numerous examples of airlines using them like that.

But even without that attribute, loyalty points are still behaving like highly targeted currencies – allowing companies to 'buy' customer loyalty by using surplus or nearly out-dated stock. What Birch and McEvoy hint at here is that information technology has changed money. It means that almost any asset, however ephemeral, can be securitized and turned into money. In fact, the year after they were writing, David Bowie turned his own future copyrights into a kind of money with Bowie Bonds. Can money ever be the same again?

※   ※   ※

What, then would make these schemes better for both companies and their customers? A smart card carrying Air Miles or Safeway's ABC Points would be the best of both worlds: consumers could pass the tokens amongst themselves (just like paper notes) using widely available devices and could redeem them in person over the Net.

What widely available devices? Smart-card readers will be ubiquitous for a number of reasons, including the appearance of smart credit and debit cards, the shift towards smart telephone cards and so forth. Consumers will have ready access to devices that enable them to either spend their tokens or pass them on to someone else: 'you don't have enough Air Miles for the holiday in Rome! Here, darling, take some of mine'. What government would risk 'taking away' people's Air Miles or ABC Points? If we make the basic assumption that the extension of loyalty schemes is the natural migration path to private currency, it then becomes interesting to consider whose money consumers might find acceptable.

While banks and insurance companies seem the natural choices, a September 1995 MORI poll found that one third of UK consumers would be happy to trust supermarket chains or Marks & Spencer with their money. By extension, then, if a consortium comprising Norwich Union and Marks & Spencer began issuing transferable loyalty points for cross-accepting within their consortium (the currency *keiretsu*) they could provide an acceptable currency for transactions and lock consumers into their group. There's no need to assume a 'big bang' to private currency: it will happen because of the dynamics of the marketplace. If you believe that Marks & Spencer will always redeem your points and that those points will keep their value then you're happy to accept them in payment. . .

In the Internet marketplace, the distinctions between consumers, retailers and banks become hazy. An individual or organization of significant reputation might buy things from one web site, sell things to another and issue their own money. Their copy of Microsoft Money, or whatever, could easily manage these transactions: any device connected to the Net has access to all of the information (and markets) it needs in order to establish the desirability of a currency. Once people can use the Net to send cash around, then a market will develop in the different kinds of offer. Someone with an excess of ABC Points puts up a page offering to trade them for Talking Points: foreign exchange brokers (eg Thomas Cook) then become web sites that will sell you the URL of a counterparty for your trade. All of this can be done in seconds and with a vanishingly small overhead.

Here, then, is a practical example. Alice asks Bob to write a report on the Manchester United vs Tottenham Hotspur game for her magazine. They agree a fee of 100 minutes of BT [British Telecom] Long Distance (100 Busbys), which has become the standard unit of account for people with Internet access. Bob writes the article, Alice loves it, and now it's time for payment:

- Alice's PC (Alice's Quicken controlling her electronic purse card) contacts Bob's PC (Bob's Microsoft Money controlling his electronic purse card) and says 'I owe you 100 Busbys: how would you like it?'
- Bob has set the preferences on his Microsoft Money to go for Safeway ABC Points, since that's where he does his shopping, so his PC asks for that.
- Alice's PC contacts the Thomas Cook PC and trades 100 Busbys for 1000 ABC Points and sends them to Bob, with a digital receipt signed by Thomas Cook stating the exchange rate.
- Bob generates a digitally signed receipt for Alice, and her Quicken neatly files this away for tax purposes. Neither Bob nor Alice have had to think about the different currencies or exchange rates: they agreed a mutually acceptable unit of account and foreign exchange market (not bank: Forrester Research predict that non-banks will have at least one-quarter of the Internet payments market by the year 2000).

In his excellent book (which cannot be too highly recommended), The history of money from ancient times to the present day, Professor Glyn Davies notes that improvements in the technology of the means of exchange – from ingots, to coins, to paper, to plastic cards – have always diminished the power of the government over the monetary system. Is it time for them to give up completely?

MERVYN KING

A FUTURE FOR CENTRAL BANKS? (1999)

The wildly excitable 1990s, thrilled with the possibilities of what became known as the 'new economy', saw money reformers – especially in the USA – discussing whether any kind of government control was necessary over the money system at all. Free market think-tanks like the Cato Institute in Washington ran conferences to discuss it, and a new philosophical amalgam between internet economics and Darwinian biology emerged – led by the magazine *Wired* – that campaigned for a world free of central banks.

What made Mervyn King's intervention in this debate so well known was that he came from the other side of the fence: King (1948–) was not just an economics professor, he was also deputy governor of the Bank of England. He also raised the possibility, as he put it, that 'the successors to Bill Gates would. . . put the successors to Alan Greenspan out of business.'

It wasn't so much that he was advocating an outcome like that – far from it – just that he was using his speech at the 'New challenges for monetary policy' conference in August 1999 to discuss whether it was possible. It was organized by the Federal Reserve of Kansas City in Jackson Hole, Wyoming and the speech caused a flutter among the world's media, especially among those who believed in the exciting prospects of electronic money. But in fact King went further than simply suggesting that electronic money would take over. He was imagining a day when real-time transactions could make money unnecessary, and reaching back to some of the ideas originally discussed 30 years before by Fischer Black (see p155).

*　*　*

Looking further ahead, the future of central banks is not entirely secure. Their numbers may decline over the next century. The enthusiasm of governments for national currencies has waned as capital flows have become liberalized and exchange rates more volatile. Following the example of the European Central Bank, more regional monetary unions could emerge. Short

of this, the creation of currency boards, or even complete currency substitution, might also reduce the number of independent national monetary
authorities.

But much more important is the potential impact of technological
innovation. At present, central banks are the monopoly supplier of base
money — cash and bank reserves. Because base money is the ultimate medium
of exchange and of final settlement, central banks have enormous leverage
over the value of transactions in the economy, even though the size of their
balances sheet is very small in relation to those of the private sector. For years,
economists have had difficulty in incorporating money into rigorous general
equilibrium models. To the elegance of the Walrasian model of an exchange
economy has been bolted on an assumption about the technology of making
payments such as a 'cash in advance' constraint.

These untidy ways of introducing money into economic models are not
robust to changes in institutions and technology. Is it possible that advances
in technology will mean that the arbitrary assumptions necessary to introduce
money into rigorous theoretical models will become redundant, and that the
world may come to resemble a pure exchange economy?

Electronic transactions in real time hold out that possibility. There is no
reason, in principle, why final settlements could not be carried out by the
private sector without the need for clearing through the central bank. The
practical implementation of such a system would require much greater
computing power than is at present available. But there is no conceptual
obstacle to the idea that two individuals engaged in a transaction could settle
by a transfer of wealth from one electronic account to another in real time.
Pre-agreed algorithms would determine which financial assets were sold by
the purchaser of the good or service according to the value of the transaction.
And the supplier of that good or service would know that incoming funds
would be allocated to the appropriate combination of assets as prescribed
by another pre-agreed algorithm. Eligible assets would be any financial assets
for which there were market-clearing prices in real time. The same system
could match demands and supplies of financial assets, determine prices and
make settlements.

Financial assets and real goods and services would be priced in terms of
a unit of account. The choice of a unit of account (perhaps a commodity
standard, which would produce broad stability in the price level) would be
a matter for public choice and regulation, along the lines of existing weights
and measures inspectors. Final settlement could be made without any
recourse to the central bank. As Henckel et al have noted, the key to a central

bank's ability to implement monetary policy is that it 'remains, by law or regulation, the only entity which is allowed to "corner" the market for settlement balances.'

Without such a role in settlements, central banks, in their present form, would no longer exist; nor would money. Economies of this kind have been discussed by Black. . . The need to limit excessive money creation would be replaced by a concern to ensure the integrity of the computer used for settlement purposes. A regulatory body to monitor such systems would be required. Existing regulators, including central banks, would no doubt compete for that responsibility. Moreover, in just the same way as the internet is unaware of national boundaries, settlement facilities would become international.

The key to any such developments is the ability of computers to communicate in real time to permit instantaneous verification of the credit worthiness of counterparties, thereby enabling private sector real time gross settlement to occur with finality. Any securities for which electronic markets exist could be used as part of the settlement process. There would be no unique role for base money, hence the central bank monopoly of base money issue would have no value. Central banks would lose their ability to implement monetary policy. The successors to Bill Gates would have put the successors to Alan Greenspan out of business.

As a central banker interested in information technology, should I regard this prospect as a dream or a nightmare? Perhaps the answer is that central bankers should enjoy life today. I shall place my faith in the words of Walter Bagehot who, in *Lombard Street* (1873), wrote that 'Nothing would persuade the English people to abolish the Bank of England; and if some calamity swept it away, generations must elapse before at all the same trust would be placed in any other equivalent.'

PART VI INTRODUCTION
CREATE YOUR OWN: REAL MONEY

I take for myself and my colleagues of other days whatever degree of blame and burden there may be for having accepted their advice. But what has happened? We have had no reality, stability. The price of gold has risen since then by more than 70 per cent. That is as if a 12-inch foot rule had suddenly been stretched to 19 or 20 inches. . .

SIR WINSTON CHURCHILL SPEECH TO THE HOUSE OF COMMONS IN 1932, ABOUT HIS DISASTROUS DECISION SEVEN YEARS BEFORE TO RETURN THE POUND TO THE GOLD STANDARD

But money should always be money. A foot is always twelve inches, but when is a dollar a dollar? If ton weights changed in the coal yard, and peck measures changed in the grocery, and yard sticks were today 42 inches and tomorrow 33 inches (by some occult process called 'exchange') the people would mighty soon remedy that.

HENRY FORD, MY LIFE AND WORK

This is what a bond document began like in 1780, in the emerging new United States of America at a time of economic – as much as political – upheaval and uncertainty:

In Behalf of the State of Massachusetts-Bay, I the Subscriber do hereby promise and oblige Myself and Successors in the Office of Treasurer of said State, to pay unto Charles Steward or his Order, the Sum of Three Hundred and seventy three Pounds 3/9 on or before the First Day of March, in the Year of our Lord One Thousand Seven Hundred and Eighty one with interest at Six per cent per Annum: Both Principal and Interest to be paid in the then current Money of said State, in a greater or less Sum, according as Five Bushels of Corn, Sixty-eight Pounds and four-seventh parts of Beef, Ten

Pounds of Sheeps Wool, and Sixteen Pounds of Sole Leather shall then cost,
more or less than One Hundred and Thirty Pounds current Money, at the
then current Prices of said Articles. . .

And so on. The point is that when dollars don't yet exist and when pounds might mean nothing the following year – in other words, when conventional money isn't reliable – people could still define value in terms of something basic. We are so much more dependent on money now that it's hard for us suddenly to use sheep's wool or corn as a standard of value. But at various times over the past few centuries, radicals have tried to base money on something more appropriate – anything from human labour or vegetables to energy. And as currencies increasingly set themselves adrift from gold and precious metals in the 20th century, and when the inability of governments to control their Keynesian money supplies became serious in the 1970s, the clamour for real money became much more strident.

National currencies are now almost entirely 'fiat' currencies – from *'fiat lux'*, the Latin words at the start of the Book of Genesis meaning 'let there be light'. Central banks simply assert the existence of their currencies and underpin their value with government debt. The majority of our money is now underpinned by our collective belief that our governments will pay their debts. It isn't very reliable, as the increasing number of global currency crises implies.

Of course, whatever you base the value of money on becomes valuable in its own right. The solutions here include new forms of mutual credit – where money is based on the goods or services of whoever is engaged in the transaction – pioneered by the anarchist Pierre-Joseph Proudhon (see p181). They include a determination to force banks to get out of the money creation game altogether, so that they are simply loaning money out of their deposits, as Irving Fisher suggests (see p192). And they include using local products like vegetables to back the issue of a new currency in the form of local notes, as proposed by Bob Swann, Susan Witt and others (see p211) – part of a tradition of currency reformers that stretches back via Borsodi and others. They also include proponents of a new international currency, backed by commodities around the world, which would help keep everyone's currency stable.

It will be obvious straight away that real money advocates are not necessarily enthusiasts about state control, like Soddy (see p184). Nor are they necessarily anarchic types committed to local power, like Proudhon, Borsodi or Swann. They could be internationalists like Graham (see p196) or a combination of all of those like Lietaer (see p221). Some want to create new kinds of currency; some want to improve the functions of the money we already have. What holds them together is a determination that money should be real enough to be useful and safe for ordinary people to use, so that it doesn't disappear from the local economy for speculation, or disappear from a catastrophic loss of belief.

Real money advocates are emphasizing the function of money as a store of value, but not exclusively so. Money which is just value and based on something scarce becomes elitist; it becomes available only to the rich, and creates a sclerotic society where nobody can better themselves. But even Winston Churchill recognized in the quote at the start of this part that – just because your currency is based on the value of gold – it doesn't necessarily mean it's reliable. It was a lesson learned by the British Treasury the hard way during the late 1920s.

That's why the insights of people like Swann and Lietaer, who recognize that money also needs to be widely available, are so important. The truth is that money needs to retain something of all its functions – standard of value, medium of exchange and store of value – for it to work. It just doesn't have to retain it in exactly the same balance as it has at the moment.

PIERRE-JOSEPH PROUDHON

PEOPLE'S BANKING (1848)

What underpins the currency? For people worried about the vagaries of paper money distributed by banks or the state and backed by little or nothing – and in these days, primarily by government debt – it doesn't necessarily have to be something solid like gold. It could be a basket of other raw materials or, maybe, as in this case, by the products that are on sale.

That is the basic idea behind the People's Bank, the brainchild of the pioneering French anarchist Pierre-Joseph Proudhon (1809–1865), whose ideas were taken up by socialists, anarchists and nationalists alike, dreamed up in the excitement of the 1848 overthrow of the Louis Philippe regime. Proudhon spent part of the period in hiding after his attack on the newly elected president Louis Napoleon – shortly to seize power himself as Napoleon III – but managed to register the People's Bank in January 1849.

The idea was that the bank would issue it's own money in the form of vouchers, backed by the products they were about to buy – 'real' money only existed once it was offered for exchange. It was a revolutionary idea, and borrowed in the same way from Robert Owen as Karl Marx had for his Labour Theory of Value. It never raised the necessary capital and was wound up after a few months, but not before a staggering 27,000 workers and small tradespeople had joined.

This passage is taken from 'Solution du Problème Social', in *Selected Writings of Pierre-Joseph Proudhon*, translated by Elizabeth Fraser.

*　　*　　*

Only products may be exchanged for products. Nobody today disputes this maxim of political economy. Socialists and economists alike accept it *de jure* and *de facto*, and it provides a common ground on which opposing theories may be reconciled and opinions meet to form one doctrine.

Exchange is either direct or indirect.

The chairmaker in Paris needs a cask of wine at the same time as a Bordeaux wine merchant needs chairs. The two producers can exchange their respective products by sending them to each other. This is direct exchange.

But let us suppose, as is usually the case, that one of the two people involved in the exchange does not need the other's product. For example, the Bordeaux wine merchant, instead of requiring chairs, requires calico; then exchange is no longer possible. The Parisian will pay for his wine with money, and the citizen of Bordeaux will use this money to have the material he requires sent from Mulhouse. This is indirect exchange.

Now this exchange, which is necessarily indirect because of the lack of any common credit link, would operate directly and without intermediaries were it possible for all those who wished to exchange goods in a country — all those who needed to buy and sell — to know one another. Let us imagine, for example, that the Parisian, the citizen of Mulhouse and the citizen of Bordeaux know at the same moment that each needs something: the first, a cask of wine, the second, chairs, and the third, a length of calico. It is clear that in this case the goods can be exchanged without any money having to be used. The Parisian will send his chairs to the manufacturer in Mulhouse, who will then send his calico to the producer in Bordeaux, and he in turn will send his wine to Paris. Substitute a hundred thousand people involved in exchanges for these three and it will still be the same, the exchange will still be direct.

What then must we do in order to allow direct exchange to take place — not simply between three, four, six, ten or a hundred people, but between a hundred thousand, or between all the producers and consumers in the world?

Something very simple. We must centralize all commercial transactions by means of one bank that will receive all the bills of exchange, money orders and promissory notes which represent the traders' invoices. Then we must generalize or convert these liabilities into vouchers that would be their equivalent and that consequently would be guaranteed by the products or real values that these liabilities represent.

Bank vouchers formed in this way would have all the qualities of the soundest bills.

They would not be subject to depreciation, since they would only be delivered against actual values and acceptable bills of exchange. Thus they would be based on the products manufactured, but on those sold and delivered, and for which, consequently, repayment could be claimed.

There would be no problem of over-issuing since the voucher would only be delivered in exchange for bills of the first quality, that is to say, when there is a genuine and certain promise to repay.

Nobody would refuse to accept them since, as a result of the centralizing of all exchanges, and because all citizens would patronize the bank, they would represent for each person a value equal to the one that he would soon have to pay in bank vouchers.

THE REMEDY (1926)

Sir Frederick Soddy was the Nobel prize-winning chemist who became so enraged with the way that banks create money that he tried to take the Bank of England to court (see p97). This passage, taken from his 1926 book *Wealth, Virtual Wealth and Debt: The solution to the economic paradox*, outlines his solution: banks should be forced to hold 100 per cent of any loan as backing. There was to be no more 'funny money', no more creating money out of nothing as debt; if they handed over money, they handed over the ownership of it as well. It was a design for a fundamentally safe economic system.

In that respect, at least, Soddy was ahead of his time. The years between the First and Second World Wars was the great age of the 'real money' debate. They were the years of the Wall Street Crash and the Great Depression, where money seemed to slip through people's fingers because it seemed to be based on nothing. But Soddy was writing in the mid-1920s. His book pre-dates the Crash by three years, but was a reaction more to the miserable post-First World War conditions that Britain was facing compared to the USA – with the wage cuts and strikes that followed Winston Churchill's decision to fix the pound again to the gold standard.

Soddy also prefigured very similar proposals from one of the greatest economists of the age, Irving Fisher (see p192), who published it in his book *100% Money* – except that Fisher said the banks should be compensated, while Soddy said they should be prosecuted. Politicians, he said, have 'abdicated the most important function of government and ceased to be *de facto* rulers of the nation'. Via Fisher and the Chicago economists, Soddy also influenced the early days of monetarism and the ideas of Milton Friedman.

* * *

The State, having decided to recover its lost prerogative of issuing money legislates to that effect, and notifies the banks that henceforth, after a reasonable interval, they must not lend money in current account, but only money surrendered into their keeping for a definite period under a proper deed of transfer or other authorized legal form. A suitable scale of stamp duties on such deeds could be devised, so that it was not profitable for them to be taken out for finicking periods, in order to avoid the intentions of the Act being made a dead letter by some new development of the system of purely fictitious loans.

The situation then is:

1 The banks now lose one of their sources of income and must be conducted on the same principles as other business services, charging their clients for keeping their accounts.

2 The debtors – owing the banks £M2000 in aggregate, and owning for the most part collateral securities or other property against which the loan has been issued – must either sell their securities or find someone who has the money – either individuals or the State – genuinely to lend it to them.

3 The State has ultimately to issue £M2000 of new national money, and with it buy back and cancel £M2000 worth of National Debt.

4 This new money has in future to be held by the banks, pound for pound of deposits in current account, so that instead of their keeping a *safe* proportion of their depositors' money as at present, they must keep the whole.

There is no difficulty or danger to be feared in carrying out this operation, provided it were conducted with ordinary financial prudence and acumen. The banks themselves could, with the cooperation of their clients, no doubt easily provide the whole £M2000 of national securities to be liquidated. It represents less than one-quarter of the amount in existence, and, if they had not so much in their possession already in the form of collateral securities, it would be a simple Stock Exchange matter to exchange other non-national collateral securities for them to the requisite amount. Mr. Withers' office-boy in the City no doubt would be able to explain if consulted.

The position, then, is that all purely fictitious loans have been terminated. The amount of money in the country has not been affected by the transaction, and, indeed, the general public would only know that it had been carried out by the consequent reduction of taxation.

The banks are now solvent in foul financial weather as well as fair. Not a single legitimate feature of their business as moneylenders has been touched. They can lend money at interest as before provided they, or the owners of the money lent, genuinely do transfer the ownership of it to the borrower and give up the use of it. In so far as the loans to industry were due to simple deficit of legal tender, they will have been repaid and industry freed from the incubus by the sale of collateral securities in the debtors' possession. In so far as they are not, they would have continued as genuine and legitimate transactions between the industries and the lending public.

R O B E R T   E I S L E R

THE MONEY MAZE (1931)

Many of the ambiguities of the current money system stem from the different functions that money is expected to have, so it's not surprising that many of the people featured in this book should be trying to create different kinds of parallel money – each one more focused on fulfilling specific monetary functions a little bit better. The Austrian polymath Robert Eisler (1882–1947) imagines a solution whereby *current money* is used for simple exchanges of cash, but *money banco* – kept to a steady value by using a Retail Price Index – is used as a store of value. The basic underlying value of money is therefore a basket of services, like public transport and education, that it can buy.

Eisler published only two works on economics in English, but on both occasions, he managed to persuade directors of the Bank of England to write a preface. It was in one of these that Vincent Vickers made his unusual admission at the top of Part III. This was pretty good going for Eisler, a man whose main distinction was that he was a decorated Austrian war hero, and who wrote not just about money but about astrology, archaeology, biblical studies, art and history, and whose first book – *The Theory of Values* – was written when he was just 20 years old.

Still, his monetary ideas did attract attention. So did his constant pleas for stability by linking currencies either to stable commodities or other currencies – hence his campaign for a common currency for the British Empire, and hence his creation with Fisher (see p192) and another Bank of England director, Lord Stamp, of the Stable Money Association. He had, after all, been profoundly influenced by the hyperinflation that hit Germany after the First World War, which he mentions in this passage. At the height of that crisis in 1923, Germany created the stabilizing *festmark* linked to the US dollar. The previous year, the Polish *zloty* had been linked to the Swiss franc.

Both of these were early examples of double currency systems, and have been coming back into vogue more recently. Argentina, for example, linked its currency to the US dollar, with disastrous results, because permanent linkages of this kind tend to muddle the information that currencies can provide (see Jacobs, Part III, p100).

The idea was nearly disastrous for Eisler too. When he suggested that Austria should join the sterling zone, he was arrested by the Nazis and found himself serving 15 months of forced labour in Dachau and Buchenwald. International pressure led to his release and he went to live in England. This passage is taken from *The Money Maze: A way out of the economic world crisis*, published in London in 1931 by Search Publishing Company.

❊   ❊   ❊

All contracts concerning wages, salaries and appointments, all stipulations concerning insurances, bank deposits or credits, loans or mortgages, rent or interest on such, all deeds of sale, all commercial bills, etc – shall be carried out with due regard to the actual purchasing power of the national money at the time when the payment stipulated is effected, the temporary purchase power of the money being ascertained by means of index numbers representing the average retail price of a fair number of consumable goods, the height of rents, rates, taxes, local transport fares and the cost of elementary education at that particular moment in terms of the respective monetary unit.

Such legislation would be tantamount to redefining the monetary unit according to the following tentative draft:

1 The monetary unit of the <u>United Kingdom</u> is the <u>pound sterling</u>
USA   US dollar

2 The <u>pound sterling</u> is the <u>Bank of England</u>
    USA dollar   Federal Reserve Bank

note equivalent to <u>122.839</u> grains of fine gold
23.22

at the London gold price of 18 September, 1931.

3 The <u>pound sterling</u> note is legal tender to the
US dollar
extent of its actual purchasing power.

4 The term 'actual purchasing power' is defined as the reciprocal value of the cost of living index obtaining at the day of payment.

5 The cost-of-living index is calculated on the basis of the average price of the following commodities . . . of local transport, rents and taxes, and expenses for elementary education.

Through such a law the two functions of money – to serve as a medium of exchange (legal tender) and as a means of accumulating capital (purchasing power) or contractual income for future use – will henceforward be separated still more completely than now. Henceforth legal tender, called a pound or a US dollar of '*current* money' or money proper (£*cr*, or $ *cr*) – as opposed to bank or contract money of account, called a pound or a dollar *banco* (£ *b* or $ *b*) obtained through including a contract about a future payment of money proper or through depositing 'current money' with a bank or similar institution – will be exclusively used for small transactions between persons not sufficiently known to one another or not in possession of a bank account, especially for the payment of wages, transport fares and occasional retail purchases, while all other payments will be effected by means of bank-money, that is cheques or traveller's cheques or transfers of money *banco*.

All prices in the better-class shops will be marked in money *banco*, the index multiplicator of the week being affixed at the cashier's desk, who will calculate by means of simple multiplication tables published by the Sunday papers the sums due in 'current money'. This is how retail business, inn and hotel-keeping was done in Germany at the height of inflation in 1923 when the 'stable mark' was introduced as a money of account alongside the paper mark used as 'current money'.

All bank and business accounts will be calculated without any additional complication in money *banco*, current money being exchanged against bank money by special tellers only in so far and as soon as a client wants to pay in or draw out current money. In each country the external exchanges between the national and the foreign bank moneys will be pegged, but a variable internal exchange rate between current and bank money will be determined by the cost-of-living index.

Current money will, of course, slowly but constantly depreciate through the expansion of credit and currency necessary to meet the requirements of increasing production and consumption, the rate of increase being no longer limited but by the necessity of expanding the expenses of the various countries in due proportion to their actual spending power as measured by the volume of their present gold standard currencies and by the physical limits of production. This will force commercial and clearing banks to diminish as far as possible their cash reserves by increasing their deposits at National Banks, and all private people to spend or to deposit current money as quickly as possible. In this way the velocity of monetary circulation which is now one of the most intractable factors of monetary instability will always be maintained at its maximum value, that is, stabilized as far as possible, and the maximum of available credit will be automatically placed at the disposition of the producers.

JAN GOUDRIAAN

How to Stop Deflation
(1932)

Jan Goudriaan (1893–1974) was a professor at Rotterdam University when he came to write the pamphlet *How to Stop Deflation* (Search Publishing, London, 1932) but it was one of those slow-burning ideas that carried on gathering momentum, and was soon taken up by a new tradition of economists looking for ways that money could be made more reliable, first by Benjamin Graham (see p196) and Jan Tinbergen, and in recent years by the former central banker and money innovator Bernard Lietaer (see p221).

The idea was that banks should intervene in the commodity markets and use raw materials as backing for the value of currencies rather than gold. Gold has bizarre other effects, after all, and Keynes had recently called it a 'barbarous relic'. This is how Goudriaan explains how the banks would be able to minimize the commodities they would actually have to hold.

*   *   *

Taking raw materials into the cover of the circulation banks does not lead to high storage and transportation costs. From the foregoing it may be clear that the amount of raw materials in the possession of the circulation banks can be regulated by their own credit policy: a liberal credit policy (by raising the price level of manufactured goods somewhat, that is, by raising the profits and wages in the production of manufactured goods and by raising the costs in the production of raw materials) will tend to diminish these stocks; a policy of credit restriction, on the other hand, will tend to increase them. The really necessary amount is determined by the amplitude of the national fluctuations, which occur in the volume of agricultural and mining production; therefore this amount has not to exceed about 25 per cent of the annual production, and may be, on average, about 10 to 12 per cent.

The storage and transportation costs are to be borne by the bank; they can, however, be shifted to the producers by determining that the bank only buys locally and at a certain discount for average storage charges; it sells only locally, and at a rate allowing a small percentage for storage charges.

This will mean that the intervention of the bank in the commodity markets only takes place when the general price level in these markets has fallen a certain percentage below, or has risen a certain percentage above the fixed level. These margins cannot exceed a few points, and a fluctuation of the price level of raw materials between these two levels cannot have a disastrous effect on economic life.

The main thesis is that certain limits exist, whilst the catastrophe of the moment is caused by the general feeling that the price level can fall without any limitation at all, and just because of that quite reasonable feeling it falls still further.

The role of the raw material cover in the adjustment of international payments are chiefly effected by buying and selling bills of exchange, and gold transports only take place when the stock of bills at a certain moment is exhausted, and therefore the rate of exchange has fallen to such an extent that the costs of gold transport are paid – so the transport of raw materials for international payments will only take place when, firstly, the stock of foreign bills has become exhausted and the rate of exchange has fallen still further. This will only occur in pathological conditions, the stock of raw materials being small with respect to the gold stocks (for the whole world: gold stocks, $12 billions; raw materials stocks at 1928 prices, about $5 billions). We may expect that by consolidating the general price level, the financial situation of the producing countries will at the same time be consolidated.

The fall in the rate of exchange of the producers' countries, which now is the almost inevitable consequence of the fall in prices of their products, will only occur in cases of real mismanagement.

A stabilization of the rate of exchange between producer and consumer countries will not only be of economic significance; it will restore and maintain peaceful relations between colonies and home countries, between the Far East and Europe; it will be a permanent safeguard against the dislocating policy of Soviet Russia on the commodity markets.

IRVING FISHER

100% MONEY (1935)

The Wall Street Crash of 1929 cost Professor Irving Fisher (1867–1947) dearly. He lost a fortune himself, earned from his invention of a card index system, but he also lost a reputation too. Not long before, he had been reassuring about the markets, claiming that they had reached a 'permanently high plateau'. From then on, although he was the most famous economist in the USA, Fisher sounded just a little like a maverick.

It wasn't just that he failed to oppose Roosevelt's New Deal, like his Yale colleagues did. It was that he was prepared to embrace some radical ideas to rescue the banking system and reflate local economies. The local economic idea was his Stamp Scrip currency (see p238), but he also campaigned vigorously to force banks to keep a 100 per cent reserve requirement – to make sure that all the money in circulation really *was* safe from the bank crashes that were taking place at the time all over the USA. That made him, by implication, a supporter of Soddy's proposal (see p184) that banks should no longer create money. It should be done instead, said Fisher, by a Currency Commission.

It seems such a strange idea today, but at the time it was also then supported by the Chicago economists, and was famously adopted as an idea in 1960 by the father of monetarism, Milton Friedman – even popping up as a serious proposal by economists in the 1980s. Now it is proposed less as a method of securing banks and making money real, than as a proposal for democratic reform (see Robertson and Huber, Part IV, p133).

As well as his card index system and his economic theories – Fisher resurrected the Quantity Theory of Money in 1911 and is the man most responsible for inflation indices, fanatically collecting statistics from his home in New Haven. He was also a vegetarian and enthusiastic promoter of eugenics. His most successful book was actually a self-help volume of health advice called *How to Live*. He was, as the following passage from his 1935 book *100% Money* shows, much more than just an academic – he was a campaigner with a mission.

*   *   *

Let the Government, through an especially created 'Currency Commission', *turn into cash* enough of the assets of every commercial bank to increase the cash reserve of each bank up to 100% of its chequing deposits. In other words, let the Government, through the Currency Commission, issue this money, and, with it, buy some of the bonds, notes, or other assets of the bank or lend it to the banks on those assets as security. Then all cheque-book money would have actual money – pocket-book money – behind it.

This new money (Commission Currency, or United States notes), would merely give an all-cash backing for the chequing deposits and would, of itself, neither increase nor decrease the total circulating medium of the country. A bank which previously had $100,000,000 of deposits subject to cheque with only $10,000,000 of cash behind them (along with $90,000,000 in securities) would send those $90,000,000 of securities to the Currency Commission in return for $90,000,000 more cash, thus bringing its total cash reserve up to $100,000,000 or 100% of the deposits.

After this substitution of actual money for securities had been completed, the bank would be required to maintain *permanently* a cash reserve of 100% against its demand deposits. In other words, the demand deposits would literally be deposits, consisting of cash held in trust for the depositor.

Thus, the new money would, in effect, be *tied up* by the 100 per cent reserve requirement.

The chequing deposit department of the bank would become a mere storage warehouse for bearer money belonging to its depositors and would be given a separate corporate existence as a Cheque Bank. There would then be no practical distinction between the chequing deposits and the reserve. The 'money I have in the bank', as recorded in the stub of my cheque book, would literally *be* money and literally be *in the bank* (or near at hand). The bank's deposits could rise to $125,000,000 only if its cash also rose to $125,000,000, by depositors depositing $25,000,000 more cash, that is, taking that much out of their pockets or tills and putting it in the bank. And if deposits shrank it would mean that depositors withdrew some of their stored-up money, that is, taking it out of the bank and putting it in their pockets or tills. In neither case would there be any change in the total.

So far as this change to the 100% system would deprive the bank of earning assets and require it to substitute an increased amount of non-earning cash, the bank would be reimbursed through a service charge made to its depositors – or otherwise.

Advantages

The resulting advantages to the public would include the following:

1 There would be practically no more runs on commercial banks; because 100% of the depositor's money would always be in the bank (or available) awaiting their orders, In practice, less money would be withdrawn than now; we all know of the frightened depositor who shouted to the bank teller, 'If you haven't got my money, I want it; if you have, I don't.'

2 There would be far fewer bank failures; because the important creditors of a commercial bank who would be most likely to make it fail are its depositors, and these depositors would be 100% provided for.

3 The interest-bearing Government debt would be substantially reduced; because a great part of the outstanding bonds of the Government would be taken over from the banks by the Currency Commission (representing the Government).

4 Our Monetary System would be simplified; because there would be no longer any essential difference between pocket-book money and cheque-book money. All of our circulating medium, 100% of it, would be actual money.

5 Banking would be simplified; at present, there is a confusion of ownership. When money is deposited in a chequing account, the depositor still thinks of that money as his, though legally it is the bank's. The depositor owns no money in the bank; he is merely a creditor of the bank as a private corporation. Most of the 'mystery' of banking would disappear as soon as the bank was no longer allowed to lend out money deposited by its customers, while, at the same time, these depositors were using that money as *their* money by drawing cheques against it. 'Mr. Dooley,' the Will Rogers of his day, brought out the absurdity of this double use of money on demand deposit when he called a banker 'a man who takes care of your money by lending it out to his friends.'

In the future there would be a sharp distinction between *chequing* deposits and *savings* deposits. Money put into a chequing account would belong to the depositor, like any other *safety* deposit and would bear no interest. Money put into a savings account would have the same status as it has now. It would belong unequivocally to the bank. In exchange for this money the bank would give the right to repayment with interest, but *no chequing privilege*. The savings depositor has simply brought *an investment* like an interest-bearing bond, and this investment would not require 100%

cash behind it, any more than any other investment such as a bond or share of the stock.

The reserve requirements for savings deposits need not necessarily be affected by the new system for chequing deposits (although a strengthening of these requirements is desirable).

6 Great inflations and deflations would be eliminated; because banks would be deprived of their present power virtually to mint cheque-book money and to destroy it; that is, making loans would not inflate our circulating medium and calling loans would not deflate it. The volume of the chequing depositors would not be affected any more than any other sort of loans increased or decreased. These deposits would be part of the total actual money of the nation, and this total could not be affected by being lent from one person or another.

Even if depositors should withdraw all deposits at once, or should pay all their loans at once, or should default on all of them at once, the nation's volume of money would not be affected thereby. It would merely be redistributed. Its total would be controlled by its sole issuer – the Currency Commission (which could also be given powers to deal with hoarding and velocity, if desired).

7 Booms and depressions would be greatly mitigated; because these are largely due to inflation and deflation.

8 Banker-management of industry would almost cease; because only in depressions can industries in general fall into the hands of bankers.

Of these eight advantages, the first two would apply chiefly to America, the land of bank runs and bank failures. The other six would apply to all countries having cheque-deposit banking. Advantage '6' and '7' are by far the most important, that is, the cessation of inflation and deflation of our circulating medium and so the mitigation of booms and depressions in general and the elimination of *great* booms and depressions in particular.

BENJAMIN GRAHAM

COMMODITIES AND CURRENCY (1944)

Benjamin Graham (1894–1976) has been described as the father of modern investing, and as the teacher and mentor of the most successful contemporary investor in the world – Warren Buffett – is probably as responsible as anyone for the modern obsession with markets and fluctuations. That might imply that Graham was somehow responsible for the current market instability, but the reverse is true. In his book before this one, *Storage and Stability*, he came up with a plan to produce and store raw materials to increase living standards and stabilize prices.

This passage is taken from its sequel, *World Commodities and World Currency*, published by McGraw-Hill in New York in 1944, where he applied the same idea to currencies in a post-war economy. Graham offers a more global analysis of the systems that could reduce dangerous cycles of price instability in order to make a post-war economy more stable. A range of commodities would be bought and stored around the world, to stabilize currency values and prices, provide reserves in the case of crises, and to achieve a balanced expansion of the world's output and consumption of useful goods.

Floating currencies – as we have them now – are thoroughly dangerous, he warned, because they are not based on anything. The Asian currency crisis – and all the other sharpening currency crises over the past half century – seems to have proved his point.

His idea was that an international agency called the International Commodity Corporation (ICC), a subsidiary of the then just proposed International Monetary Fund, should hold a basket of 15 commodities around the world – buying them when their value falls below the set price and selling when they're above. They would hold them as commodity units which would be in effect a world currency, stablize world prices and provide a backing to the value of money.

The idea is just as relevant today as it was then, as the recent proposals by Bernard Lietaer (see p221) demonstrate. But it also betrays the way leading economists were leaning in the increasingly frenetic negotiations as the Second World War drew to a close, about the shape of the post-war financial world. Fear of a post-war famine in Europe lay behind Graham's plan, just as it informed the rival plans by John Maynard Keynes for the British and Harry Dexter White for the Americans for a new financial system.

✳   ✳   ✳

I THE COMMODITY UNIT

A tentative 15-commodity unit is outlined in the appended table [not appended], which indicates also the method of derivation of the relative quantities. The relationship of the 15 commodities selected from the entire field of raw materials is developed statistically in Appendix [not included here]. Nine commodities on our list are of major rank with respect both to the value of world production and value of world trade. These are wheat, corn, sugar, cotton, wool, tobacco, petroleum, coal and wood pulp. One, pig-iron, is of first rank in world production but not in world trade. The remaining five – coffee, tea, rubber, copper, and tin – are of first rank in world trade, though not in world production. About five-eighths of the unit is made up of agricultural products and about one-third represents food.

The number of commodities in the unit might ultimately be considerably larger – say 25 to 30. It would seem best to operate the system at the outset with a readily manageable number of products, and to expand the group gradually – say at the rate of one commodity per year – after the plan has been well tested by experience.

2 PURCHASES OF THE COMMODITY UNIT

We shall assume that world prices for the component commodities are calculated fob at principal ports of shipment, in dollar equivalents. These will thus be export prices familiar to world trading operations and easily determinable. When the composite price falls to 95 per cent of the base, ICC will buy appropriate amounts of all 15 commodities in the world export markets, including therein purchases on the commodity exchanges. The operations will be patterned as closely as possible upon the commercial purchases regularly made by importing nations. Purchases in the various primary markets should ordinarily be proportioned to the related production or possibly exports, contingent, however, on storage arrangements discussed in the next section. Futures contracts may be bought in place of spot-delivery commodities, whenever the former are obtainable at a discount.

3 STORAGE ARRANGEMENTS

It is suggested that storage expense be distributed between producing nations, holding nations, and participants generally on some rational basis. The storage burden should fall upon the vendor nations that will benefit most directly from the purchase operations. Perhaps each nation should agree to provide free storage of commodities sold by it to ICC, for a period of not more than two years. This storage burden may in turn be assumed by the producers or even the commodity exchanges, subject to government supervision. If the commodity is provisionally stored in the interior, the producing country must complete delivery to the port of shipment when requested.

Nationals holding deposits with the IMF, who thus have helped finance the purchase of the units, should have the privilege of holding up to the equivalent amount of units in their own custody. This they may wish to do for their general protection. In such case they must pay delivery costs from the nearest available port of shipment and assume the cost of storage thereafter. They will then hold the units as agents for ICC, and will have the privilege of drawing out individual commodities and replacing them by future contracts whenever this is advantageous. Alternatively, creditor nations may be given the right to purchase units from ICC at 100% of base value, thus cancelling an equivalent amount of their money claim.

Unit commodities still held in the producing country two years after purchase will then be stored at the expense of ICC at the most economical rate. Storage arrangements will include suitable rotation to preserve the commodities in merchantable condition.

E C RIEGEL

The Valun System (1954)

If anyone pioneered the idea that inflation would be the major challenge for economics in the middle of the 20th century, it was the iconoclastic American philosopher Edwin Clarence Riegel (1879–1954). Just as Ralph Borsodi (see p202) was trying to arouse Americans to the danger of Keynesianism, Riegel was doing the same. Both published their most important diatribes on the subject in the middle of the Second World War, Riegel in his book *Private Enterprise Money* in 1944. Both were pioneers of the local currencies that emerged after their deaths.

Both have also been seriously neglected since. It's all very well to be a prophet, but as the novelist C P Snow pointed out, those prophets that are more than a couple of minutes ahead of their time are often dismissed as cranks. Riegel, in particular, could reasonably claim to have foreseen the way the modern free market would eventually work. But at the time of his death from Parkinson's Disease, desperately working to finish the manuscript *Toward a Natural Monetary System* from which this passage is taken, it seemed very much that his warnings about inflation had fallen on completely deaf ears. The book, *The Flight from Inflation*, wasn't actually published for another two decades.

Riegel's solution was a new currency he called the *valun*, which he had been writing about since the 1930s. It would be a private currency – this written a good 20 years before Hayek made the idea widely known (see Part V, p157) – and issued as a kind of mutual credit system by participating organizations, in the form of cheques, notes and coins.

The key is to provide some kind of money that is backed by something real, he argues. Labour is the most logical commodity, but different kinds of labour have different values. Commodity goods, as proposed by Graham (see p196) and Kaldor (see p204) are too unwieldy. The valun would be backed by the products and services that they were being exchanged for, and it wouldn't bear any interest either – its whole purpose was to cut the cost of money. No money would be issued that wasn't covered by goods and services.

Ironically enough, Riegel – the great pioneer of free market economics – seems to be suggesting something very similar to Proudhon's People's Bank (see p181), but such are the ironies of money 'heresy'. His philosophy was based on deep suspicion of Roosevelt's New Deal and of big government and big business generally. His social security card sums it all up: having refused to reveal to officials what his middle name was, it read 'Edwin Controversy Riegel'.

*　*　*

The *valun* system would be governed on a mutual participation basis. A board of governors would license the participating banks, and the board and member banks would be served by a separate service organization which, like the banks, would be organized and operated for profit. . .

The board of governors would be a non-capitalized, mutual association of participating banks in which all members would have one vote. With the bank stocks, in turn, being held by personal enterprisers, the whole monetary system would thus be truly of, by and for personal enterprise. The banks would pay stipulated fees to the board, and any surplus accruing would be redistributed among the banks in proportion to their volume of valun business, probably with cheque clearances being the criterion.

The board would license new and existing banks to operate under the system, without distinction as to nationality or the monetary unit in which the latter normally transacted business. Valun banking would require merely a separate set of books. The operating licences would stipulate rules of practice and provide for periodic examinations. Through its control of the name *valun*, the board would guarantee adherence to uniform standards by all banks in the system. The board would also authorize the printing of bills and minting of coins and provide for surveillance against counterfeiting of valun currency.

A chief responsibility of the board would be with respect to credit policy. The board could set what it deemed to be the most conservative policy and provide therefore a minimum percentage to be charged for loss insurance, and from there up graduations of more liberal policies, with appropriate percentages for loss insurance for each. Thus there would be no more need for standardizing the basis of credit in the valun system than in the present banking system. Each bank could choose its own credit policy. The appropriate loss insurance percentage would then be added to the cheque clearing charge made to the customers. In this way, customers of the various banks would pay more or less as the policy of their bank was less or more conservative. The insurance fund this set up against defaults would be held by the board, subject to draft by any bank to cover any 'loss' from credit default.

The service organization would be a profit corporation with capital adequate to promote the adoption of the system by banks and their depositors. In addition to negotiating licences for the board, it would supply the banks with cheques and other forms required by them, as well as any mechanical equipment desired. It would also supply valun currency in bills and coins, as authorized by the board. In view of the national and international potentialities of the valun system, it can be seen that the service organization would have the possibility of becoming a very profitable enterprise, expanding both in capital and income with the growth of the valun system.

The function of the banks would be to administer, for an appropriate service charge, the mutual credit of their account holders. The banks would provide credit facilities for the issuance and redemption of valuns by personal enterprisers, and would clear cheques and render other appropriate banking services. There would, of course, be no interest charge for lines of credit, since the banks would take no credit risks. The credit would be extended by traders to one another, and the banks would not be involved except as administrators.

Hence, under the valun system, credit would be free, but not printing, book-keeping, insurance and other expenses; service costs would be paid for by the account holders. The small percentage charge stipulated by the board of governors to set up reserves against credit 'losses' might range from $1/20$ th to $1/10$ th of a per cent per month. Thus the valun system would save business the tremendous sums paid in interest under the speculative political monetary system.

RALPH BORSODI

The Escondido
Memorandum (1972)

Ralph Borsodi (1888–1977) was a key figure in the world of monetary innovation in the middle years of the century. He warned of inflation a good quarter century before it became a problem, he predicted the post-war flight of population out of the cities on both sides of the Atlantic. He also worked with Irving Fisher during the Depression to help him develop his 'Stamp Scrip' (see p238).

By the 1970s, enraged by growing inflation around the world – which he regarded as a government fraud on the public – he was fascinated with the practicalities of creating a new kind of money that would be able to keep its value because it was based on something real. In 1973, he launched his own experimental currency in his home town of Exeter, New Hampshire.

What was revolutionary about the *constant* was that, by tying its value to a basket of commodities, it had a constant value – backed by US$100,000 of his own money, on deposit in banks in Exeter, Boston and London. The main problems Borsodi had to solve were how to choose these commodities, how to buy them as backing, and how to store them. You clearly couldn't put $100,000 worth of oil and wheat in the bank, let alone your garage – even on the scale of American garages. He decided to arbitrage them instead, organizing a team of supporters to arbitrage shiploads of the chosen commodities while they were at sea in tankers, and sell them straight on – and make a profit while they were about it.

By February 1973, the University of New Hampshire Press was printing 275,000 *constants* in different denominations up to *C100*. Exeter's local council even started accepting them as payment for parking fines. Having proved that it was a success – but failing to incite public fury at the Federal Reserve when they saw the dollar dropping in value – Borsodi wound up the experiment.

This passage was the document he wrote in Escondido, California on 3 March 1972, that led to the Exeter experiment, inspired by a fit of rage at the age of 85 at growing inflation. It was known as the Escondido Memorandum. It belongs in that hothouse atmosphere of threatened social collapse that so characterized the 1970s, but the questions remain meaningful today.

* * *

1 Can a stable 'measure of value' be computed using index numbers for the purpose? Can the margin of error in such a 'measure of value' be kept down to one per cent and minus?

2 Can a 'basket of currencies' be used in place of gold to provide a reserve for the backing of a stable monetary unit? Can confidence in such a monetary unit be created and maintained? Can provision be made to guard against the devaluation and even the repudiation of its currency by a major power?

3 Can a 'basket of currencies' be used to provide such a reserve? How much will it cost to provide for the storage of such a basket?

4 Can provision be made so that a 'money of account' based upon such a reserve can be used as 'legal tender' for all practical purposes in a national currency – specifically in the dollar?

5 Can an experiment be conducted – say for a year – in circulating through our banks and clearing through the Federal Reserve System – the notes representing such a stable 'money of account'? Are there any legal roadblocks which need to be removed to make such an experiment possible?

6 Can the cost of issuing such a 'money of account' by an international institution organized for that purpose be earned by it since it will have no taxing power; because resorting to taxing power would nationalize and politicalize it?

7 Can arbitrage be used to provide for its expenses of operation? Can debentures be used to create a 'revolving fund' which can earn enough to provide for such expenses? How much would have to be paid to investors in interest in addition to its inflation-proof feature on such debentures?

8 Can the various currencies in which such debentures would have to be sold be invested through such a 'revolving fund' so as to earn the expenses of the issuing institution?

9 What other income is possible to cover the cost of maintaining not only the staff of economists, statisticians, and accountants, but also an advisory board or committee of outstanding economists, bankers and businessmen?

10 How much will it cost to fund such an experiment for a year?

NICHOLAS KALDOR

ECONOMIC STABILITY (1975)

'Because of the absence of money-value-measures, economics (in many respects) is a pseudo-science – something of patches, of expediency, and of compromise in which all-too-fallible human judgement essays to do its best – too often contriving to do its worst.' That is how the economist St Clare Grondona introduced his book *Economic Stability is Attainable*. A modest statement for an economist, no doubt, but it does sum up the problem of currencies that have no backing. Real wealth, he argued, was in the basic commodities, raw materials and foodstuffs which human life depends on.

International currencies had been on the agenda since Keynes put forward his plan for one called the *bancor* during the war, but as Keynesian economics became eclipsed after the war, so did talk of an international currency. The idea of a bancor backed by commodities hasn't gone away, and was taken up in the 1960s by the leading Keynesian economists Albert Hart, Jan Tinbergen and Nicholas Kaldor (1908–1986).

Once the old Bretton Woods agreement had unravelled in the 1970s, Kaldor returned to the theme, and this passage is taken from his preface to Grondona's new commodity currency proposal *Economic Stability is Attainable*, published in London in 1975 by Hutchinson. The idea is still for an international currency, backed by stores of commodities, and stabilizing the prices of all currencies – as well as making the producers of basic foodstuffs as critical as the gold producers were under the gold standard. Growing grain would also then be producing the basis for money – and that now seems a pretty revolutionary idea.

The IMF does actually have an international currency. It's called Special Drawing Rights (SDR), and it's intended to provide support for other currencies – four countries even peg the value of their currencies to it. But its value is determined by a basket of other currencies, reviewed every five years, so this is not the commodity-backed international currency that Kaldor wanted.

* * *

I have for many years supported the idea of stabilizing prices of basic commodities by means of international buffer stocks, tied, if possible, to the creation of a new international currency.

As I see it, the major attraction of a scheme of this kind, for which it would be difficult to find a substitute, is that it spreads the courses of 'money-making power' far and wide – among the commodity producers of the world – and would thereby tend to generate the maximum attainable rate of growth in world economy, and under conditions of stable prices, at least for basic materials. By ensuring that any increase in the output of basic commodities will generate a corresponding increase in the purchasing power of the producers, it will also ensure, through adequate 'multiplier' and 'accelerator' effects, that the growth of commodity absorption will proceed fast enough to match the long-term rate of growth of commodity production which, under the automatic functioning of the system, would gradually be brought into balance.

Those who object to schemes of this kind on the ground that they might generate too much money and too much income in the hands of the primary producers, and would therefore be 'inflationary' in their effects, fail in my view to understand the true nature of inflationary processes. These are to be found, as the experience of the last two years should have made evident, in a *shortage* of basic commodities relative to the need for them, and not in any super-abundance of such commodities. Inflationary pressures arise whenever the growth of demand for food and basic materials – which is governed by the *growth* of industrial activities – tends to outrun the growth of availabilities of such goods: the opposite case, when the growth of availabilities intercedes faster than demand (and which would require an acceleration of the growth of industrial production) is a cause of world-wide *deflationary* trends – as was shown by the experience of the years following 1929.

Mr Grondona's proposal would create a powerful automatic stabilizer for adjusting the growth of demand to the growth of supplies of primary products through its repercussions on the effective demand for industrial goods. When production exceeds consumption, world investment in commodity stocks would automatically rise: this would imply a supplement to incomes derived from current sales to consumers, and thereby stimulate the absorption of primary products through increased production and employment in the industrial regions. A shortage of commodities would cause a depletion of stocks; this would reduce producers' incomes relative to the consumers' outlay on such commodities; it would thereby reduce the effective demand for industrial goods until the excess demand for basic commodities was eliminated.

Over a longer period it is of course quite inevitable that the flow of production and of consumption of basic commodities should be kept in balance, either through adjustments on the side of production, or of consumption, or both. Mr Grondona's scheme has the tremendous benefit of making it possible for adjustments to proceed smoothly and continuously, without upheavals that now accompany this process; and it would do so by adjusting the rate of consumption to the limits set by production possibilities, and not the other way round.

In other words, in the longer run it is the supply of basic materials which would set the limit to the rate of growth of world industrial production and now, as now, the rate of growth of effective demand, emanating from the advanced countries, which governed the trend rate of growth of investment and production of primary commodities.

Looking at the matter from another angle, the Grondona system would enormously enhance the effectiveness of monetary policy. For the Central Banks of the world would then come to regulate the supply of money through open market operations in commodity markets (and thereby ensure that such operations have a *direct* and *powerful* effective demand and on incomes) and not in the market for high-grade substitutes for money (such as Treasury bills) the income effects of which are both slow and highly uncertain.

SHANN TURNBULL

KILOWATT HOUR CURRENCIES (1977)

Ah yes, but what if the whole business of storing great quantities of oil and grain is just too much to stomach, and arbitraging it while on the high seas doesn't really seem reliable enough? The innovative Australian thinker Shann Turnbull suggested an interesting alternative – basing a new currency on the value of locally produced renewable energy. The costs of producing it are relatively stable throughout the world – or so he argued – and the costs of transporting it are pretty prohibitive, so this really isn't a commodity with which any corporate raider could corner the market.

Ironically, Turnbull was actually a corporate raider himself, working for the Australian financier Robert Holmes à Court. Since then, he has devoted his career to working out ways to make the financial world socially sustainable. He is also an influential adviser to the president of the World Bank and is one of the foremost authorities in the world on new kinds of money.

The first version of this idea was published in *The Australian* in 1977, but it reached a wider audience as one of the 'Tools for Community Economic Self-reliance' presented in the USA by the E F Schumacher Society at a series of seminars from 1982 to 1984.

Even so, it betrays its origins in the 1970s in its tone – the determination that money should be real and that the solution should have something to do with energy: inflation and energy provided the 1970s with their twin crises. Nobody has yet taken up the Turnbull plan, but the energy crisis on the horizon might provide an extra spur.

* * *

Another option for basing a currency system is provided by services. Generally, these can only be produced as they are consumed and so avoid wide changes in value and the cost of storage associated with physical commodities. The most obvious service to consider is human labour. An individual could create a contract note to provide specified hours of a specified service. If these services were deliverable to the bearer of the note, then the note could be exchanged (sold) by the creator of the note for other goods or services.

The number of situations where such arrangements could be practical is quite limited. As one hour of one person's time may not be worth one hour of another's, a currency based on labour hours does not provide a useful unity of value. There is an additional problem created in modern societies where the output of goods and services produced by an hour of human labour depends very largely on the technology employed. The level of technology thus determines the value of labour. . .

With much modern technology the volume of output is quite independent of human labour except that required for repair and maintenance. The automatic elevator is an example of labour in the form of attendants being entirely eliminated. These examples are becoming more and more common as machines replace people and robots replace and repair machines and even run factories. Today there now exists the opportunity for any community in the world to produce electrical energy without any human labour on a continuous basis by the use of wind, solar, hydro, or wave generators.

The production of electrical energy has now become a basic activity for all modern communities. Modern technology, using renewable energy sources, has made the cost of production relatively constant throughout the world. The technology of power production from renewable energy sources has diseconomies of scale and so favours small discrete autonomous communities. For this reason, the unit of electrical power, the Kilowatt-hour (Kwhr) has much appeal as a universal unit of value for an autonomous community banking and monetary system.

The owners of the power generator would create money. It would be in the form of a voucher or contract note to supply a specified number of Kwhrs at a specified time in the future. These notes would be created and issued by the owners of the generator to pay for its purchase and installation. The value of notes that could be issued for redemption in any given time period would be limited by the output of the generator. The notes with a specified maturity date would represent the 'primary' currency. Such currency notes would mainly be held by investors, investment banks, and banks.

Commercial banks would hold the primary currency notes as a reserve currency in like manner to a bank holding gold or a merchant banker holding grain or other commodities. Similarly, the commercial bank would issue its own 'secondary' notes, which would be based on the primary notes and which the holder could convert cash in to the primary notes or reserve currency (to be used to pay his power bills at the time specified). The secondary notes could be denominated in Kwhrs but without any specified redemption time. They could be used as hand-to-hand money in the community. . .

The renewable energy dollar would be far more democratic than gold dollars, as sun, wind, and/or wave energy is available to all communities in the world, whereas gold is not. It is also very democratic within communities since each individual could own his own renewable electrical energy source to supply his own needs and/or to supply to others.

In the United States, legislation known as PURPA (Public Utility Regulating Practice Act) compelled power utilities to buy and distribute power from individuals or groups who invest in generators to produce power from renewable energy sources. In principle, requiring the existing electric utilities with distribution facilities to pay a 'fair' price allows decentralized small producers to sell power on a competitive basis. This legislation provides a mechanism for facilitating the creation of community-based renewable energy dollars.

The total volume of paper primary energy dollars that could be created is directly related to the total installed capacity of electrical generators. The total installed capacity of electrical generators is, in turn, related to the total activity in the community. The volume of primary currency that could be created has physical limitations, which are related to the total volume of goods and services traded for money within the community. No such constraints and relationships exist with a gold-backed currency.

While some communities may have natural advantages over others in their ability to produce cheap electrical power, such differences would neither be as great or as volatile as that with gold or agricultural commodities. The community that produced the cheapest power would have the 'hardest' or most valuable dollar in terms of its ability to purchase more goods and services in other communities. While one community could sell its cheaper power to another community, the cost of transmitting energy creates a natural limitation to encourage independent autonomous community production. Gold is not so limiting in this regard because it can be cheaply transported.

The possibility of using electrical energy as a basis for creating money has only emerged in the current century. In recent decades, this option has been considerably reinforced by advanced technology, which permits small renewable power generators to compete with large centralized generators using non-renewable energy sources. Non-renewable power sources are less suitable for defining units of value since a substantial proportion of their costs are fuel and labour, the value of which (relative to the original investment cost) may change over the life of the plant. Further technological advances could make small, decentralized, environmentally compatible energy sources even more competitive and so suitable as a universal democratic basis for defining a unit of value.

The new option provided by electrical power generation to create a unit of value and the attractions it offers are not presented with the idea that it should be the only basis for creating community currencies. A number of other options could also be used simultaneously and in competition. Some individual and/or communities may prefer to create and/or use other commodities as a basis for creating a currency.

However, the renewable energy dollar would appear to present a highly competitive option in providing a reference unit of value, whether or not it is also used to carry out the other functions of money in providing a medium of exchange and a store of value. If a community preferred to adopt a currency system based on gold, agricultural commodities, oil, or labour services, then kilowatt-hours of electricity could provide a universal reference unit of value between communities of the world and within communities.

BOB SWANN AND SUSAN WITT

REGIONAL CURRENCIES

(1995)

The green critique of economics has dovetailed with the currency reformers mainly through the efforts of the influential American pacifist and social innovator Bob Swann (1918–), who with Susan Witt (1946–) has been running the American E F Schumacher Society since its inception in 1980. Swann made a special trip to visit Schumacher in the UK in 1967, long before his fame as the author of *Small is Beautiful*, and encouraged him to write the series of articles that formed the basis of the book. Swann had also helped Borsodi (see p202) with his *constant* experiment in 1973, and his Society has formed a close relationship with Jane Jacobs (see Part III, p100), whose analysis they share. Their alliance with Paul Glover (see Part II, p73) has also led to their strong support for the new 'hours'-style currencies that sprang up in North American towns in the mid-1990s.

Swann is a fascinating figure. He spent two years in prison as a conscientious objector during the Second World War, much of it in solitary confinement because he refused to accept the prison's racial segregation rules. During that time, he came under the influence of an associate of Gandhi and found himself thinking deeply about money.

As you might expect from a close colleague of Borsodi's, Swann has been concerned primarily about the issue of underpinning the value of money – but also of making it more available by basing its value on local products that are universally available, rather as Turnbull suggests with locally produced energy (see p207). Regional currencies, he suggests in this passage taken from the essay he wrote with Susan Witt, '*Local Currencies: Catalysts for sustainable regional economies*', can provide real help for farmers and small business people if they are based on the value of products. This could be farm produce, as in one of the pioneering experiments they describe in this passage. It could be food sold by a local restaurant, as in the famous *deli dollars* currency they describe here. It could be chickens or wood, but it has to be real.

The basis for the experiments, which began in 1989, was their very successful small loans programme known as Self-Help Association for a Regional Economy (SHARE), which was intended also as a basis for a local currency. Their more ambitious plans for a currency called BerkSHARE – they are based in the Berkshires region of Massachusetts – have yet to come to fruition. SHARE used the idea, pioneered by the Grameen Bank in Bangladesh, of a circle of supporters to guarantee their loans to small business – which was adapted to create new currencies called *farm notes*.

Swann and Witt occupy a fascinating position, because of all this pioneering work, between the real money advocates and the free money advocates. They seem to have developed a way of using the best of both traditions, by rooting their currencies firmly to the value of something that is widely available locally. The idea of using farm produce as backing for money actually goes back to the Populist Party (see Donnelly, Part I, p31). The leader of the Texas Farmer's Alliance, Charles Macune, proposed back in 1889 that the US government set up county warehouses to store crops after every harvest as the backing for money to be lent to farmers. Macune's ideas were watered down and emerged as the Federal Reserve system in 1913. By then, there was no sign of the vegetables.

*   *   *

Frank Tortoriello is the owner of a popular deli on Main Street in Great Barrington. He turned to SHARE when the bank refused him a loan to move his restaurant to a new location. But Frank didn't need SHARE's circle of grandmothers; he already had a circle of his own in his customers. SHARE suggested that Frank issue Deli Dollars as a self-financing technique. The notes would be purchased during a month of sale and redeemed after the Deli had moved to its new location.

A local artist, Martha Shaw, designed the note, which showed a host of people carrying Frank and his staff – all busy cooking – to their new location. The notes were marked 'redeemable for meals up to a value of ten dollars.' The Deli would not be able to redeem all the notes at once after the move, so SHARE advised Frank to stagger repayment over a year by placing a 'valid after' date on each note. To discourage counterfeiting Frank signed every note individually like a cheque.

We recommended that the notes be sold for ten dollars each, but Frank thought that would be too good a deal for the Deli. With his customers in mind he sold ten-dollar notes for eight dollars and raised $5000 in thirty days: contractors bought sets of Deli Dollars as Christmas presents for their construction crews; parents of students at nearby Simon's Rock College knew Deli Dollars would make a good gift for their kids; the bankers who turned down the original loan request supported Frank by buying Deli Dollars.

The notes even showed up in the collection plate of the First Congreg-
ational Church because church-goers knew the minister ate breakfast at the
Deli. Regular customers were pleased to help support what they saw was a
sure thing – they knew first-hand how hard Frank worked and believed in
his ability to make good on redemption. Frank repaid the loan, not in hard-
to-come-by federal notes but in cheese-on-rye sandwiches.

Jennifer Tawczynski worked at the Main Street Deli and carried the idea
home to her parents Dan and Martha Tawczynski, who own Taft Farm, one
of two farm markets in the area. The Tawczynskis came to SHARE with the
idea of issuing 'greensbacks' to help them meet the high cost of heating their
greenhouses through the winter. Customers would buy the notes in the late
fall for redemption in plants and vegetables come spring and summer.

At around the same time the other farm market in town, the Corn Crib,
was damaged by fire. Customers of the Corn Crib came to SHARE with
the idea of issuing notes to help owners Don and Ruth Zeigler recover from
the ravages of the fire. SHARE suggested that the two farms together issue
a Berkshire Farm Preserve Note. Martha Shaw designed the note with a head
of cabbage in the middle surrounded by a variety of other vegetables. The
notes read 'In Farms We Trust' and were sold for nine dollars each.

The Massachusetts Commissioner of Agriculture travelled from Boston
to purchase the first Berkshire Farm Preserve Note, and five national
networks showed our farmers using Yankee ingenuity to survive a difficult
winter. The Berkshire Women with Infants and Children (WIC) programme
purchased Berkshire Farm Preserve Notes in order to give them to families,
part of a local initiative to supplement the federal food programme. The
notes do not carry the food-stamp stigma, and the Berkshire agency knows
it is supporting local farmers at the same time it is supporting local families.

The notes could be purchased at either farm and were redeemable at either
farm. At the end of the redemption period SHARE acted as the clearing
house for the notes. The farmers received the income (ranging from $3000
to $5000 per farm per year) from the sale of the notes, and they found a
committed base of customers who would travel out of their way to buy from
their local farms rather than purchase the jet-lagged vegetables from supermarket chains. Deli dollars started a consumer movement in the Berkshires.
The Berkshire farm preserve notes, Monterey general store notes, and Kintaro
notes that followed gave Berkshire residents a way to vote for the kind of small
independent businesses that help to make a local economy more self-reliant.

The popularity of the scrip inspired the Southern Berkshire Chamber of
Commerce to work with the Schumacher Society staff to issue Berk-Shares

as a summer promotion. Customers were given one Berk-Share for every ten dollars spent in a participating business over the six-week summer period. During a three-day redemption period customers could spend their Berk-Shares just like dollars in any of the seventy participating stores.

The success of the Berk-Share programme depended on the energy and cooperation of a small group of merchants and in large part on the sense of community among consumers. Of the seventy-five thousand Berk-Shares handed out (representing three-quarters of a million dollars in Berk-Share trade) twenty-eight thousand were spent during the three-day redemption period! Some families pooled their Berk-Shares for a gift for one member of the family. People who were going away over the redemption weekend were sure to give their Berk-Shares to a neighbour who would use them. A spirit of festivity and excitement filled Main Street that weekend as people chatted about how they planned to use their Berk-Shares.

Although the Berk-Shares and Deli Dollars and Farm Preserve Notes represented a major shift in local attitudes toward an alternative exchange and captured the imagination of both consumers and producers, they were not yet the year-round local currency the organizers had envisioned. A suggestion from several area banks pushed the effort forward to its next stage. The Berk-Share organizing committee proposed that the five local banks participate in a Berk-Shares zero percent loan programme during the winter holidays. Spending that would normally flow to catalogue stores and malls would instead go to the locally owned stores that accepted Berk-Shares, helping to secure local jobs and keeping local dollars local.

The committee presented the idea at a meeting with the bankers, who in turn proposed that the committee create a year-round Berk-Share which would be a 10 percent discount note. Customers would come to the banks and purchase one hundred Berk-Shares for ninety dollars and redeem them at local stores for one hundred dollars worth of goods and services. The merchants would then deposit their Berk-Shares at local banks at ninety cents per share.

But how to clear the Berk-Share accounts among the five banks? The Federal Reserve system moves dollars (cheques) between the receiving bank and the issuing bank. This clearing system is automated and keeps the national currency moving. A local currency needs a local system. The bankers at the meeting came up with the solution. They said, 'Well, we can just walk down the street to one another's banks and make the exchange, the way we used to with cheques.' It gave these individual bankers, who are caught up in a highly centralized and fast-paced system, great pleasure to imagine recapturing in a small way the early days of banking when transactions had a warmer, more community-spirited tone.

The Schumacher Society and the Main Street Action Association of the Southern Berkshire Chamber of Commerce are cooperatively seeking funds to staff the first year of issue. When the programme is in place and local businesses and their customers are familiar with the Berk-Share as a year-round scrip, Main Street Action and the Schumacher Society will work with local businesses to develop a commodity backing for the Berk-Share. Eventually, loans can be made in Berk-Shares at an interest rate as low as three percent – the cost of servicing the loan.

Unlike the current SHARE programme, which relies on borrowed dollars, a loan in Berk-Shares would carry no profit costs. A three per cent loan could encourage new business ventures like local food processing that otherwise couldn't compete because investment capital is too expensive. A local scrip can empower Berkshire residents to shape their own economic futures unfettered by high interest rates and credit decisions made in far-away money centres. Each town can be a money centre, and local economic problems will have local solutions.

In the summer of 1991, Paul Glover heard a radio interview with Schumacher Society staff about the Deli Dollars and Berkshire Farm Preserve Notes. The story inspired him to issue Ithaca Hours in his hometown of Ithaca, New York, as a way to create more local jobs and more security for Ithacans who are underemployed. Ithaca Hours has grown from its small grass-roots beginning to include over a thousand individuals and stores.

The scrip can buy food items, construction work, professional services, health care, and handicrafts. Each Ithaca Hour is worth ten dollars – the average hourly wage in Tompkins County – so the five thousand Ithaca Hours (or $50,000) in circulation have increased local economic transactions by several hundred thousand dollars annually.

A local currency may be dollar-denominated or measured in chickens (as Wendell Berry once suggested for his part of Kentucky) or hours or cordwood, as long as people know they can spend that chicken cash, that cordwood note. Confidence in a currency requires that it be redeemable for some locally available commodity or service. The Schumacher Society recommends the following policies to maintain confidence over the long haul:

- The issuing organization should be incorporated as a non-profit so the public understands that providing access to credit is a service not linked to private gain. The organization should be democratic, with membership open to all area residents and with a board elected by the members.

- Its policy should be to create new short-term credit for productive purposes. Such credit is normally provided for up to three months for goods or services that have already been produced and are on their way to market – credit for things which pay for themselves in a very short time.
- The regional bank or currency organization should be free of governmental control – other than inspection – so that investment decisions are independent and are made by the community.
- Social and ecological criteria should be introduced into loan-making. (Community investment funds also use a positive set of social criteria particular to their own region. These funds could join with hard-pressed local banks to initiate regional currencies.)
- Loan programmes and local currencies should support local production for local needs.

Local currencies can play a vital role in the development of stable, diversified regional economies, giving definition and identity to regions, encouraging face-to-face transactions between neighbours, and helping to revitalize local cultures. A local currency is not simply an economic tool; it is also a cultural tool.

Community groups in Kansas City, Eugene, Boulder, and in Little Philmont, New York, are issuing their own currencies, and each is uniquely tailored to the people, culture, and products of the region. Each community has its own tale of how and why people first organized and what they hope to achieve by their efforts.

A Schumacher Society member who was visiting Ithaca looked in *Ithaca Money* for a way to spend his scrip before leaving town. He decided on a craft item that a woman made and sold in her home. The daughter who answered the door understood that the visitor was not from Ithaca and asked, 'What does your hometown currency look like?'

DAVID FLEMING

DOMESTIC TRADABLE QUOTAS (2000)

Shann Turnbull's proposal that money should be based on the value of renewable energy (see p207) is not the only one of its kind. When the greenhouse effect threw up the idea of tradeable carbon emissions permits – now the basis of the international climate change negotiations – it provided a whole new possible basis for money.

Imagine, said the policy analyst David Fleming (1940–), that those emissions permits are not just credited towards nations, and traded by them, but credited to all of us as individuals and ordinary businesses – rather like wartime ration coupons. In fact it was Fleming's childhood experiences with sweet rations that gave him the idea that the permits or coupons could be held on a personal smart card and either spent or traded, just as nations do. The idea, introduced for the first time in an article in *Country Life* in 1996, would provide a kind of basic income to every individual, as of right.

The background to the scheme is our rapidly dwindling worldwide stocks of fossil fuels, and Fleming's Domestic Tradable Quotas (DTQs), developed with Richard Starkey of the Centre for Corporate Environmental Management at the University of Huddersfield, are intended also as a method to involve everyone in reducing our carbon emissions. The idea was the subject of a European Commission workshop in 1998. This passage is taken from the Domestic Tradable Quotas website.

And in case you don't believe something so elusive could provide the basis for anything that could be bought and sold, it's happening already – and not just in the Chicago exchange that has pioneered carbon trading. Green energy producers on continental Europe are already unbundling the energy from the 'green-ness' – and selling on the green aspect to electricity suppliers in the UK who want to sell green energy but haven't enough windmills yet to provide it.

✼   ✼   ✼

DTQs are an economic instrument to enable national economies to reduce their carbon emissions. They are designed for application within the economy; they are to be distinguished from international instruments designed for trading between nations. They allow national authorities to take control over the rate at which fossil fuel consumption is reduced, while allocating the available resource fairly, and maintaining price flexibility so that the economy can distribute it efficiently.

The nation implementing the scheme sets an overall Carbon Budget that is reduced over time. The 'carbon units' making up this budget are issued to adults and organizations. All adults receive an equal and unconditional entitlement of carbon units; organizations acquire the units they need from a tender, a form of auction modelled on the issue of government debt. There is a national market in carbon units in which low users can sell their surplus, and higher users can buy more.

It is a hands-off scheme, with virtually all transactions being carried out electronically, using the technologies and systems already in place for direct debit systems and credit cards. The scheme has been designed to function efficiently not only for people who participate in it, but for those who do not participate – for example for overseas visitors, for the infirm and for those who do refuse to cooperate. The advantages claimed for the scheme are that it is effective, equitable and efficient.

HOW THE QUOTA MARKET WORKS

The *numéraire* of the model is the 'carbon unit,' defined as one kilogram of carbon dioxide (or CO_2-equivalents in the global warming potential of nitrous oxide and methane). . .

There is a rolling annual issue of carbon units – with an initial issue for one year, topped up each week. Carbon units are issued into the market in two ways. First, there is the *Entitlement* for all adults. The share of emissions accounted for by households (about 45 per cent in the UK) is issued to all adults on an equal per capita basis. (Children's carbon usage would be provided for in the existing system of child allowances.) The remaining share (55 per cent) is issued through the *Tender* to commercial and industrial companies and to the public sector, using the system already established for the tender of government debt. It is distributed by the banks to organizations using direct credit (for the units) and direct debit systems (for the payments).

When they make purchases of fuel or energy, consumers and firms surrender quota to the energy retailer, accessing their quota account by (for instance) using their QuotaCard or by direct debit. The retailer then surrenders carbon units when buying energy from the wholesaler. Finally, the primary energy provider surrenders units back to the Register (QuotaCo) when the company pumps, mines or imports fuel. This closes the loop.

Some fuel purchasers will not have any carbon units to offer at point of sale – for example, foreign visitors, people who have forgotten their card, people who have used all their quota, and small firms and traders that do not bother to make regular purchases of units through their banks. All these must buy quota at the time of purchase, in order to surrender it.

Individuals who cash in all their quota when they receive it and who then have to buy quota to cover their fuel purchases pay a cost penalty for this: they have to buy carbon units at the market's offer price and surrender them at the (lower) bid price – and the difference between these two prices is the cost of their non-participation.

Carbon units can be bought and sold on the secondary market. People who use less than their entitlement can earn a revenue from the sale of their surplus, and people who use more must buy their additional requirement. The government receives a revenue from the tender. Trading revenues are earned by the market-makers – quoting bid and offer prices. Purchases and sales of quota are made through automatic teller machines (ATMs), over the counter of banks and post offices and energy retailers, or by direct debit arrangements with energy suppliers.

ADVANTAGES OF DTQS

1 Effectiveness

It is claimed that DTQs are an effective instrument, first, because they are set up within a framework of collective motivation, integrating private preferences with public goals, and integrating the programme of reducing carbon emissions within the set of social values and priorities for which there is a broadly-based support and commitment.

Secondly, they provide a long term signal, giving the economy clear information about the quantity of fossil fuel that will be available for all users in the future. The short-term elasticity of demand for fossil fuels is low; the long-term elasticity of demand is high. DTQs build a framework in which the economy can take action now in the knowledge that this is the only way in which it can cope with the reduced supply conditions which – it knows for certain – will exist in the future. Such a signal is only possible if it is tolerant to sharp and unpredictable changes in the price of fuel: the Carbon Budget builds price flexibility into the model of DTQs.

2 Equity

Equity is a necessary condition for political acceptability. Unless the instrument used is clearly equitable, then there will be no public and political acceptance for it, and the task of reducing carbon emissions on a significant scale within a democratic society is likely to prove to be impossible.

The instrument gives consumers themselves a central role in the reduction of carbon emissions. It does not act over their heads; it involves them. It is therefore transparent: it is clear to consumers how the scheme works, and how prices are set. There is no sense that there is some anonymous government body setting the prices for them. It is citizens' own scheme; there is a sense of justice.

3 Efficiency

If the claim that DTQs effectively stimulate collective motivation is correct, there are positive efficiency implications: for any given quantity of carbon emissions, the fuel price (ie fuel + quota/tax/other) is likely to be lower under a DTQ regime than under alternative regimes. Cost savings in the transition to a low-carbon regime would have major economic advantages, with positive benefits for real incomes and employment.

BERNARD LIETAER

THE TERRA (2001)

I've remarked already how strange it is that so little research is being done about the money system, compared to the dead weight of research about other areas of modern economics. So perhaps it wasn't surprising that, when Bernard Lietaer (1942–) calculated that as much as 97 per cent of the foreign exchange trading every day (about US$2 trillion) is speculation, the mainstream political world wasn't terribly interested.

Lietaer has emerged as one of the most interesting and authoritative contributors to the growing debate about the future of money. He was a successful currency trader himself, and in that respect – like Soros (see Part II, p80) – is poacher turned gamekeeper. As a top executive at the Central Bank in Belgium, he became one of the originators of the ECU, the convergence mechanism that led to the euro. Again like Soros, he has become concerned at just how unstable the main money system has become with currency crises of increasing seriousness and with increasing regularity.

To tackle this, his book *The Future of Money* (published by Century in 2001) included a proposal for a new currency that retains its value anywhere in the world – not instead of national currencies like the euro, but as a complementary currency, operating in parallel with all the others. Lietaer's reference currency, the *terra*, would have a demurrage charge – the negative interest rate proposed by Silvio Gesell (see Part I, p233) – and it would be based on stocks of commodities as proposed by Benjamin Graham (see p196), to which some standardized services would be added.

Using the *terra* means that the reserves that the country could rely on would be much larger than its current stock of hard currencies and gold. As he points out, it could be started unilaterally or even privately, because the necessary international commodity exchanges already exist. But the bottom line is that it would be much more stable than any of its single components, and also more stable than any other convertible currency in the world. This passage is adapted from his book *The Future of Money: A new way to create wealth, work and a wiser world.*

✻   ✻   ✻

I will call a Global Reference Currency (GRC) the generic concept of a currency which is not tied to any particular nation state, and whose main purpose is to provide a stable and reliable reference currency for international corporate planning, contracts and trade.

Furthermore, I will propose as unit of account for one particular type of GRC the *terra*, which aims at firmly anchoring that currency to the material/physical world. Remember, one of the reasons that the global currency casino can churn as wildly as it does is the disconnection between the financial world and physical reality, a link that was severed by President Nixon in 1971. In this role, the *terra* would be akin to the gold standard in the 19th century.

The *terra* is defined as a standard basket of commodities and services particularly important for international trade, and their relative weight in the standard basket would ideally reflect their relative importance in global trade.

For instance, the value of the *terra* could be defined as:

1 *terra* = $^1/_{10}$ barrel of oil (for example Brent quality and delivery).
+ 1 bushel of wheat (Chicago Mercantile Exchange delivery)
+ 2 pounds of copper (London Metal Exchange delivery)
+ . . .etc
+ $^1/_{100}$ ounce of gold (New York delivery)

(Note: the specific commodities, their quality, delivery standards, and their respective weights in the terra unit are proposed here as simple examples. In practice, this would be part of a negotiated agreement among participants. This standard could also include services, or indices aiming at increasing further its stability.)

The *terra* has the following main characteristics and effects:

- The currency can be made inflation-proof by definition. Inflation is always defined as the change in value of a basket of goods and services, therefore to the extent that the basket composing the *terra* can be made representative of global trade automatic inflation-proofing is obtained.
- The value of this new currency could easily be translated into any existing national currency. Anybody who wants to value the *terra* in his own national currency just has to look up the prices of those internationally traded commodities that are part of the basket. These prices are already published in the financial sections of all the major newspapers in the world. And are available in real-time on the Net everywhere.
- More importantly, this currency is also automatically convertible into any existing national currency without the need for any new international

treaty or agreement. Anybody who is paid in this currency would have the option just to receive the value of the basket of commodities delivered in pre-arranged facilities (such as the already existing delivery places for the different futures markets, for example). We should expect that – as the system proves reliable and credible – fewer and fewer people would feel the need to go through this process of cashing in the receipts. But this linkage with existing commodity markets guarantees the full integration of the proposed currency with the 'real' economy in all its aspects.

- The *terra* would be an ideal mechanism to re-launch the world economy out of a simultaneous recession, as is a major risk today. The reason is that during a recession, there is invariably a glut of raw materials, and raw material producers would have a strong incentive to exchange their excess inventories for *terra*. The demurrage feature of the *terra* would ensure that this currency is not hoarded but rather actively circulated. Therefore, the additional liquidity in the form of *terra* injected in the world markets would have a stronger stimulating effect than what happens with conventional currencies. In a boom period, when raw materials are scarce, the reverse would happen: corporations would tend to cash in the *terras* to take delivery of the underlying raw materials (notwithstanding a two per cent transaction fee). This would reduce the amounts of *terras* in circulation, thereby cooling off the economy at such high points in the cycle.

- A 'sustainability fee' would be 'naturally' embedded in the money system. A sustainability fee, also called demurrage, is a small time-related charge on hoarding a currency. It is called sustainability fee because it would realign financial interests with long-term thinking. Indeed a demurrage charged currency inverses the discounting of the future that occurs automatically with interest-bearing currencies. Notice that in the case of the *terra* this sustainability fee is not a new cost (in contrast with for example Gesell's proposals). There are indeed real costs already associated with storing commodities, and being factored in the costs of goods sold today. The sustainability fee would simply be the cost of storing the basket of commodities agreed upon. These storage costs (and therefore the sustainability fees) have been estimated in a detailed study for a Commodity Reserve Currency at 3 to 3.5 per cent per annum. What is proposed is simply transferring these existing costs to the bearer of the *terra*, thereby giving them the useful social function of a sustainability fee.

- The *terra* would be a public service project, with profits earned by the *terra* alliance mechanism transferred to a non-profit foundation that would fund projects for sustainable development globally.

- From a legal viewpoint, the *terra* would in fact be an inventory receipt that can be used as a medium of exchange. From a technical viewpoint, it would introduce a standardization in countertrade, the name for international corporate barter. Countertrade represents now over $1 trillion per year, or 15 per cent of global trade.

- Last, but not least, the *terra* is a win/win mechanism for all parties. The raw material producers would benefit by reducing their storage costs; *terra* users would benefit from having a more stable international reference compared to today's national currencies; and even the banking system would win. Because of the standardization countertrade transactions would become bankable just like foreign exchange accounts today (one can have *terra* accounts and electronic transfers done by a bank, in contrast with today's countertrade transactions). All parties and society at large would also benefit from the counter-cyclical effects of the *terra* mechanism, and the better chances of a sustainable future.

In short, the *terra* would be an inventory receipt that can be used as a supra-national planning and trading currency. Its unique characteristics of being inflation-proof combined with the demurrage charge would realign financial interests with longer-term concerns, thereby eliminating the conflict between financial concerns and long-term priorities. It would not only provide a much-needed short-term kick-start to the present world economy, but effectively address four other critical systemic issues as well, including:

- International currency instability;
- The lack of an international standard of value; and
- The short-term thinking that haunts most of our financial decision-making.

CREATE YOUR OWN: FREE MONEY

Market economics values what is scarce — not the real work of society, which is caring, loving, being a citizen, a neighbour and a human being. That work will, I hope, never be so scarce that the market value goes high, so we have to find a way of rewarding contributions to it.

EDGAR CAHN, ON THE THINKING BEHIND TIME DOLLARS

Hours is money with a boundary around it, so it stays in our community. It doesn't come to town, shake a few hands and then wander out across the globe. It reinforces trading locally.

PAUL GLOVER, ON THE THINKING BEHIND THE ITHACA HOURS LOCAL CURRENCY

Advocates of free money are by their very nature keen on reflating the economy. 'Sound' economists have traditionally disapproved of this as inflationary chaos, just as they disapproved of the 'greenback' notes the American government issued during the Civil War. But, as Galbraith explains in his 1975 book *Money*, the idea of rather loose controls on money creation — by governments or banks — served the pioneering Wild West very well by making capital available, turning it into farms and businesses and eventually into sound economic success. Maybe the banks had disappeared when it came to redeem the money; maybe 'wildcat banking' shouldn't really be a model we should emulate — but it's effects weren't all bad. 'Then as still,' he wrote, 'what is called sound economics is very often what mirrors the needs of the respectably affluent.'

That implies that free money advocates are always with us, but that isn't quite true. To some extent, they are also creatures of their own time and economic environment. It isn't any coincidence, for example, that there are no passages in this part from the heady years of Keynesianism. The demand for free money rather went to sleep between the end of the Great Depression and the birth of monetarism in the 1980s. But then, once again, we could see all around us the consequences of too little money in circulation – people available to work, people needing the work done, but no money to bring people, needs and resources together.

What became increasingly clear during the 20th century was that you could have places that were awash with money right next door to places that were starved of it. So for money radicals from Irving Fisher (see Part VI, p192) in the 1930s onwards, the key idea was to provide new kinds of money that could circulate locally without seeping away into the pockets of the already rich. That was the idea behind Fisher's Stamp Scrip in the 1930s, just as it was the idea behind Michael Linton's LETS in the 1980s (see p263).

If you could target the 'free money' in the form of local currencies that didn't travel – Paul Glover's hours currency (see Part II, p73) became known locally as the 'Untraveller's Cheque' – then there was some chance that it would reflate the right bits of the economy, the parts with spare capacity, without causing inflation elsewhere.

That kind of free money, local currencies produced in parallel to conventional fiat currencies, is the stuff of revolution – or so the central banks saw it in the 1930s. They don't necessarily see it that way now: the Federal Reserve has given Ithaca hours its blessing, though the Isle of Wight County Council was prosecuted in 1997 for issuing its own coins. It is certainly not the stuff of closer state control over the currency, as many currency reformers want. It means extending the right to create money from the banks to communities, and thence to all of us. It means extending the idea behind baby-sitting tokens into something more ambitious.

Also, as trade becomes more global, there appears to be an equal trend towards the local. Consumers are increasingly demanding fresh food, traditional services and local production. It seems likely that local currencies – some backed by local authorities and other local organizations – could be used to protect local economies against the uncertainties of the international markets, especially as in Ithaca by supporting local farmers. They can also be used increasingly as methods of providing start-up finance to small businesses and encouraging local production, especially of fresh food.

On a large enough scale, regional currencies could float independently. At the same time, small currencies will remain neighbourhood systems enhancing local life, but linked to excess capacity in the main system which mainstream currencies can't recognize as valuable.

But the increasing use of loyalty points on smart cards in the 1980s — which, in the shape of *air miles* or the now defunct internet points *beenz*, have grown into currencies in their own right — has raised the possibility of other kinds of currency emerging, targeted in different ways. Edgar Cahn's time dollars (see p24) are designed to rebuild local relationships between neighbours, or make institutions like health centres share the professional load, by measuring and rewarding the efforts people put in for each other. Like loyalty points, time dollars shouldn't be inflationary in themselves, because they are giving a value to spare capacity that has no value in the market.

This seems to imply a future of multiple currencies — some international for facilitating trade, some local for repairing local economic links, some social for repairing human links. It doesn't necessarily mean those currencies will have to compete, as the free market radicals would like, but there's bound to be some competition around the edges as the various different kinds of currency expand to take in other aspects of life.

At the very least, the freedom to create new kinds of money will mean experimenting with different designs for money. Free money implies that the medium of exchange function takes precedence over money as a store of value. Free-money enthusiasts tend to agree with the poet Ezra Pound or the Buddhist writer Alan Watts that for a government to say it hasn't got enough money to build a road is like a carpenter saying he's run out of inches. The same image was made more familiar to a contemporary audience by Michael Linton (see p263). On the other hand, money that has no store of value function at all is just worthless and of no value to anyone.

So the logic of free money seems to drive us towards a multi-currency world with different kinds of money to underpin different aspects of our lives, but with competition between these currencies too on the basis of different mixtures between 'free' and 'real'. The danger, as always through the centuries, is that the 'real' money goes to the rich, while the infinite shells on the beach — the free money used for measuring and nothing else — is left for the poor.

ARTHUR KITSON

A SCIENTIFIC SOLUTION

(1 8 9 4)

Like so many of the critics of money creation in this book, Sir Arthur Kitson (1861–1937) approached it from the point of view of science. Like Soddy, Douglas and others, he believed that logic of scientific efficiency could provide an answer, hence his book *A Scientific Solution of the Money Question*, published in 1895 in Boston. Kitson was a well-known lighting inventor and industrialist, particularly respected for his work developing arc lamps for lighthouses – in fact he made his 'Mariner's Friend' lamp available to lighthouses for free. Like his American contemporary Henry Ford, he had become deeply suspicious of banks, and also like Ford, this suspicion came to verge on anti-Semitism.

Reading it now, it looks pretty conventional stuff – though that is mainly because the kind of world he envisaged: decoupling the value of money from precious metals has actually come to pass – and has failed to bring us into the kind of Garden of Eden he predicted. In fact, money has increasingly taken over from the precious metals as a commodity in itself.

But behind all that, there is a strand of radicalism here that was to make Kitson an inspiration to the 'free money' radicals that came after him. Like them, he wanted to divide up the functions of money and remix them differently – and the function of money he identified as causing all the trouble was its ability to provide a 'standard of value'. Get rid of that, and nobody can corner the market in whatever standard it is based on, and nobody can restrict the money supply either – a sin that Kitson believed was a restriction on liberty. And if money is limitless, you can't charge interest on it.

Well, it hasn't quite happened like that. One of the perennial accusations thrown at free money radicals is that they will cause inflation. It's hard to see how Kitson could have avoided that fate, except that he was searching for that touchstone of radicalism – a mechanism that provides a perfect balance between money supply and need.

Kitson was one of the few industrialists invited to give evidence to the Cunliffe Currency Committee after the First World War. It was chaired by the governor of the Bank of England, Lord Cunliffe, packed with bankers — and despite Kitson's best efforts — it came out strongly for deflation and a return to the gold standard, which finally took place in Britain in 1925, with disastrous results.

* * *

The solution of the money question, like the solution of the tariff question, is to be found in the removal of all restraints which governments have placed upon exchange and its mechanism. It is, in short, but enlarging the field of human liberty. Having acknowledged the right of all men to life, we have to acknowledge their right to support life; in fact, the one implies the other. But laws that restrict trade, that interfere with the issuance of money, deny this right. 'Commerce,' says Proudhon, 'exists only among free men.' We can transpose this aphorism and assert that men are only free where commerce is free; and as we have seen, commerce is only free where the mechanism of exchange is free. Practically considered, two distinct operations are necessary; one of demolition, the other of reconstruction. The work of demolition consists merely in abolishing that fiction known as the standard of value, and repealing all laws relating to the issuing and tendering of money. In other words, *the solution of the money question will be found in free exchange; exchange freed from tariffs and taxes of every description, unobstructed by custom houses and licensed banking houses, by law makers and usurers. . .*

Those who see in the present system of tariffs the evils, oppression and unjust privileges which its operation gives rise to, and who fail to perceive the inequity in a governmental control of the currency, are strangely blind to principle. Of what benefit is it to a nation to abolish its customs houses, so long as the medium of exchange is left to the control of a few government-licensed banking houses? Tariffs are taxes levied upon certain *special* commodities, and affect *special* exchanges; but a restricted currency, whether it be limited by the supply of a special commodity such as gold, or by the arbitrary rulings of a government, is a tax upon *all* exchanges, a burden placed over the *entire* field of industry. *Industrial commerce is impossible with a restricted currency. In other words, free trade is only possible with free money.*

The prevailing idea that a nation's currency must necessarily be restricted in volume, is entirely due to the fallacy that money is necessarily something valuable; or, as it is commonly stated, money must be 'intrinsically valuable' — a fallacy which, as we have already seen, is attributable to a false conception of the term value. *Money is not, scientifically speaking, a thing of value; it is not wealth.*

It is the symbol of wealth, the evidence of debt, a convenient means of reckoning and expressing the values of commodities. *Money is not a standard of value, nor a measure of values, neither is it a commodity.* It is a common denominator of values and a measure of purchasing power.

I have shown how impossible it is, scientifically speaking, to make money a commodity. I have shown how physically impossible it is to make of any material a common denominator of values. Gold can no more 'measure' values than a bushel basket can square the circle.

And now let us see what would be the effect of demolishing the standard of value. The one great result it would accomplish, would be to divorce money from its unnatural alliance with the precious metals. The only plea urged by economists and legislators for basing money upon specie, is that it is necessary to do so in order that money may perform the function of a standard of value. Abolition of this so-called function, removes at once all necessity and every excuse for the specie basis. The question arises, what will take its place? What will the monetary system be? To begin with, the nomenclatore would be the same. A dollar will still remain the monetary unit; but instead of being determined by a certain fixed weight of gold, it will simply be a unit of purchasing power. *It would represent no fixed amount or quantity of any particular commodity*, its power would be represented in all commodities. Goods would still be prized by the dollar system. The market reports would be printed in similar terms as now, the only difference being that prices of commodities would not be subjected to the fluctuations of gold or silver. These metals might be hoarded, exported, imported, cornered or thrown upon the market with the utmost impunity, without affecting the prices of any other commodities in the slightest degree. Every commodity would then stand upon its own base. A general fall or rise in prices would be utterly impossible. At the present time, under our present inequitable and unscientific system, the price of every commodity is dependent, first, upon supply and demand of commodities themselves; and second, upon supply and demand of money.

Variations in these two classes may occur separately or simultaneously, and the fortunes and lives of men are affected far more by the second than the first. The former are controlled by the latter, and bankers control to a large extent the destinies of producers and merchants. Today, a merchant may find the value of his stock suddenly diminished one-half, without any change having taken place in the cost of production or supply of the goods themselves, merely through the conjoint action of a number of bankers in cornering the supply of money. Observe, for instance, how the cornering of gold precipitated the general panic known as Black Friday! No cornering of commodities could possibly create a general panic, so long as money is not confined to any particular commodity.

Under the system I propose, variations in supply and demand of money could have no effect upon prices, because the supply would be always ample to meet the demand. By making all commodities equal, that is, putting them on the same footing, all would be alike monetizable. Industry, trade and commerce would then assume their natural position and would become independent of finance. The fortunes of manufacturers and merchants would cease to be the shuttlecocks of money brokers and speculators.

A dry-goods merchant would find it as easy to monetize his stock, and the builder his house, as the gold miner his gold. With freedom to monetize all commodities alike, the monopolization of money would be as impossible as the monopolization of *all* commodities. Further, the supply of money would be so abundant that interest for the use of money would rapidly disappear. *Interest is only possible with a restricted currency.*

SILVIO GESELL

Demurrage Money (1913)

As described in Part I, Silvio Gesell (1862–1930) has been one of the most influential money heretics of the 20th century, just as Keynes predicted he would be. His argument that money is unnatural because it grows in value when it isn't being used – whereas most commodities in the world lose value, whether its from mould or rats – was taken on board by a string of monetary reformers. He deeply influenced Irving Fisher (see p238), who in turn influenced his assistant Ralph Borsodi (see Part VI, p202). Bob Swann (see Part VI, p211), in turn, worked with Borsodi during the Constant experiment, and Paul Glover (see Part II, p73) was advised by Swann.

This passage taken from *The Natural Economic Order* published by Peter Owen in 1958, outlines some of the details of Gesell's alternative of what he called '*demurrage*' money – money which rusts, and loses value. The idea that people would have to fix a stamp to each note for it to keep its value, creating negative interest cash, was widely put into practice during the Great Depression on both sides of the Atlantic – with spectacular results.

The big question, these days, is whether people would be prepared to queue up every Wednesday, as Gesell suggests, just for the fiddly business of sticking stamps on all their notes. Alternative money, if it's going to succeed, is going to have to be at least as convenient as the stuff we have now. And if there is any competition between positive interest money and negative interest money, then I know which one I would prefer to receive. Even so, Gesell has hit on something here – and when other kinds of money are desperately scarce, as they were in the 1930s, demurrage money does seem to provide an answer to keeping the money in circulation.

*   *   *

I Free-Money is a stabilized paper-money currency, the currency notes being issued or withdrawn in accordance with index numbers of prices, with the aim of stabilizing the general level of prices.

2 Free-Money, decimal currency, is issued in 1/5/10/20/50 and 100 dollar (franc, mark) notes (bills). The monetary authority also sells, through the post-office, currency stamps value 1/2/5/10/20 and 50 cents.

3 Free-Money loses one-thousandth of its face value weekly, or about five per cent annually, at the expense of the holder. The holder must keep the notes at their face value by attaching to them the currency stamps mentioned above. A ten-cent stamp, for example must be attached every Wednesday to the $100 note [not illustrated], which is shown as it will appear during the week 4–11 August, 31 ten-cent stamps ($3.10) having been attached to it, on the dated spaces provided for the purpose, by its various holders, one stamp for each week since the beginning of the year. In the course of the year 52 ten-cent stamps must be attached to the $100 note, or, in other words, it depreciates 5.2 per cent annually at the expense of the holders.

4 For small change up to one dollar (1/2/5/10/20/50 cents) the current stamps themselves could be used, in which case they would not be reissued when paid in at public offices, but replaced by fresh stamps. The currency stamps would be sold in small perforated sheets resembling a page from a postage-stamp booklet, the total value of each sheet being one dollar.

5 At the end of the year the fully-stamped currency notes are exchanged for fresh notes, for circulation during the following year.

6 Everyone of course tries to avoid the expense of stamping the notes by passing them on – by purchasing something, by paying debts, by engaging labour, or by depositing the notes in the bank, reducing the rate of interest on its loans. In this way the circulation of money is subjected to pressure.

7 The purpose of Free-Money is to break the unfair privilege enjoyed by money. This unfair privilege is solely due to the fact that the traditional form of money has one immense advantage over all other goods, namely that it is indestructible. The products of our labour cause considerable expense for storage and caretaking, and even this expense can only retard, but cannot prevent their gradual decay. The possessor of money, by the vary nature of the money-material (precious metal or paper) is exempt from such loss. In commerce, therefore, the capitalist (possessor of money) can always afford to wait, whereas the possessors of merchandise are always hurried. So if the negotiations about the price break down, the resulting loss invariably falls on the possessor of goods, that is, ultimately, on the worker (in the widest sense). This circumstance is made use of by the capitalist to exert pressure on the possessor of goods (worker), and to force him to sell his product below the true price.

8 Free-Money is not redeemed by the Currency Office. Money will always be needed and used, so why should it ever be redeemed? The Currency Office is, however bound to adapt the issue of money to the needs of the market in such a manner that the general level of prices remains stable. The Currency Office will therefore issue more money when the prices of goods tend to fall, and withdraw money when prices tend to rise; for general prices are exclusively determined by the amount of money offered for the existing stock of goods. And the nature of Free-Money ensures that all the money issued by the Currency Office is immediately offered in exchange for goods. The Currency Office will not be dormant like our present monetary administration which with indolent fatalism expects the stability of the national currency from the mysterious 'intrinsic value' of gold, to the great advantage of swindlers, speculators and usurers; it will intervene decisively to establish a fixed general level of prices, thereby protecting honest trade and industry.

THE FREE MONEY EXPERIMENT (1933)

Worgl is a small skiing town in the Austrian Tyrol, but in the mid-1930s it was briefly famous for being one of the first places to try out Gesell's plan (see p233) – catching the eye of Irving Fisher (see Part VII, p238) as it did so. The experiment had a dramatic effect, as this contemporary magazine cutting explains.

But there is something poignant about it too. The article describes how Mayor Michael Unterguggenberger – whose plan it was – was about to go before the courts at the instigation of the Austrian National Bank to explain himself. He did, and – as in the USA – the national bank won and the scheme was wound up. Only four years later, Austria was annexed by Nazi Germany, and such flashes of local independence became impossible.

Worgl remains important in the folk memory of currency reformers, partly because it influenced Fisher, partly because it worked and partly because the central bank moved so fast to suppress it. Unterguggenberger was among a range of currency experimenters in the 1930s who came close to turning local money upside down. Only one of the great 1930s experiments is still running: the WIR system in Switzerland, a highly successful mutual-credit currency scheme widely used by the building industry and the restaurant sector. WIR started in 1934, the brain-child of Werner Zimmerman and Paul Enz, two followers of Gesell. By 1993, it had a turnover of £12 billion and 65,000 corporate members.

The Week, the news-sheet in which this article appeared on 17 May 1933, was set up in that year by the journalist Claud Cockburn to campaign against the appeasement of fascist leaders, and was eventually suppressed by the British government in 1941.

*   *   *

WORGL: Unprecedented and widely significant is a case – just coming before the Austrian courts – arising out of the alarm of the Austrian National Bank over the financial revolution which has brought prosperity to the little Austrian town of Worgl, and which the Bank fears is going to compete with its own monopoly powers.

Worgl had been moving rapidly to bankruptcy since the beginning of the crisis. Its factories closed down one after another and unemployment rose daily. Nobody did any business and scarcely anybody paid any taxes. Then Unterguggenberger, Burgomaster of Worgl, proposed the following plan, which was adopted. The town authorities issued to the value of thirty thousand Austrian *schillings* notes in denominations of one, five and ten schilling, which were called tickets for services rendered.

Special features of these notes was the fact that they decreased in value by one per cent every month. Anyone holding one of these notes at the end of the month had to buy from the local authorities a stamp of sufficient value to bring the note up to face value. This he affixed to the back of the note, and the proceeds of the stamps went to the poor relief fund. The result was that the notes circulated with unheard of rapidity. They were first used for the payment of wages for the building of streets, drainage and other public works by men who would otherwise have been unemployed.

On the first day when the new notes were used, eighteen hundred schilling worth was paid out. The recipients immediately hurried with them to the shops, and the shopkeepers and merchants hastened to use them for the payment of their tax arrears to the municipality. The municipality immediately used them to pay the bills. Within twenty-four hours of being issued, the greater part of this money had not only come back to the municipality in the form of tax payments, but had already been passed on its way again. During the first month, the money had made the complete circle no less than twenty times.

There was no possibility for anyone avoiding the one per cent stamp tax on any note he happened to hold at the end of the month, since, without a stamp to bring it up to face value, the note lost its entire value. Within the first four months after the issue of the new money, the town had accomplished public works to the value of one hundred thousand schillings. A large proportion of tax arrears had already been paid off, and there were even cases of people paying taxes in advance. Receipts of back taxes were eight times greater than in the period before the introduction of the new money. Unemployment is now reduced enormously, the shopkeepers are prosperous.

The fame of the Worgl miracle spread. Irving Fisher, American economist, sent a commission of enquiry to Worgl, and the system has since been introduced in a score or more of American townships. The Austrian National Bank, however, was highly disturbed by the whole proceeding. Now Unterguggenberger is being brought before the courts to explain himself and his plan.

IRVING FISHER

STAMP SCRIP (1934)

At the height of the Great Depression, Professor Irving Fisher of Yale University (1867–1947) was – apart from Keynes – probably the most famous economist in the world. Having slightly dented his reputation for economic savvy by losing an absolute packet in the Wall Street Crash, Fisher nailed his colours firmly to the mast of reflation, but also backed with enthusiasm the new kind of local demurrage currency inspired by Silvio Gesell (see p233).

When communities run short of cash, they start swapping things they need, and he watched as some of the most active exchange organizations started printing their warehouse receipts in money denominations – and soon you didn't need to want what the other person had. Within months, about 300 US communities were printing their own negative interest money, watched with fascination by Fisher. Bob Swann (see Part VI, p211) tells how he met the former editor of *The Springfield Union* in Massachusetts, who remembered the scrip issued by his newspaper in the 1930s, when he was just a copyboy. The then publisher, Samuel Bowles, paid his newspaper employees in scrip which could be spent in the stores which advertised in the paper, and the stores would then pay for adverts with the scrip, thus closing the circle. The scrip was so popular that customers began to ask for change in scrip: they would see Bowles around town and had more confidence in his local money than in the federal dollars.

Then on 4 March 1933, it was all over. President Roosevelt – advised that the monetary system was in danger – outlawed any more scrip systems, and gave the existing ones a short time to wind themselves up. Though, as he did so, he also created the conditions for a final flurry of activity. Fearing a complete collapse of the American banking system, he closed all the banks – and all over the country, communities and companies had to provide some kind of alternative to money. 'I care not what kind – silver, copper, brass, gold or paper,' said one senator from Oklahoma. One community in Tenino in Washington State even produced its own wooden money.

But Roosevelt, who famously declared that day in March that 'we have nothing to fear but fear itself,' was also trying to reassure the fears of his 'sound money' bankers and economists. As a result, local money disappeared for two or three generations. Still, it was the velocity of the money that appealed to Fisher. If the American government couldn't persuade banks to risk lending people's savings, then you can set up local money which didn't disappear into the banks of the wealthiest – but kept circulating. Stamp scrip was money like blood.

Fisher managed to be both a reflation enthusiast, and – in his book *100% Money* (see Part VI, p192) – a real money enthusiast too. They don't, after all, have to be contradictory ideas. His main legacy now is the Retail Price Index and monetarism, but his foray into Stamp Scrip cost his reputation dearly among contemporary mainstream economists. This passage is taken from *Mastering the Crisis*, published in London in 1934 by George Allen & Unwin.

✲   ✲   ✲

What is the secret of this extra speed on the part of Stamp Scrip? The secret resides in each stamp due on a Wednesday. You learn to watch Wednesday coming; and, realizing that Wednesday is tax day, you buy what you want before that day, on Thursday or Friday or Saturday or Sunday or Money or Tuesday – and so does the net recipient, unless you 'stick' him late on Tuesday night. That is, you do your buying, so far as possible, in the intervals between stamping days (Wednesdays) in order to escape the two cent stamp tax which you would otherwise have to pay.

Of course, if there is nothing which you ought to buy, you can invest the scrip in any enterprise, or deposit it in any bank, which is a party to the initial agreement to use the scrip.

Meanwhile the extra speed is of the utmost benefit in a depression when everyone is afraid to spend real money.

I have spoken of the stamp as constituting a sort of ambulatory tax. Please note that even the best people always dodge a tax if they honestly can. . . In Stamp Scrip we have, for perhaps the first time in history, a tax which the taxing authority *wants* to see avoided – by the maximum number of people. For, by passing the tax on to the next fellow you speed the scrip, and that is the chief purpose. Moreover, the more you speed it, the more you divide the burden per capita without in the least diminishing the return to the city. Suppose, for instance, that a grocer during a certain week (of six business days) receives and pays out sixty dollars of scrip. Fifty of these dollars may have come and gone on the five business days intervening between Wednesdays. Thus he is taxed, not two cents per dollar of sales but perhaps one-sixth of two cents, which amounts to a sales-tax of one-third of one per cent on the sales put through with the help of the scrip. And most of these sales are extra. The grocer is taxed for new business *which only the scrip could bring him.* This tax is not only painless but helpful.

The efficiency of money is its volume multiplied by its speed. What is the speed of the scrip? At the very least, the average scrip certificate will be unloaded twice a week – a speed that is four times the speed of an average dollar in normal times. In *depression* times, the average dollar circulates only about a third as fast as usual so that a turnover of twice a week becomes twelve times the depression average for conventional money.

This of course, does not mean that actually 12 times the business will be done; for Stamp Scrip never becomes a large proportion of the total circulation. Moreover, a fraction of the conventional currency will *withdraw* from circulation in favour of the Scrip.

Thus, the stamp is more like a tax on hoarding than a sales tax. Hoard, and the tax is heavy; spend (or invest or deposit) and the tax is light. . .

Charles Zylstram the enterprising man who first introduced Stamp Scrip to America (in a small western town) tells this story. A travelling salesman stopped at a hotel and handed the clerk a hundred dollar bill to be put in the safe, saying he could call for it in twenty-four hours. The clerk, whose name was A, owed $100 to B and clandestinely he used this bill for the liquidation of his debt, thinking that before the expiration of 24 hours he could collect $100 from his own debtor, whose name was Z. So this 100 dollar bill went to B, who, greatly surprised, used it to pay his own 100 dollar debt to one C, who (equally surprised). . . and so on, and so on, all the way down to Z, who, with much pleasure, returned the bill to A, the clerk, who, in the morning, restored it to the salesman. And then did A, the clerk, stand petrified with horror to see the salesman light a cigar with it.

'Counterfeit,' said the salesman, 'a fake gift from a crazy friend, Abner; but he didn't put it over, did he?'

Let us now look at the collective result. At the end of the year, the town has a new street, paid for with scrip which (through the stamps) was paid for by the citizens who used the scrip – and will use the street too.

The scrip cost the citizens perhaps one-third of one per cent on mostly new business, while the street cost the city (in the sense of the city treasury) nothing at all. But, of course, the city *is* the citizens; so that means various statements boil down to this: The citizens have bought a new street out of a self imposed tax on mostly new business, and it was a tax less heavy and more spread out than any other tax they ever paid.

E D G A R   C A H N

TIME DOLLARS (1986)

The pioneering law professor and former Kennedy speech-writer, Edgar Cahn (1935–), is one of the sharpest critics of the money system in the USA. But his interest comes from the point of view of what it does to the social fabric. Cahn is, in other words, a communitarian in the mould of Amitai Etzioni and Robert Putnam – but with a major difference. While Putnam suggests the problem will sort itself and Etzioni has no obvious prescription, Cahn has a solution. His currency *time dollars* are a new 'free' money, earned by people helping out in the community and spent when they need help themselves – and aimed not so much at building the local economy, but at measuring and rewarding people's efforts in the local community.

At first sight, time dollars resemble LETS, but LETS are an explicitly economy-building tool, with spin-off effects that can also bring people together. While LETS are a mutual credit system, using a barter currency, time dollars are more like loyalty points – distributed through a 'bank' to encourage a specific kind of behaviour and to build a system that might be better described as 'mutual volunteering.'

Time dollars – or time banks as they are known in the UK – have now spread into more specific remits, like tackling failing schools in Chicago or collapsing youth justice system in Washington DC (see Cahn, 1986, p260). They have also spread to the UK – the UK government zero-rated time 'credits' for tax in 1999 and benefits in 2000 – but more widely in Japan and China, with their serious problems of an ageing population.

Cahn hit on the idea during a prolonged stay in hospital after a heart attack in 1980, and persuaded the healthcare foundation Robert Wood Johnson to launch six experimental schemes in the USA in 1987. But the theoretical work was done by him on secondment at the London School of Economics in 1986. The result was the first academic statement of what were then known as 'service credits', published in a pamphlet called *Service Credits: A new currency for the welfare state*. This passage is taken from the opening remarks.

Note the emphasis on the legal basis of service credits, as you might expect from a lawyer. The economists were not convinced, which is why the time dollars idea had to go back to the USA to prove itself before finally arriving in the UK in 1998, 12 years later. But the tone of the passage betrays when it was written: it was six years into the monetarist policies of Margaret Thatcher and Ronald Reagan, when public spending was being seriously curtailed and unemployment was rising. Cahn had a particular horror of the word 'redundant', which he first heard applied to unemployed people during his visit to the UK.

The result is a parallel currency, much more medium of exchange than store of value – though people can and do use time banks as a long-term insurance policy – that is focused specifically on making neighbourhoods work better and restoring trust. Conventional money uses too complex a set of signals to work in this way, but new kinds of money can make the necessary connections. The launch of networks of time banks in St Louis and London opens up the possibility that time dollars can become widely recognized regional currencies.

*　*　*

When a society has vast unmet needs at the same time that there are large numbers of healthy, energetic productive human beings for whom the society can find no use – even though they would like to be useful – then something is wrong. There was a time when we addressed the problems of unmet needs and utilization of human potential with expanding expenditures of public funds. At present, the indications are that unmet needs will increase and human resource potential will remain untapped, but no increase in public funds commensurate with need is in prospect. In theory, private market mechanisms are supposed to supply what people want. Money functions as the medium of exchange enabling the market (or the public sector) to match supply and demand and to harness productive capacity in order to meet consumer demand. So far as the people this society has designated 'redundant', the medium of exchange, money, is not doing the job.

The approach this paper develops is simply this: *create a new currency*. I call this new currency 'service credits'. It has been created by law in three jurisdictions in the United States, is being tested (so far successfully) in five, is under consideration by the legislatures of seven more states.

How does it work? The basic concept is simple: purchasing power earned by producing service is then expended to consume services produced by others earning service credits.

The initial experiment took place in Missouri: persons over sixty earn service credits by providing 'respite care' (to relieve or 'provide respite to' the primary care giver) for older persons; they can then spend those service credits to purchase respite care or homemaker care for themselves or for someone in their family. One might call that the Blood Bank model – (Give now,

Drawn down later if needed) – except 'time', not blood, is being 'saved'. There are other, more far reaching models, in various stages of planning and implementation:

- Older persons earn service credits staffing a pre-school day care programme. The parents pay with service credits earned in a driver's pool serving the elderly at night and weekends.
- A congregation, union or other membership organization pledges to earn a total of several hundred hours per month in service credits to be held by the membership organization for use by its members if they need homemaker services, day care, or other agreed upon benefits.

The first model, day care, looks like an intergenerational barter programme. The second resembles a rudimentary insurance plan. In short, even though initial experiments have concentrated on the elderly, all the parameters can be expanded:

- Services Produced. These might include tutoring for students with special problems or special talents, services to the handicapped, home repair, food preparation, cooperative food purchasing, 'adult day care', removal of architectural barriers for the mobility impaired, post hospital convalescent care, shopping, escort service.
- Who Earns? Present experiments focus on the elderly; but high school children might perform shopping and chore service; single heads of households might be trained to operate a day care centre with intensive child development components; young men and women could learn basic home repair and home renovation skills.
- Who can 'spend'? Different degrees of transferability can be provided: a grandson or daughter across town could earn service credits as a gift for grandparents so that they could get help when needed; groups can combine to pool credits earned for members and their families.
- Mixed Prices. A two component price can be charged for the services. Where money must be spent to pay for supplies, materials, capital expenditure, or essential professions, the price can include a pass through charge to cover the money expenditures and a service charge credit charge to cover the service credit component.

The basic approach is this: *we can begin to address our social problems by creating a new medium of exchange that can convey presently unutilized personal time into a marketable asset that can generate real purchasing power.* The following features seem worthy of mention:

- A local currency (that can be authorized by local government) permits initiatives to be undertaken without waiting for national legislation or a national consensus.
- There is not loss of 'status' in earning a service credit whereas there might be in accepting a 'minimum' wage.
- This is a currency which can be 'designed' to target specific social problems and specific populations simply by specifying what services are to be produced and for whom; it is a currency that can be expressly fashioned to reward mutual self-help, family, extended family support systems, and various forms of 'neighbourliness'. It is a currency that might be used to strengthen neighbourhood and community.
- To the extent that societies traditionally use 'moral criteria' to determine the allocation of wealth produced by the society, this currency permits citizens to redefine themselves as contributors and producers – rather than as merely worthy receivers of alms.

The insight behind the proposal is that the real wealth of a society is its people – and the time they are prepared to devote meeting their own needs by meeting the needs of others. If time is the ultimate resource, then the question becomes how to mobilize it. Could a new currency simultaneously reclaim 'redundant' people and meet major social needs? By posing the question, we may at least have begun to alter our assumptions about the range of the possible.

MARGRIT KENNEDY

THE LOTTERY IDEA (1988)

Margrit Kennedy (1939–) is an architect, who became fascinated by money as part of her determination to design utopias. She and her husband Declan set up the eco-village in Steyerburg in Germany. Her book *Interest and Inflation Free Money* (see p103) began as a critique of the interest system, but Kennedy is nothing if not practical.

The problem with Gesell's demurrage money as she saw it, quite rightly, was that fiddling with stamps to keep every one of your notes valid really isn't practical any more. Instead she suggests a lottery system that would periodically withdraw notes of different denominations, and exchange them into other notes in return for a fee. The result would be the same: an increase in the velocity of cash, but this time without having to invent and print a whole new currency.

This passage is taken from Margrit Kennedy, with Declan Kennedy: *Interest and Inflation Free Money: Creating an exchange medium that works for everybody and protects the earth*, published in 1995 by New Society Publishers, Philadelphia.

* * *

If somebody has more cash than they need, at any time, they pay it into their bank. Depending on the length of time the money is deposited, the parking fee will be either diminished or waived. . . In the case of long-term deposits there would be no fee; cash would have the highest fee.

The hoarding of cash in the new system could be avoided much more easily than by gluing a stamp on the back of a banknote as was done in Worgl. Several suggestions have been made: one is a lottery system. It would ensure the circulation of cash by the withdrawal of one specific note denomination, in the same way as a lottery draw. . .

Based on today's eight denominations (in the case of the German Mark DM 5/10/50/100/200/500/1000), for example, the eight coloured balls representing different bank note denominations would be mixed with white balls representing no conversion in such a way that on a statistical average – a conversion of one denomination would occur once or twice a year.

Draws could take place, for example, on the first Saturday of each month. Once a denomination is drawn, the conversion period could go on until the end of the month. The drawn notes would remain legal tender and could be used for payments in all shops. However, the respective fee would have to be deducted from payments with these banknotes.

Another option is to exchange the invalid notes against the payment of the exchange fee at a bank or post office. Because no one likes to pay fees, everyone would limit their use of cash to the necessary amount, and surplus money would be paid into bank accounts.

The exchange would be facilitated by giving the new note denominations a new colour and size. New DM-100 yellow notes replace the old blue notes which go out of circulation. The concealment of overdue notes can be avoided by making the new notes slightly longer or wider so that every false note would jut out of the bundle, no matter how thick.

Unlike stickers, or stamp money, the drawing of denominations has the advantage that there is no need to print new money. We could keep the same money we have today and the actual cost of the system would be no higher than the replacement of worn out notes today.

VALUING WOMEN DIFFERENTLY (1992)

New York's Upper West Side was immortalized in Leonard Bernstein's *West Side Story*, but is now gentrified with a large group of artistic, self-employed, creative people in the local population. This is an increasingly expensive neighbourhood of flats and coffee bars: exciting for the young, but isolating for many others – especially so for women trapped in the neighbourhood with a shrinking pension.

The problem of rebuilding a community led to the project Womanshare in the Upper West Side, the brainchild of carpenter Diana McCourt and caterer Jane Wilson, who joined forces in 1991 and have created a group of about 100 people who trade computerized 'credits' – each worth an hour of work.

To that extent, the system sits midway between time dollars and LETS, but the central idea is to train, enthuse, empower and transform the lives of its members – who owe six credits to the organization as part of their membership fee. If currencies can encourage sustainability in the community, Womanshare is about psychological sustainability. 'I think it gives people permission to ask for help,' Diana McCourt told me: a key ingredient was that group members regain their self-esteem.

This passage taken from *News from Womanshare*, in February, 1993 is their statement of principles, finally hammered out in December 1992. It comes as almost a shock to think that these ambitions belong in a book about money, yet Womanshare have created a new kind of currency of mutual support that positively encourages these ideals.

*   *   *

Womanshare is a practice of a new socio-economic alternative in which the resources of each individual are valued independently of the prevailing economy. We value all work that women do, and specifically honour what is traditionally called 'women's work' – work that has been denigrated in our culture.

Womanshare recognizes *time* as a limited resource and our real wealth. In our practice of economic democracy, Womanshare credits all hours of work equally.

1 Caring Community. Womanshare is a dynamic caring community. Our intention is to find a balance between the needs of each individual member and the needs of the larger community. Every activity, whether an exchange of services, a workshop, or a membership meeting reflects this commitment. In the sharing of our individual resources, self-interest and the desire to help others converge.

2 Simple Living and Ecological Mindfulness. Womanshare honours simple living, recognizing that the misuse of our material world is destructive to our relationships with each other, the environment, and other sentient beings. We recognize our role as caretakers of this earth and are deeply committed to mindfulness and moderation in the way we live.

3 Diversity. Womanshare honours women's personal experience and thrives on our differences. The coming together of women of diverse age, ethnicity, economic and educational background, sexual orientation, and marital status enriches our lives and strengthens our purpose.

4 Linking. Womanshare acknowledges the importance of linking with other groups who share our values in order to create a strong network of alternative communities.

5 Trust. Womanshare is committed to creating an environment in which each women's privacy, integrity and well-being are protected.

6 Joyous Living. Womanshare regards joy as the birthright of every human being. We nourish that spirit and encourage its expression in our community.

7 Empowerment. Womanshare encourages women to reclaim their rightful roles as leaders, healers, mentors, and visionaries. The quality of life on this planet and even our ultimate survival depend on our recognition of our collective power and the willingness to take necessary action to bring our vision into being. We women are a force.

These principles articulate the vision that inspired the creation of Womanshare and provide the foundation for its continued evolution.

JOEL HODROFF

COMMONWEAL (1999)

The twin cities of Minneapolis and St Paul have been playing host to an interesting variant on time dollars, linking them to the vast over-production in the mainstream economy. The idea, from former political activist Joel Hodroff (1951–) was somehow to direct some of that over-capacity at the places – often right next door – that need it most. In this passage he describes how people can earn *business dollars* by helping out in the neighbourhoods, but spend them in a range of restaurants, shops and other services which have agreed to accept them in part payment – usually at off-peak times.

That means a restaurant which has to employ cooks and waiters and heat the place all afternoon for the benefit of a handful of customers can fill its tables for business dollars, plus enough dollars to cover their costs. Businesses signing up when the project launched in the Lyndale neighbourhood in 1998 included Camp Snoopy – Charlie Brown came from Minneapolis – the theme park in the middle of the biggest shopping mall in the USA. Camp Snoopy has to stay open through busy Saturdays and quiet Wednesdays, and offering to accept business dollars means it can also attract punters on Wednesdays. In other words, the businesses can clear excess stock without expensive marketing, as well as underpin the parallel 'time' economy where people are helping neighbours.

Hodroff set up an organization called Commonweal. They provide participants with dual-track debit cards, known as Community HeroCards, and take a small percentage in dollars of each transaction to run the scheme. The idea is to use a new kind of money as an information system to direct the economy's over-capacity into the hands of people who never usually get it. It's a kind of win-win-win deal.

Joel Hodroff has patented his dual currency pricing, accounting and transaction settlement system, and is now the chief executive of DualCurrency Systems. This passage is taken from one of his most recent discussion papers about what dual currencies might mean – *Re-inventing Money for the Information Economy*.

*   *   *

A novel application of banking and transaction technologies has been devised to bridge the gap between underutilized business capacity and the limited financial resources of many consumers and communities. The new form of exchange is called dualcurrency commerce (dc-commerce). The simple premise behind dc-commerce is that cash resources can be stretched or supplemented – without causing inflation – through the use of a non-cash currency.

As the name suggests, dualcurrency transactions are priced and settled in two currencies simultaneously. For example, a $10 restaurant meal might cost $5 cash and $5 in the second currency, while a $40 pair of pants might cost $34 cash and $6 in the second currency. In theory, the second currency can expand trade and commerce, much the way that paper currency at first augmented gold coins. This article introduces *Business Dollars* as one such companion currency.

A brief overview of several non-cash currencies will help give a context for *Business Dollars*. Barter dollars allow businesses or individuals to trade when cash is in short supply. Corporate scrip was historically a privately issued business note that could be redeemed for a company's product or service. Today, scrip is used primarily as a marketing tool in customer loyalty programmes such as frequent flyer miles or as promotional currency such as Disney Dollars. Service Credits, sometimes known as Time Dollars, are a community economic development tool helping individuals to trade services with one another on an equal, hour for hour, basis.

Technologically simple, dualcurrency commerce enhances transaction banking products, such as credit cards, debit cards and smart cards. It can also be applied to e-commerce on the Internet. An enhancement means that with little modification and expense, *transaction companies and banks can turn the very cards that consumers use today for spending into earning cards as well.*

The dualcurrency system also utilizes standard retail point of sale terminals. It can therefore reduce the inconvenience and expense for consumers and merchants of cash, cheques, discount coupons and incentive point programmes. The entire transaction process is automated and hassle free – simply swipe and sign a standard transaction receipt. The patented dualcurrency technology checks balances and approves transactions, as well as credits and debits cardholder accounts with dollars and *Business Dollars*.

There are numerous ways to introduce *Business Dollars* into circulation, including employee incentives, wage subsidies, social security supplements, investor dividends, volunteer rewards, charitable gifts, foundation grants or tax rebates. Along with the inevitable risks, early adopters of dc-commerce may enjoy a degree of freedom to experiment and innovate. Laws and regulations governing dc-commerce will likely evolve over time through industry initiatives, regulatory agencies and federal lawmakers – much like the laws and regulations that govern banking, credit cards, insurance, investing and other financial products and services.

Imagine yourself a restaurant owner participating in dualcurrency commerce. You must first determine an enticing, yet profitable, ratio of cash to *Business Dollars* at which to offer your meals. You must also decide upon any limitations on times at which you will accept *Business Dollars* and whether discounted specials will be included or excluded. These considerations are similar to the rules of '2 for 1' dining coupons or senior citizens' discounts.

A representative of your local dualcurrency business alliance will help you to design a promotional campaign aimed at dualcurrency cardholders. There is also an orientation for your employees. Right from the start, you would enjoy an influx of new customers and a modest, incremental cash profit with every dualcurrency sale. Your business would receive dualcurrency statements from your transaction processor – Visa, MasterCard etc – while cardholders receive dualcurrency statements from their banks and credit card issuers.

Your cash revenues are distributed in the traditional way – towards materials, labour, overhead and profit. However, *Business Dollars* are distributed through the dualcurrency business alliance as a dividend. While each dualcurrency business alliance may operate somewhat differently, the one in our example gives each employee an equal dividend of B$350 per month, prorated for a forty-hour work week. The figure is calculated by the dualcurrency business alliance based upon the underutilized capacity in the business community and the number of participating employees.

When you and your employees go to spend your B$, here is what you find: an evening at the movies costs $2 cash and B$4 for tickets, and half cash-half B$ for refreshments; a $100 bag of groceries costs $95 cash and B$5; a flight from Minneapolis to New York City costs $200 cash and B$150; $2000 in tuition and books for a semester of college is available on a sliding-scale fee ranging from $500 cash and B$1500 to $1800 cash and B$200.

A dualcurrency business alliance would operate much like the Visa system. Visa is cooperatively owned and managed by its member banks, which set policies and control operations through representative boards. Within the framework of Visa regulations, individual banks control their own portfolios of cardholders. The primary difference is that the dualcurrency business alliance is composed of retailers, employers, employees and consumers, as well as banks and transaction companies.

Most consumer and business decisions in a dualcurrency network would look the same as they do today. Business owners and managers would make decisions about products and services, hiring and compensation, distribution of profits, etc. The market would determine prices, but with a new factor. Consumers would also consider, 'What part B$ can I pay?' Individuals would still choose where to work, as well as how and where to spend their pay-cheques. Labour unions would play their traditional roles, only with labour-management relations enhanced by a bigger economic pie and an inherently more co-operative economic set up. Lastly, a dissatisfied customer would have the same recourse that they now have with cash transactions – calling on the local Better Business Bureau or similar agencies. . .

The first inkling of dualcurrency pricing is appearing in the airline industry, with special offers for airline tickets on a part-cash and part-frequent flyer miles basis. As well, large trades in the commercial barter industry are commonly made on a part-cash, part-barter dollar basis.

In Minneapolis, Minnesota, a demonstration project established by Commonweal Inc is underway utilizing a dualcurrency cash and Community Service Dollar system. The Commonweal HeroCard Programme rewards youth volunteers for work in their communities. Lastly, the newly integrated economies of the European Economic Community offer a perfect appli-cation for dc-commerce, where products and services could be priced partly in one or another national currency and partly in euros, the new common European currency. . .

The story is told that Henry Ford doubled the wages of his employees, so that they could afford to purchase his Model-T Ford – an unequivocal win-win proposition for the company and its workers, and perhaps a useful model for today. We also know of the legacy of the Carnegie family in building a network of public libraries across the land, when education beyond the grade school level was still a privilege for the upper classes. That legacy benefits thousands of communities and millions of people to this day. How much greater could be the legacy of the banking and transaction industry, arguably the most powerful institution in the history of the world? How much more powerful an economic engine would the profit motive be if it were harnessed to serve businesses, employees and communities alike? With a little imagination and courage we can find out.

RICHARD DOUTHWAITE

STARTING A REGIONAL
CURRENCY (1999)

Richard Douthwaite (1942–) was a British government development economist
working in the West Indies, and since then has been a great popularizer of new
ideas in economics, and a considerable part of his book *Short Circuit* was devoted
to new kinds of money. His main criticism of the sustainability of Ithaca hours –
the local currency introduced by Paul Glover (see Part II, p73) – was that it would
be hard to withdraw the notes from circulation if necessary. The following passage
– taken from *The Ecology of Money*, published in 1999 by Green Books, Dartington
– is partly his answer to the problem.

The background was a decision in 1997 by the European Commission to
sponsor four experimental regional currencies that could be used by organizations,
charities and small businesses as an alternative to cash. The four new currencies, in
rural Scotland, County Mayo, Madrid and Amsterdam, were planned as the basis
for large mutual credit schemes along the lines of the WIR system in Switzerland
(see p236). All four were launched in 1998/9, but only one – the Scotbarter
system, run by the Scottish/Dutch currency consultancy Barataria (called after a
mythical island invented by Gesell (see p233) – is still in existence.

But the Irish currency, designed partly by Douthwaite – though he implies here
the role of an entirely objective observer – was very different. It was known as roma
(ROscommon-MAyo), and it took the form of currency notes, sponsored by local
businesses and issued by them into the local economy. The idea was developed by
the Irish community leader Gerry McGarry, but was informed by the progress of
a similar project using electronic cash pioneered by Michael Linton as 'Community
Way' in British Columbia (see p263). The roma is an example of a highly innovative project that required more time and money to turn its initial success into
something more sustainable.

✳ ✳ ✳

The *roma* currency system was invented by Gerry McGarry, an Irish engineer, cinema owner and social activist, to encourage the businesses in his area to do more trade among themselves and to raise the money for local charities. The first notes went into circulation in a small Irish town, Ballyhaunis, in 1999 and were withdrawn as planned two months later. The experiment raised £1000 for good causes.

Although *romas* can service as short-term currency to raise money for a community cause, their potential is far greater as a low-cost, low-risk, way of developing a system equivalent to the WIR. They work as follows. Members of voluntary organizations approach businesses in their area asking for gifts of *romas* to support their activities. If the trader agrees, the local manager of the *roma* system overprints the required number of notes with the name, address and logo of the donor and that of a good cause to which they are being given. The business sponsoring the notes promises to supply goods and services to the value of one pound for every note presented at its premises. It also agrees to honour notes issued by other sponsors.

The notes are overprinted with a date a few months from the time of issue after which holders can present them to organizers for conversion into cash at a rate of one roma to the Irish pound. The cash to cover the conversion comes from the sponsors. If a business has backed, say, £500-worth of *romas* that matured last month, it can cover the cost of its sponsorship by paying organizers £500 in cash, or handing over 500 mature *romas*, no matter who issued them. If the business has gained more than 500 mature *romas*, it will be paid one pound for every one above the 500 mark.

The reason for converting mature notes into cash and withdrawing them from circulation after a few months is to create space for later issue of notes in favour of other voluntary organizations. Otherwise, the benefits to the good causes would only occur in the early stages of the currency's develop-ment while the amount of *romas* in circulation was continuing to expand. Notes that aren't presented for conversion within a month of maturity lose their value altogether. This to allow the accounts for a particular note issue to be closed.

Firms get major advantages from giving their donations in *romas* rather than conventional money. For example, when a firm gives cash, the amount involved comes straight out of its profits for the year because it is paid from the proceeds of sales that have already been made. A gift of *romas*, on the other hand, comes out of the profits to be made on future business which the new money will help to generate. Moreover, the fact that a firm's name appears on the note in association with a local good cause is not only good advertising but builds a lot of goodwill. And, finally, the system is very tax-efficient because the notes are treated as discount vouchers when they are used to make a purchase from the firm that issued them. Consequently the amount of the gift is free of VAT. McGarry thinks that if firms find that supporting local organizations with *romas* is beneficial then they will be much more generous to them.

The voluntary organizations spend their notes in the local area just as if they were a national currency. In Ballyhaunis, 92 out of the 95 local traders were happy to accept them. The public, too, was happy to earn them, or to take them as change, as they knew that by doing so they were helping the good causes named on them and that they could always spend the notes at the next shop.

The plan is to set up a user-owned cooperative to run the system which will steadily increase the amount of *romas* in circulation until saturation is reached and people begin to be reluctant to handle more. Other towns in the area will be brought into the system and the stage should quickly be reached at which notes are being issued and withdrawn every month. . . After two or three years, when confidence in the *roma* as an exchange currency is sufficiently high, the cooperative will open cheque accounts for businesses to allow them to pay each other in *roma* instead of Irish pounds. These accounts will be operated in the same no-interest, service-charge-only bases as the WIR, and participating firms will be required to give security for overdrafts above a certain amount. There will also be stringent safeguards to ensure that firms spend as many *roma*-days in credit as in debit.

When this stage is reached, the ability to accept payments in *roma* should give local businesses a competitive advantage within their own area over firms from outside who will have to insist to 100 per cent payment in Irish pounds, or by then, euros. It will also mean that the people of the area will no longer have to earn money outside the district before they can do business among themselves. The most remarkable thing about the *roma* system, however, is that it is simple to set up and cheap to operate and could be developed over a period of years into a fully-fledged regional currency.

DAVID BOYLE

WHY LONDON NEEDS ITS OWN CURRENCY (2000)

At first hearing, the idea of London issuing its own currency sounds as if it flies in the face of the modern world. With the euro struggling across the Channel and Argentinians pegging their currency to the dollar, we seem to be in a world of big currencies. London money raises the spectre of having to change coins and notes every time we cross the M25 – not an attractive prospect. But it's simply because currencies are getting so big – with interest rates that can only possibly suit a few of us – that the future might also include a number of little ones.

The problem is the sheer diversity of London, and it is getting more diverse every day that goes by. Yet all of us who live here – from nurses to currency traders – have to get by using the one currency, the value of which is decided by tens of thousands of youthful traders in Wall Street and the City. That's fine for the international economy and the financial services sector. But there are at least two more levels of the economy in London – one a local economy, untouched by financial services and the other, perhaps not strictly an economy at all, is the neighbourhood level of mutual support, known these days as 'social capital'.

The international economy brings in executives from all over the world, whose employers will pay their housing expenses no matter what – forcing up the value of London homes beyond anywhere else in the country, and pricing London services beyond the other economies altogether. That's why London struggles to employ nurses or teachers or bus conductors, because they can't afford to live there, so the basic services suffer. We can all see the symptoms – expensive theme bars, yuppie online travel agents, but no local shops.

How do you help those other hidden economies to thrive? The answer, according to this passage, taken from *Why London Needs its own Currency*, published by the New Economics Foundation in 2000, is to give them their own currencies. For the social economy, London could have a city-wide time currency along the lines proposed by Edgar Cahn (see p24), and the new London Time Bank launched in

2001 exists to do just that. But for London's interlocking local economies, well – read on. . .

✻   ✻   ✻

Imagine for a moment that your tickets for the London Underground were electronic digits on a smart card. You may not have to imagine it for long: the underground has already embarked on a £1.8 billion project for just such a card. But imagine a little further – that you could buy these units in small shops all over the capital and could exchange them easily, along the lines of a Mondex or Visacash card – from card to card.

Imagine, like Mondex, that you could download them onto a card in a mobile phone. Mondex and Visacash are experimental electronic versions of pounds which can be held on cards, downloaded over the phone or via computer direct from your bank. The technology has advanced so much that you can now pay parking meters or drinks dispensers in Finland simply by phoning them up. In five years time, the chances are that this technology will have reached even London underground enough for us to download tube payments direct from the station over the phone and onto a smart card.

Now imagine that these units also circulated around London's local economy, swapped from card to card by card readers in shops and pubs or kept in a handbag or pocket. Imagine that, as well as paying the price of an underground journey, you could also use them to buy what you need in the local economy. Let's call this new electronic currency 'tubes'. London underground may then find they have created a *de facto* regional currency, which can be redeemed in journeys - and is therefore not subject to the same inflation as pounds or euros – but which we can also use to buy a range of other things in the informal and maybe formal economy too.

Tubes could be bought in the normal way, of course. But they could also be issued into the economy in no-interest loans to small business – in return for a fee – and then earned by people providing a range of services in the local economy, ranging from building work to informal baby-sitting. The underground would get the fees and some benefit from 'float' – because it may be months before the *tubes* are redeemed by journeys. . .

Why shouldn't bars have a particularly happy hour when they accept part payment in *tubes*? Why shouldn't we launch a range of new babysitting circles and 'favours' groups that exchange *tubes*? The currency would be trustworthy and able to underpin a range of semi-economic activities that are simply not viable in an international currency like euros or pounds. The underground would be a bank for the local London economy, underpinning a network of smaller business as WIR does in Switzerland. . .

There may be a range of reasons why *tubes* are not, after all, the answer. Maybe a sclerotic institution like the London underground isn't the right body to preside over this innovation. Maybe a currency that devalued every January when the underground prices go up might not be the most appropriate – though there are advantages in a currency that 'rusts': people don't hoard it. It would depend how the new smart-card system worked whether this would be a currency that rusts or one that inflates when the fares go up in price – and the consequences for the way the currency worked would, of course, be very different.

Maybe instead the new Mayor of London organizes a bond issue to pay for the upgrading of the underground – as many of the candidates have suggested. Maybe instead of large denomination bonds, sold to pay the enormous costs and paid off by charging cars driving into the centre, they could be converted also in very small denominations which circulate around the local economy – backed by the promise of London government to repay them at a set date. The point isn't that these specific brainstorms should be adopted, but that experiment is possible in a range of fields.

The point is also that the tools and infrastructure, and certainly the technology, are available to us to invent new currencies that can circulate around London's local economy. They are unlikely to be accepted by the big retailers who bundle up their takings every night and send them electronically to city accounts. They are more likely to provide a kind of local multiplier effect for London's less advantaged neighbourhoods. And if they are widely accepted, they open up the possibility of zero-interest or very low interest loans that would make small businesses viable, when a loan at six per cent wouldn't.

Probably the best contender would be a new currency based on the LETS or Scotbarter system, allowing small business to exchange their goods and services without using scarce pounds or euros, but using a new mutual credit currency. Small businesses would accept the currency from each other and from customers, knowing that they could use it by buying locally. A London website would allow people to use it more easily. Trades and exchanges would be featured regularly on local media. London's currency would be the subject of some pride – even if it didn't float independently on the world's stock markets.

What should we call the new currency? It needs to sum up the history of London, to catch the imagination of Londoners, and to emphasize that as a zero-interest currency – its whole purpose is to flow. I suggest we call it a *thames*.

London business would be able to earn it by providing services or goods for *thames*, or partly for *thames*. They could get very low interest or no-interest loans in it from the Thames Bank in return for a fee. They could buy the services they need in *thames*, whether or not they have *thames* in their account, by going into debt to other participants – itself a small interest-free loan. Local authorities can play a key role in its distribution. If they agree to accept it as a proportion of council tax, fines and other charges, it immediately gives the currency a value. That means that they must also spend it – perhaps as part of payments to contractors and maybe even staff, but certainly in grants to local charities and in zero interest loans – for a fee in pounds – to small business.

The new local currency will provide a lifeblood of money and connection – bringing together people with time and skills with the work that badly needs doing, and which even in the richest places still seems undone. By staying circulating in London's local economy, without being siphoned off into the international economy, the London currency will provide more work for people and business on the margins.

It would be taxable if it is used as part of business: this is not a means of avoiding tax. As things stand, the Inland Revenue would insist on this tax being paid in pounds. But since some of its circulation will be new, it might be possible to negotiate that some of the tax could be paid in the same local currency. It may be also that, since this is a local currency, its tax should be hypothecated to London – which would give an added reason for Londoners to use it.

That is for the more distant future. For anyone active in the local economy – and that's most of us – *thames* would provide an extra currency which would underpin our economic lives. We would earn it more easily and spend it more readily. It would be exchangeable on the internet and it would be the subject of local TV programmes dealing with cashless exchange and barter, which would capture people's imagination as the US auction sites like eBay have done – and as the French TV barter programmes have done on the continent. Dealing in *thames* would very quickly become a major feature of life in London.

EDGAR CAHN

No More Throwaway People (2000)

Time dollars and time banks have developed considerably since Edgar Cahn first came up with the idea of a 'social currency' (see p241). Teenage jurors in Washington or teenage peer tutors in Chicago are now cashing in their time dollars in return for refurbished computers, which have a low value in the market economy. Prisoners are earning them by keeping in touch with their children. People with depression are earning them by looking after local older people.

As many as 55 struggling schools in Chicago have been pioneering this, paying time dollars to pupils as peer tutors, which they cash in for refurbished computers. Academic results go up and bullying goes down. Residents in one public housing complex in Baltimore have been paying part of their rent in time dollars. Children in the Slovak city of Zilina have organized their own network of six time banks, and contribute to ambitious activities in their after-school club. People in Maryland and California pay for legal advice in time dollars, paid off sometimes by taking part in demonstrations outside the offices of bad employers. Women ex-prisoners in San Diego pay for aftercare services in time dollars, paid off by providing support to each other.

What's more, time dollars can have an effect on the conventional bottom line, especially as – as one academic researcher put it – 'volunteer work can inoculate, or protect, the older person from the hazards of retirement, physical decline and inactivity.' The Sentara group of hospitals in Richmond, Virginia paid time dollars to asthmatic patients creating a phone network of local people with asthma, befriending, advising and informing, and managed to cut the cost of treating asthma by over 70 per cent in two years.

Time dollars are about motivating people to make a contribution, rather as loyalty points motivate people to stay loyal to one retailer, using surplus stock to fund it. A similar innovative scheme in the Brazilian city of Curitiba issued points to people for recycling their rubbish, which are then collected enthusiastically by street children handing in litter off the streets. The points could be spent during off-peak times on the buses. The result: Curitiba is the cleanest city in Latin

America, and all paid for by spare public transport capacity. Ordinary money isn't targeted enough for that.

A new project in Rotterdam, launched in 2002, rewards people using a new credit system for recycling, or buying green or ethical products. In the same way, time dollars use spare capacity – all those people rejected by the market economy – to provide non-medical, human neighbourhood support. Again, ordinary money can't work to direct specific spare capacity at specific need in this way.

Cahn describes the process that time banks make possible as 'reciprocity'. Using time dollars means that public bodies, whether they are health centres or housing estates, can involve clients as equal participants in the business of regeneration. Because they are a currency, they make people equal, and have an energy of their own: spending them pump-primes the time economy by creating debts that have to be paid off.

In this passage from his book *No More Throwaway People: The co-production imperative* – a reference to the way that time dollars can involve people who are excluded from the mainstream economy – Cahn looks at a specific example of how a time economy can rebuild a particularly difficult neighbourhood.

☆   ☆   ☆

In Southeast Washington, DC, five-year-old Natasha understands what it takes to create social capital. She lives in Benning Terrace, a housing complex where (until cleaned up by former gang members) graffiti warned visitors that they were entering a war zone. No grass grew – only hard-packed soil, littered with cans and broken glass. Simple City, as it was called by the media was nationally notorious for the number of drive-by shootings. One year after a truce was negotiated by the Alliance of Concerned Men, former gang members were hired by the housing authority to dig up the soil, lay sod, and plant flowers.

I watched this five-year old, in her pigtails, go up to a six-foot hulk who towered over her, decorated with tattoos, gold tooth, and gold chains. She said to him pointedly, 'We have trashcans here and we use them.'

The teenager was completely taken aback. After staring at this little pipsqueak in amazement, he reached down, grabbed the litter he had just tossed on the ground, crumpled it up, stuck it in his pocket and walked away. Natasha didn't even know what raw courage her act took. She was just defending her sense of how her world should be kept. That was her Time Dollar job.

More precisely, it was *one* of her Time Dollar jobs, because she also serves on the graffiti patrol and earns Time Dollars attending storytelling sessions, listening to a senior who reads storybooks to five- and six-year-olds. Her pay was in Time Dollars, which made her a breadwinner for her family. She earns two bags of groceries each month from the Benning Terrace Time Dollar food bank.

When residents first started the Time Dollar club at Benning Terrace, a lot of the hours were earned in preparing the food served after funerals for teenagers killed in drive-by shootings. Some neighbours earned Time Dollars as look-outs, using their phones to send coded warnings or all-clear messages to beepers that neighbours took whenever they left to go shopping.

For nearly a year now, the killings have dropped to zero. Much of the credit belongs to the Alliance of Concerned Men, who negotiated a truce between rival gangs. Then the Housing Authority provided some maintenance, gardening, and clean-up jobs for former gang members. Now the money is gone and the jobs have ended; but the sense of community remains, reinforced by the social network that the Time Dollars system has helped to generate and sustain. This past year, that translated into a total of 78,560 hours at different public housing complexes.

A new kind of village is emerging. If safety and security are forms of social capital, then that's what Natasha was producing. If social capital, as Putnam tells us, is composed of equal parts trust, reciprocity, and civic engagement, surely she is producing social capital.

MICHAEL LINTON AND
ERNIE YACUB

OPEN MONEY MANIFESTO

(2 0 0 0)

The following passage brings us back into the mainstream business of finding ways
of increasing the medium of exchange in circulation, not in this case by getting the
central bank to print or borrow more of it, but by inventing a new community
currency. Michael Linton's LETSystems, are part of a wider class of mutual
exchange systems generally called LETS. The idea is not just to increase the
medium of exchange, but to improve the quality rather than just the quantity of
the economy, by creating sustainable patterns of exchange.

LETS emerged in recession-hit district of the Comox Valley on Vancouver
Island in 1982. Linton (1945-) is an Alexander Technique teacher who invented a
mutual credit money system, then called green dollars. People and businesses decide
the rate and conditions for accepting the community currency instead of normal
cash, which they can negotiate with customers. You may need cash for the tax and
the cost of materials from outside the local economy, but you can use other kinds
of money for other aspects of the purchase. Instead you issue your own money in
green dollars, and by doing so, you are 'committed' to honour it, redeem your
money, and keep your promise. The transactions are tracked, normally using a
computer programme. In the UK, where LETS spread to almost 400 schemes
during the 1990s, a series of bizarre and colourful names were used for these –
bricks in Brixton or *bobbins* in Manchester – much to the disapproval of the
originators of the idea in Canada.

Within two years in the Comox Valley, Linton's project had turned over the
equivalent of over $300,000 in green dollars trading, including vegetables, room
rents and dentistry. What was – and is – exciting about LETS is its simplicity. It
would not attract the attention of regulators and officials concerned that this
might be some kind of 'bank.' There was also no problem – as there was with
Stamp Scrip, for example – about how much should be issued. The debits and
credits on the system always exactly equalled each other: when you buy with LETS,

you create a credit that can be spent by somebody else. Unlike time dollars, it was also able to keep buying power circulating in the local economy.

Linton brought the idea with him on his 1985 visit to the UK, and the first European project was set up in Totnes – but it wasn't until the recession of the early 1990s that it began to spread rapidly across the UK and continental Europe. Maybe because LETS information was originally only available in English, there did seem something about LETS that particularly appealed to Anglo-Saxon countries, which is why it became so popular in Australia and New Zealand – especially after Linton met the inventor of Permaculture, the Australian Bill Mollison, at a conference in the USA. Australia's Blue Mountain LETS is one of the biggest local currencies in the world. But the related Système Échange Locale (SEL) systems in France have taken off recently as part of what they call the *Economie Solidaire*, and have spread from there to parts of French-speaking Africa. Similar projects have also emerged in Japan and Thailand.

LETS is normally taxable, like barter trade dollars, but governments have generally been confused about how to treat LETS for welfare purposes. New Zealand and the Netherlands are among those to have passed laws encouraging unemployed people to use their local currencies, just as UK cities like Liverpool and Sheffield have been among those experimenting with LETS as a way of building a sense of community on poverty-stricken housing estates.

But Linton has always been more ambitious for his ideas, noticing – quite rightly – that commercial barter systems often charge over ten per cent for trade dollars transaction, and that LETS or 'open money' provides a far cheaper parallel currency system to boost local spending power.

The Comox Valley system is among those that have also adopted another more complex design by Linton, known as 'community way' (see Douthwaite, p253). Here, local businesses donate community way currency (cw$) to charities, projects or individuals, and undertake to accept it as a proportion of the price of their own goods and services. Community way is able to use smart cards, as well as the phone, internet and paper registers, which make the necessary dual-currency transactions a bit smoother.

Linton stands firmly in the tradition of 'free money' – 'free as in speech, not as in beer,' he says – and the idea that the traditional functions of money can be divided. Open money is primarily a function of information – providing information about value so things can be exchanged – though it could be designed as a store of value if it's in very wide use. It provides a mechanism to link up wants and needs when cash is in short supply, or save cash for other uses when it's not. The Open Money Manifesto, the passage below, was written by Linton together with his colleague, the environmentalist and community organizer Ernie Yacub (1944–) and features on the internet at www.openmoney.org.

'We have the materials, the tools, the space, the time, the skills and the intent to build – but we have no inches today?' he writes. 'Why be short of inches? Why be short of money?' It was an insight learned from the Buddhist writer Alan Watts, but Watts didn't suggest a solution for the money system: Linton has.

*   *   *

The problems with money stem entirely from how conventional money is normally issued – it is created by central banks in limited supply. There are three things we know about this money. We know what it does – it comes and it goes. We know what it is – it's scarce and hard to get. And we know where it's from – it's from 'them', not us.

These three characteristics, common to all national currencies, determine that we constantly have to compete for a share of the limited amount of the 'stuff' that makes the world go round. This money can go anywhere, and so it inevitably does, leaving the community deprived of its means of exchange.

It is simply the nature of conventional money that by its coming and going it creates conditions of competition and scarcity, within and between communities.

So we have to scramble for money to survive, we are forced to compete for it, often ruthlessly. Intent on getting the most for the least, we strive for the best bargains, as individuals, businesses, non-profits, governments, and nations.

As a society, as a generation, it seems we are determined to have everything ourselves no matter what consequences our excesses and negligence bring for others, now and in the future.

We rely on this money. It seems there isn't much choice, despite its evident failings. Some people have little or none and cannot do what they need to live in this world – some people have vast amounts of it and yet it seems to do them, and the world, no good.

And what's it all about? A money that is scarce, runs away in all directions, and comes from 'them'. This money of theirs comes with many problems.

- The problem of supply – how much money in circulation is 'right' for the economy? Nobody seems to know how to keep the balance between too much and too little.
- The problem of distribution – where is it? Who has it and who hasn't? Is it where it's needed? Clearly not.
- The problems of cost – costs of creation and security, operations and accounting, the costs of interest, the costs of the courts.

But above all, at a cost beyond counting, our monetarily-driven behaviour has utterly disastrous effects on our society and the global environment. That's the bad news, but you probably knew it already. Now here's the good news – all these problems can be fixed with money that's better designed.

Money is just information, a way we measure what we trade, nothing of value in itself. And we can make it ourselves, to work as a complement to conventional money. Just a matter of design.

There is no good reason for a community to be without money. To be short of money when there's work to get done is like not having enough inches to build a house. We have the materials, the tools, the space, the time, the skills and the intent to build – but we have no inches today? Why be short of inches? Why be short of money?

Open moneys are virtual, personal and free. Any community, network, business can create their own free money – 'free' as in free speech, free radical, freely available – but NOT free as in free lunch, or free ride. It's not something you get for nothing.

Open money is money that must be earned to be respected. When you issue it, you are obliged to redeem it – your money is your word. It's just a matter of your reputation in your community.

Open money is flat money. It confers no power of one *over* another, only one *with* another. Exploitation is no problem; when you have your own money, you can't be bought and sold so easily. You can choose what you do to earn your money. And there's no monopoly, all systems co-exist in the same space. Flatter than flat – open money is superflat.

Open money is virtual and not limited. Physical things exist in space and time – which makes them limited – in number, mass, place. Virtual things don't exist and need not respect any such limits.

So any and all things are possible in open money space – any form at all. It's just a matter of devising a scoring system for those who consent to using it – money is simply a social arrangement.

Of course, a system won't work as a money unless it's well designed. A scoring system that nobody wants to use isn't a working money. So while there's no limit to the moneys that can be conceived, not all moneys will work.

The new money that will work will be created by us, in sufficient supply to meet our needs, and in an open context so that all can contribute and be acknowledged. Open money will circulate within the networks and communities it serves, quite legally and virtually free, by design.

We believe that the problems that come from conventional money can be resolved with open money systems.

- Where conventional money is scarce and expensive, the new money is sufficient and free.
- Where conventional money is created by central banks, new money is issued by us, as promises to redeem — our money is our word.
- And where conventional money flows erratically in and out of our communities, creating dependencies that are harmful to the economy, society and nature, the new complementary money re-circulates, enabling business and trade.

So let's fix the money problem and for the rest of the problems that we face in our world, let's see what follows. Just imagine:

- Imagine having enough money, sufficient to meet all our needs.
- Imagine a society and economy operating without any of the familiar monetary problems of poverty, exploitation, homelessness, unemployment, fear and stress.
- Imagine a world where everyone can have work and pay, work and play.
- Imagine clean air, water, and food — enough for all.
- Imagine human society living in balance with the environment.

Too good to be true? Or maybe not? Maybe worth checking out?

These are our beliefs about open money, our ideas for developing open money systems, and our intent to act now to implement our beliefs — we invite you to sign on.

INDEX